THE WRONGS OF THE RIGHT

The Wrongs of the Right

*Language, Race, and the Republican Party
in the Age of Obama*

Matthew W. Hughey and Gregory S. Parks

NEW YORK UNIVERSITY PRESS

New York and London

NEW YORK UNIVERSITY PRESS
New York and London
www.nyupress.org

© 2014 by New York University
All rights reserved

References to Internet websites (URLs) were accurate at the time of writing. Neither the author nor New York University Press is responsible for URLs that may have expired or changed since the manuscript was prepared.

For Library of Congress Cataloging-in-Publication data, please contact the Library of Congress.

ISBN 978-0-8147-6054-3

New York University Press books are printed on acid-free paper, and their binding materials are chosen for strength and durability. We strive to use environmentally responsible suppliers and materials to the greatest extent possible in publishing our books.

Manufactured in the United States of America

10 9 8 7 6 5 4 3 2 1

Also available as an ebook

CONTENTS

ACKNOWLEDGMENTS

We are grateful to the many hands that helped bind this book. Our research assistants, Bianca Gonzalez-Sobrino, Rachel Lord, Kara Matejov, Michael Norsworthy, Janak Padhair, and Jennifer Skinner, were all a boon to our endeavor.

We remain indebted to our academic homes for providing the space and sustenance that helped bring this work to fruition. First, the research librarians at the University of Connecticut and Wake Forest University were most helpful guides. Second, our respective departments were instrumental in this book's completion. At the University of Connecticut, we are thankful to Bandana Purkayastha (head of the Department of Sociology) and to William Jelani Cob (director for the Institute for African American Studies). At Wake Forest University, we are appreciative of Blake Morant (dean of the School of Law) for his unwavering support.

This book came to New York University Press through the foresight and assistance of Deborah Gershenowitz. Her keen editing and numerous conversations helped to redirect earlier drafts. The project then passed to Clara Platter, acquisitions editor for history and law, who has served as a windfall of support in terms of refining and polishing our final version. Constance Grady has served as a relentless assistant and resource for our every need and question. To the remainder of the people at New York University Press, its editorial board, its support staff, and the anonymous reviewers, we are most gratified by your backing and professionalism.

Introduction

On November 5, 2008, the nation awoke to headlines, such as that of the *New York Times*, that read "OBAMA. Racial Barrier Falls in Heavy Turnout." For many, the near-prophetic election of an African American to the highest position in the land is a watershed moment that confirms the declining significance of both race and racism in the nation. Accordingly, a wide variety of activists, cultural critics, and political pontificators issued pronouncements to that effect. Just after the election, Adam Geller of *USA Today* wrote, "The principle that all men are created equal has never been more than a remote eventuality in the quest for the presidency. . . . [T]hat ideal is no longer relegated to someday. Someday is now." Approximately a year later, just after Obama's January 2010 State of the Union speech, MSNBC's Chris Matthews blurted out, "I forgot he was black tonight for an hour. . . . I said wait a minute, he's an African American guy in front of a bunch of other white people."

Despite the utopian proclamations that we now live in either a "color-blind" or a "post-racial" country, social-scientific research illuminates the grim reality that racial biases are more entrenched than ever. For example, white hate groups like the Ku Klux Klan have been on an unprecedented rise, which many scholars attribute to the outcome of the 2008 election. In early 2011, Donald Trump built a run for the Republican Party's presidential candidate almost exclusively on the racist and xenophobic notion that Barack Obama was not born in the United States and that his educational entrance to, and accomplishments at, Columbia and Harvard were neither merited nor authentic. By the fall of 2011, the *Washington Post* broke a story that GOP candidate Rick Perry's family rented Texas property with "Niggerhead" painted across a large rock that sat at the property's gated entrance. By February of 2012, a federal judge sent an admittedly racist e-mail about

Obama from his official courthouse e-mail account to several friends, and in June of 2012 the head of a Tea Party group in Arkansas stepped down after telling a racist joke at a political rally.

If all of these events are taken together, the core conclusion appears paradoxical. On the one hand, a positive change in dominant attitudes dislodges Jim Crow ideology and now calls for integration and equality. On the other hand, stereotypes of and prejudices toward African Americans pervade the populace. Thus, deep polarization over the appropriate social-policy response to racial inequality yields an ongoing legacy of tension and division.

In this book we set the "post-racial" claims into relief against a background of pre- and post-election racial animus directed at Barack Obama, his administration, and African Americans in general. In specific, we examine how racial fears, coded language, and explicit as well as implicit (automatic/subconscious) racism are drawn upon and manipulated by the political Right. Racial meanings are reservoirs rich in political currency, and the Right's replaying of the "race card" still serves as a potent resource for "othering" the first black president in a context rife with nativism, xenophobia, racial fatigue, and white backlash.

We pay particular attention to racial discourse among those on the political Right and to how that discourse is employed to oppose and hinder the presidency of Barack Obama. Certainly, this unprecedented opposition, if not obstruction, on the part of one political party toward a president of the United States might be seen as a result of the staunch opposition to his policies and the direction in which he points the country. Some, certainly many on the political Right, will argue that race is an insignificant issue in our supposed "post-racial" era—or that, if it is an issue, it is one that works to Obama's benefit. While American voters elected Obama president, some also cast a ballot as much for the washing away of what Condoleezza Rice termed America's "birth defect" (slavery) and all that flowed from it. To counter this reading, we provide an analysis of the political Right and its opposition to Obama from the vantage point of its rhetoric, a history of the evolution of the two-party system and its relation to race, and social-scientific research on the relationship between race and political ideology. What we conclude is that while political conservatives may certainly disagree with Obama's policies, their disagreement does not seem to account for the outright hostility toward Obama expressed by both grass-roots conservatives and their political leaders. Accordingly, now Obama must govern a "post-racial" country that is anything but—one in which the opposition party, from the bottom up, may be heavily influenced by race and racial animus toward Obama.

Let us take a moment to clarify our intention in this book. We stand as neither hard-line apologists for, nor avid critics of, the Obama administration. From our standpoint, there is much about Obama's policies to both celebrate and castigate. In some ways, Obama is the black face of American empire and hierarchy. He has stepped up imperialist policies in Afghanistan and other nations, supported drone attacks that violate constitutional freedoms and rights for citizens, engaged in mass immigrant deportation, stalled on the closing of Guantanamo prison and on ending "extreme interrogation methods," and put forth a health care reform policy that will help some black and brown people (and those of any color among the lower class) but is a policy that was previously advocated by the Republican Party and that reflects some of the least progressive health-care legislation put on the table in quite some time. And in terms of race, he has moved gingerly and even in a reactionary way, no doubt fettered by his right-wing opponents, who would pounce on any racially progressive statement from his mouth. Hence, in his address to the NAACP centennial convention in July 2009, Obama stated that the United States possesses "structural inequalities" and is mired in a "legacy of discrimination" and yet bookended those realities with the conservative talking point that those barriers can be overcome with enough focused willpower and that "your destiny is in your hands." Obama's presidency represents a double helix, the national DNA of race. His presidency is polarized by boot-strapping hyper-individualism on the one hand and a robust commitment to collective equality on the other. For example, after the arrest of African American Harvard professor Henry Louis Gates Jr., Obama said that the police acted "stupidly." Days later (after outcry from the Right), he changed tack and said that he should "have calibrated those words differently," and then days after that—in a moment of flaccid multiculturalism divorced from consideration of asymmetrical race relations—Obama called a "beer summit" at the White House with Gates, the arresting officer, and his vice president.

There is much to critique in Obama's "post-racial" persona. Our point is neither to uncritically support Obama or the Democratic Party nor to single out the GOP for criticism. Our analysis is not hampered or bounded by the divisions of electoral politics. Rather, we draw attention to the fact that in spite of Obama's tightrope act on the question of race, coupled with many of his right-leaning policies, the Right has actively critiqued him—and from a place of implicit racial bias. Now, it is certainly a mistake to focus *all* of our attention on the Birther movement, the Tea Party, and the radical right wing of the GOP. After all, an October 2012 poll by the Associated Press found that 51 percent of Americans express explicit antiblack attitudes (a rise from 48 percent in a similar 2008 survey). And when implicit racial attitudes were measured, the number of Americans with antiblack sentiments jumped to 56 percent—a 7 percent rise from 2008. Still, these antiblack biases were inflected by political worldviews. While 32 percent of Democrats expressed explicit racial prejudice against blacks and 55 percent held implicit antiblack biases, those numbers rose to 79 percent and 64 percent, respectively, for Republicans. Accordingly, our analysis dives into the heart of antiblack prejudice and should not be read as a dismissal of the subtle or liberal forms of racism among the Left and independents.

Grass-roots opposition to Obama has found expression and growth through implicit and explicit race baiting from the Right. The rise of the Birthers, and that of their cousin the Tea Party Movement, together signal the rise of a Second Southern Strategy—a replaying of the 1940s, '50s, and '60s GOP strategy of winning elections by exploiting anti–African American racism and fears of a growing federal government among southern white voters. As one of the key strategists for Nixon, Kevin Phillips, stated in 1968, "Who needs Manhattan when we can get the electoral votes of eleven Southern states?" Those eleven states were the Old Confederacy. Phillips continued, "Put those together with the Farm Belt and the Rocky Mountains, and we don't need the big cities. We don't even want them. Sure, Hubert [Humphrey] will carry Riverside Drive in November. La-de-dah. What will he do in Oklahoma?"[1]

Over the past forty-plus years, the ground to nurture this strategy has already proven fertile. For example, during the 2008 primary and general election, there was already a strong rejection of Obama in counties (concentrated in the South) with high proportions of "unhypenated

Americans"—whites who claim no foreign ethnic ancestry and identify simply as "American." Right-wing grass-roots activism has relied heavily upon this voting bloc in mounting opposition to Obama and the Democratic Party. Such racial fear and apprehension is deeply embedded in our national culture. For centuries people have argued that blacks lack the capacity to govern. Right-wing reactions to the election of Obama, especially within the Birther movement, certainly have many facets, but at their core resides the implicit conflation of whiteness and citizenship that ipso facto marginalizes and "others" nonwhites from being the most cherished citizen in the land—citizen president, representative, and leader. Simply put, Barack Obama does not fit most Americans' implicit idea of an authentic American.

Viewing the matter in this light, it would be a mistake to dismiss the Right as either ignorant, irrational folks on the fringe or a cadre driven by intentional and conscious racial animus. Racism is neither the domain of a few irrational people nor is it predicated upon conscious intentions. Rather, a proper analysis looks to the ways political movements both rely upon and reproduce racist imagery, representations, and symbols (such as apes, witch doctors, fried chicken, watermelons, etc.) under the pretense that their cause is racially neutral or even color-blind.

For example, in December 2008, Chip Saltsman—candidate for chairman of the Republican National Committee—sent a compact disc to committee members featuring the song "Barack the Magic Negro," a parody of the Peter, Paul, and Mary song "Puff the Magic Dragon." In October 2008, the Chaffey Community Republican Women of Upland, California (an area in San Bernardino County) mailed a newsletter to two hundred club members that depicted Barack Obama on a ten-dollar "food stamp." Also on the food stamp was a bucket of fried chicken, a piece of watermelon, spare ribs, and a pitcher of Kool-Aid—all stereotypes of "black" food that carry the racist connotation that blacks cannot control themselves from overconsumption of these items. The organization's president, Diane Fedele, indicated that she had no idea why anyone would take offense to the image, stating, "It was just food to me. It didn't mean anything else." Around the same time, Los Alamitos, California's Republican mayor, Dan Grose, was pressured to resign from his position after sending a racially coded e-mail labeled "No Easter egg hunt this year." The e-mail contained the picture of the White House lawn being decorated as a watermelon patch, rather than with the traditional colored eggs associated with Easter. Watermelons have been, since at least the nineteenth century, associated with blacks, as it was commonly believed that blacks could not resist them and would steal them given the chance. Grose, however, acted shocked that the e-mail was taken to be racist and claimed that the e-card was a commentary on the president's fiscal plan.

Even those with presidential aspirations got into the mix. In the spring of 2011, Donald Trump cast himself as a Birther—questioning the legitimacy of Obama's national origin—and also questioned whether he was a mere affirmative action beneficiary and not intellectually equipped to compete at Columbia University and Harvard Law School, Obama's two alma maters. Prior to announcing his final position on whether or not he would run for the presidency, Trump launched an attack against Obama concerning his birthplace. By adopting claims made previously by other skeptics about the legitimacy of Obama's constitutional rights to the presidency, Trump framed the focus of his presidential announcement. After forcing the release of not only the president's Certification of Live Birth but also the Long Form Birth Certificate, Trump took pride in this "accomplishment" and in finally ending the controversial topic that prevented media highlighting of potential political agendas. Before these topics would be approached, however, Trump also insisted on testing the validity of the documents due to the president's hesitancy about a public release. As the majority of conspiracies were disproven with the release of the two official birth documents, Trump moved from citizenship to academics. Now Trump, within months and even within days of the November 2012 election, demanded that the president's transcripts be released in order to disprove Trump's claims of Obama's academic mediocrity and to dispel the supposed mysteries surrounding his educational background.

These brief examples are part of a trend in which conservative voices engage in opposition and obstruction toward a president of the United States. By "conservative," we mean Republican, Libertarian, Tea Party, and other officially unaffiliated, yet decidedly right-wing, groups and individuals, and we outline the way they use racialized fears, code words, and animus to advance a specific political cause. That cause is often detailed by a political agenda supportive of brands of evangelical Christianity (that favor school prayer and oppose both abortion and homosexuality), principles of limited regulation (that desire small government, low taxes, and free-enterprise capitalism), and generally support restrictions on immigration, favor a strong military, and are skeptical of scientific thought.

In specific, in this book we move step by step through the process by which racialized discourse is used in subtle and sometimes overt ways, generally reproducing a dangerous and white-supremacist ideology and practice. This process has at least four dimensions. First, people of color, especially African Americans in general and Barack Obama in specific, are reconstructed as dysfunctional, pathological, social pariahs that threaten the very foundations of Western democracy and civilization. Second, specific performances of white racial identity are deemed the manifestations of morality and are often conflated with authentic and moral forms of US citizenship and patriotism. Third, whites are constructed as the proper administrators and caretakers of an increasingly diverse society. Here, whiteness emerges as the paternalistic savior of the nation, if not the world, and whites should be left to their own devices to govern and decide what is best for others. Fourth, white people and white culture are framed as the embattled victims of a politically correct and totalitarian society in which whites can't simply speak their mind or exercise basic human rights under the leadership of Obama. These dimensions of black dysfunction, white patriotism, white paternalism, and white victimhood together reveal the existence of a *Herrenvolk* (white master race) democracy in the midst of the supposed "post-racial" era of Barack Obama.

To explore how these dimensions have played out in conservative discourse about Obama, we present a multifaceted approach. Chapter 1 presents a brief overview of race and the Republican Party that covers the evolution of the US two-party system and the central role that racial identity, conflict, and politics have played in that evolution. Chapter 2 examines the latest stage in overt right-wing responses to Obama in the forms of the Birther and Tea Party movements. Chapter 3 then takes on the right-wing media—from cable TV to conservative radio—to examine how the discursive structure of this institution maps anti-Obama racial discourse onto political debates. Chapter 4 provides an overview

of how the GOP—in the context of attitudinal support for racial equality—reengineered overt racist messaging into subtle and implicit racial
appeals throughout political campaigns over the past forty years. Chapter 5 affords a review of the social-science research on political ideology and racial attitudes to demonstrate the effectiveness of racial messages in influencing human action and attitudes. We cover how racial
bias quite often resides in the minds of even those who profess racial
egalitarianism, with 70–90 percent of whites and even 35–65 percent
of blacks harboring automatic/unconscious racial biases in favor of
whites and against blacks. And while there is little distinction between
liberals and conservatives in implicit racial attitudes, research indicates
that conservatives appear to sit more comfortably than liberals with the
racial biases they hold. In chapter 6, the penultimate in our treatise,
we make four key arguments about racial bias and the law: (1) lawsuits
alleging that Obama is not a US citizen are undergirded by unconscious
biases that more easily associate whites, versus blacks, with symbols of
America; (2) unconscious racial bias is a primary predictor of opposition to Obama's efforts to pass various forms of legislation; (3) images of
Obama associating him with various forms of primates serve to unconsciously dehumanize him among onlookers, putting him at greater risk
for assassination; and (4) Obama's election and the resulting backlash
demonstrate, more than ever, the continued significance of race in electoral politics, which likely reverberates to congressional elections. And
in conclusion, we argue that much of the aftermath of the 2012 reelection of Obama demonstrates the continued conflation of whiteness
with US citizenship.

But such racial ideology does not permeate the ether. An unvarying
form of racism does not robotically control us or lurk evenly within
all our heads. While there is some social-scientific work out there that
would come close to making such claims, we find such a view unten-
able. Expressed racial biases, whether conscious or unconscious, do
not exist in ahistorical or acultural vacuums and, as a result, are rarely
automatic. Rather, the political racism we cover in this book is indicative of a shared, intersubjective, and cultural phenomenon that is often
measurable through implicit and explicit bias tests, as well as within
the rhetoric and discourse expressed in the context of political debates,
and in the materially unequal society we call the American economy.

Racialized politics are certainly hegemonic and widely shared, but such systematic racism is institutionalized in our political processes and discourse inasmuch as it exists in our shared ideological frameworks. And on the macro and the micro levels both, racism's presence and salience vary by context, by interaction, by institution, and certainly by what different political ideologies are at play and what interests are known to be at stake.

1

The Grand Old Party and African Americans

A Brief Historical Overview

The history of the "Grand Old Party" (GOP) and African Americans is a rich and tumultuous one. And it is a relationship guided by factors put into play long before the formation of the Republican Party in 1854. Chief among those factors is the subject of race.[1] This chapter provides a brief account of the Republican Party's relationship to the black/white color line, especially how the GOP shifted to being the party of white conservatism after the political realignment of the Southern Strategy of the 1940s. In turn, we present this chapter—largely for those unacquainted with the role of race in the US political two-party system—as a historical aid to understanding the contemporary currents that undergird the political Right's relationship with Obama and its racist rhetoric.

The Political Party System of the United States

The dominant two-party system of the United States is a now-commonplace structure of modern government, but the country did not always have political parties.[2] After the American Revolution, the "founding fathers" held a series of conventions to develop a government that would connect the thirteen colonies that had hitherto operated independently of one another under the control of King George III. The Constitutional Convention of 1787 was crucial in charting the course for the country, particularly because the racialized Constitution it produced protected only a small number of the residents as full citizens under the newly formed nation-state. In particular, when the Naturalization Act of 1790 was passed, women, Native Americans, and blacks were left out of this social and legal contract—only white male property owners (approximately 15 percent of the nation's population) had the legal right to vote.[3] Moreover, out of a population of about five million, nearly one person in five was black and enslaved.[4] From the outset, people of color were looked upon as less than human; certain propertied white males were seen as worthy of citizenship and the "inalienable rights" of which Thomas Jefferson wrote in the Declaration of Independence. Those whites deemed worthy of full citizenship were thought the proper administrators of the nation—a nation conceived and built under a chattel slavery system based on racial categorization. And the early white leaders of the burgeoning United States already looked upon themselves as potential victims of a growing hoard of darker brethren due to the growing demographic size of the African American population and increasingly stringent critiques of slavery, which together threatened an end to the economic supremacy of both the industrialists of the North and the planter class of the South, as well as the social supremacy of the poor whites everywhere else.

Under this system, slavery thrived, and its importance to the American economy and social system was paramount.[5] Plantation owners and agricultural production, the maritime trade industry, textile manufacturing, even insurance companies depended on slavery for their livelihood.[6] Delegates at the Constitutional Convention retained the "peculiar institution" of slavery, yet not all were of one mind on the matter.[7] The question of slavery led to many battles, both figuratively and literally. One of the major points of contention was whether slaves should be included in population censuses for taxation measurements and congressional representation. Northern delegates argued that only the free and enfranchised population—white male property owners—should be counted.[8] If slaves were enfranchised, then southern delegates would hold sway in the House of Representatives. Hence, many southerners argued that slaves should be counted. The Three-Fifths Compromise was placed in Article 1, section 2, paragraph 3 of the US Constitution to assuage both sides.[9] It designated that three-fifths of a state's slave population would be counted in determining that state's representation in the House of Representatives.[10]

Just two years after the Constitutional Convention of 1787, George Washington became the first president of the United States. Washington set the standard for many a president, including a four-year term limit and the ownership of slaves. However, he did not set the precedent of leading, or even being a member, of a political party. While

Washington unofficially supported many of the programs sponsored by the newly formed Federalist group, he was a staunch detractor of political factionalism; Washington believed that those who occupied the presidency should avoid political party affiliation.[11] Washington's "Farewell Address" of 1796 was a stern warning against partisanship, sectionalism, and involvement in foreign wars.[12] Yet, as this address was read, a group calling themselves the Democratic-Republicans recruited Thomas Jefferson to run for president.[13] Jefferson lost to John Adams by only three electoral votes and became his vice president.

John Adams, the second president, overtly aligned himself with the Federalists. The Federalists were an influential faction that predated American political parties. Led by Alexander Hamilton, they were primarily men of considerable material means who began to operate like a political party.[14] They soon reached beyond their upper-class comrades to recruit support from local chambers of commerce, the Society of Cincinnati (a group for military officers), and rich men's societies and clubs.[15]

Jefferson opposed many of the issues supported by the Federalists. Jefferson's followers were aligned with agrarian interests, and they advocated a decentralized government (akin to the contemporary promotion of local and states' rights).[16] A showdown was brewing: Adams and the Federalists had wealth, social standing, and political sophistication; Jefferson's Democratic-Republicans had raw numbers.[17]

Jefferson rallied substantial support against Adams's second bid to the presidency.[18] Jefferson and supporters created local political clubs to be "soldiers in a national 'Republican' movement."[19] Through their efforts, in 1801 Jefferson was elected the third president of the United States as a member of the Democratic-Republican Party. Although Jefferson and the Democratic-Republicans' views on the Constitution and policy were clear, their views on race and slavery were muddled.[20] On the one hand, Jefferson officially opposed slavery; he even attempted to write a condemnation of slavery into the Declaration of Independence, but the passage critical of the slave trade was deleted by Congress—a change that Jefferson resented.[21] Jefferson unsuccessfully attempted to abolish slavery in Virginia, famously stating, "Nothing is more certainly written in the book of fate than that these people are to be free."[22] But on the other hand, Jefferson owned slaves, most likely fathered children with his slave Sally Hemings, and wrote white-supremacist interpretations of the biological and cultural differences between the races in *Notes on the State of Virginia*.[23] Furthermore, the two presidents who followed Jefferson (James Madison and James Monroe) were also slave owners from Virginia as well as members of the Democratic-Republican Party.[24]

Despite the centrality of slavery in the agrarian culture of the South and the industrial culture of the North, future presidents spoke less about the institution, at least in terms of national policy. But James Monroe did not have that option. In 1819, Missouri applied for admission into the United States as a slave state. Northern politicians were especially upset because this would alter the balance between the eleven free states and eleven slave states.[25] This resulted in the Missouri Compromise of 1820, which admitted Missouri as a slave state and added Maine as a free state. At this time, the Democratic-Republicans were virtually the only party in existence following the slow decline of the Federalist Party after the War of 1812.[26]

By the end of John Quincy Adams's term as president in 1829, the Democratic-Republican Party had split apart.[27] In the 1824 election, most of the party boycotted the caucus; only a small group backed William Crawford to run against Adams.[28] The Crawford faction included the "Radicals," "Old Republicans," and "National Republicans." These groups remained committed to states' rights and slavery and were distrustful of the nationalizing program promoted by both Henry Clay and John C. Calhoun.[29] Adams's supporters—in league with Clay and Calhoun—favored modernization, banks, industrial development, and federal spending for roads and other internal improvements—and called themselves the Democratic-Republicans.[30] In this context of a developing political bifurcation, slavery and race became key issues they used to malign and mudsling their opponents.[31] For example, in leading up to the 1824 election, one National Republican newspaper, the *Cincinnati Gazette*, published an editorial by Charles Hammond, in which he wrote, "General Andrew Jackson's mother was a COMMON PROSTITUTE, brought to this country by the British soldiers! She afterward married a MULATTO, with whom she had several children, of which number General JACKSON IS ONE!!!"[32]

This split—particularly on questions of racial difference, slavery, and nonwhite political participation—was formative of the two-party system we recognize today. The modern Democratic Party was formed in the early 1830s by factions of the Democratic-Republican Party due primarily to the efforts of Martin Van Buren and his support of Andrew Jackson, a slave owner.[33] During Jackson's administration, in 1833, South Carolina attempted to nullify the high tariffs from the federal government.[34] This action drew a battle line of sectionalism on the national map. Although the fear was not directly stated by the southern politicians, the high tariffs were seen as potentially devastating to the slave-based economies.[35]

The growing concern over slavery in the 1830s and 1840s put a strain on the newly formed Democratic Party. Abolitionists petitioned Congress to abolish slavery in 1834 and 1835.[36] But Democrat Martin Van Buren, then vice president, helped to establish the congressional adoption of a "gag rule" that required the immediate tabling of all such anti-slavery petitions.[37] Yet by 1840, the American Anti-Slavery Society had about two thousand branches and two hundred thousand members.[38] This movement assisted disgruntled members of the Democratic Party (upset at the party's being led by wealthy slave owners), abolitionists, Conscience Whigs, and advocates of land disbursements to "settlers" to band together to form the Free Soil Party in 1848.[39] They opposed slavery in every territory.

With the issue of race and power already fraying the fabric of the young nation, the Clay Compromise of 1850 attempted to quell this growing divide.[40] The compromise allowed California to enter the union as a free state, gave popular sovereignty for the remaining territories (leaving the slavery question up to the states' voters), and adjusted the Texas border. Importantly, the Clay Compromise abolished the slave trade, but not slavery itself, and provided for a tough fugitive slave law. As a result, the compromise only temporarily settled some of the division over slavery and many, if not most, remained dissatisfied.[41]

Race, Slavery, and the Birth of the GOP

By 1854, four years after the compromise of 1850, there were approximately twenty-five million people in the United States.[42] Hundreds of thousands were new immigrants.[43] Immigrants usually identified with the Democratic Party and had a large impact on local and state politics.[44] As a response, "native," Protestant, white Americans formed the "Know Nothing Party" in order to oppose immigrants and Roman Catholicism. Alternatively, members of the newly formed Whig Party were suspicious of the executive branch of government. They believed that Congress should hold the majority of power and supported internal infrastructure improvements to the nation.[45]

The questions of race and slavery began to blur party lines, and northern and southern factions began to develop among Democrats, Know Nothings, and Whigs.[46] The Kansas-Nebraska Act of 1854 proved a final straw for many. Designed by Democrat Stephen A. Douglas, the act gave Kansas and Nebraska popular sovereignty, which allowed them to choose whether they wanted slavery in their territories.[47] The act upset many northerners and abolitionists as it would allow slavery in territories above the parallel 36°30′ north line—the slave/free line passed by the US Congress in the Missouri Compromise of 1820.[48]

It was in this environment that dissident Democrats, Whigs, and Free Soilers met on February 28, 1854, in Ripon, Wisconsin, to form a "Republican" Party.[49] A second coalition of Republicans met a month later on March 20 in Jackson, Michigan, where a state convention was held.[50] Candidates were nominated and a platform was written.[51] Over the next few years, the newly formed Republican Party drew from Know Nothings and Whigs as both of those parties fell into disarray due to internal bickering.[52] Given that many of the initial Republicans were antislavery advocates who already received black support, an appeal to join the party was made to blacks.[53]

The GOP and the Civil War

Democrats in the mid-nineteenth century were the party of limited government and of white supremacy.[54] The large southern Democratic wing exclaimed that slavery was a positive good for both master and slave. Many highlighted the claim that slavery brought Christianity to the blacks, and was thus a beneficial institution.[55] Many northern

Democrats were also virulent racists. Illinois politician Stephen Douglas stated, "I do not question Mr. Lincoln's conscientious belief that the negro was made his equal and hence is his brother, but for my own part, I do not regard the negro as my equal and positively deny that he is my brother or any kin to me whatever."[56]

Conversely, the Republican Party's efforts to curb slavery were explicit. However, historians have questioned whether the Republicans were sincere opponents of slavery.[57] Republicans indicated a belief that southerners would make slavery a national institution without restrictions like the Missouri Compromise or the Kansas-Nebraska Act.[58] Republican Party leaders used antisouthernism, as much as abstract morality issues, to fuel distaste for slavery.[59] Republicans were also far from being racial saints, but worked to downplay or disguise their racial animus. For example, Abraham Lincoln voiced the opinion of many, if not most, white northerners when he said,

> I am not nor ever have been in favor of making voters or jurors of negroes, nor of qualifying them to hold office, nor to intermarry with white people; and I will say in addition to this that there is a physical difference between the white and black races which I believe will forever forbid the two races living together on terms of social and political equality.[60]

The questions of race and slavery generated a tense political environment. Some members of Congress resorted to toting pistols during a congressional debate with Republican John Sherman because he endorsed a book by a white North Carolinian, Hinton Rowan Helper, who criticized slaveholding as poisonous to the interests of all whites.[61] The Republicans used the anxiety over race and slavery to enlarge their party and increase their chances of winning the 1860 election against Stephen Douglas.[62] Consequently, Lincoln won the election and became the sixteenth president of the United States. But just after the Republican victory, and before the new administration took office on March 4, 1861, seven cotton states declared their secession from the United States to form the Confederate States of America (CSA), resulting in a Civil War from 1861 to 1865.

The Racial Politics of Reconstruction

The Reconstruction era created some political rights for African Americans in the United States for the first time. Hiram Rhodes Revels and Blanche K. Bruce, both Republicans from Mississippi, were the first and second African Americans elected to the US Senate, respectively.[63] Over a dozen African Americans served in the House of Representatives during Reconstruction—they were all Republicans.[64] Republicans who favored Reconstruction's expansion of rights for black Americans and a stringent policy toward the South became known as "Radicals."[65] However, much of the Radical Republican agenda was curtained on April 14, 1865, when Lincoln was assassinated. Lincoln's successor, Andrew Johnson (who refused to officially join a party as president), was a white supremacist who did not believe in black enfranchisement. Johnson declared, "This is a country for white men, and by God, as long as I am president, it shall be a government by white men."[66] He also opposed the monumental Freedman's Bureau and Reconstruction legislation.[67] The Radical Republican Congress upheld and increased Reconstruction efforts, but soon Democrats attacked Republicans for seeking rights for African Americans. With waning federal support for Reconstruction measures, many southern states enacted "Black Codes" in their legislatures, used violence, and voted in former Confederate officers to all levels of government, banding behind the Democratic Party.[68]

No longer as politically efficacious, the Radical Republican commitment to racial equality stalled. During the 1868 elections, Republicans decided to minimize issues surrounding race after receiving signs from northern voters that they did not endorse Republican efforts to achieve suffrage for blacks. In 1868, Democratic presidential candidate Horatio Seymour from New York, vice presidential candidate Frank Blair from Missouri, and other Democrats (claiming to be defenders of Stephen Douglas) openly declared that they wanted "a government by white men, of white men, for white men."[69] Moreover, and foreshadowing many of the political uses of race today, Democrats played the race card by accusing the Republicans of subjecting the South to "negro supremacy."[70]

As the United States slowly approached the twentieth century, the history of the Civil War and Reconstruction was being written by southern Democrats. These accounts—widely read publications

between 1877 and 1965—generally maligned Republicans as racial ideo-
logues rather than sound leaders.[71] As a response, the GOP began to
reach out to southern whites and purposefully changed some of their
policies because they no longer had enough votes from blacks due to
Black Code disenfranchisement in southern states. Hence, "lily-white
Republicans"—white Republicans who advocated white supremacy and
segregation—developed and grew in number.[72] Still, the GOP enjoyed
sustained support from African Americans because of loyalty to the
"party of Lincoln"—a loyalty that would persist for six more decades.[73]

From the Death of Reconstruction to the Great Crash, 1877–1929

The period from after Reconstruction through the Depression was especially hard on African Americans. Blacks faced virulent racism in both
the North and the South. They were offered little, if any, protection from
either the Democrats or the Republicans.[74] US presidents demonstrated
limited, if any, concern for the civil and human rights of African Americans.[75] For example, Democrat Woodrow Wilson was not a supporter
of civil rights.[76] He believed that segregation was in the best interest of
blacks, including segregation at the federal level.[77] During this period
Congress did not pass or support antilynching legislation or other civil
rights measures, despite tireless efforts from groups like the NAACP
and individuals like Ida B. Wells-Barnett and W. E. B. Du Bois.[78]

While African Americans who voted during this period usually identified with the Republican Party, black voting was difficult, to say the
least.[79] The overwhelming majority of blacks lived in the South, where
they were legally disenfranchised through methods like the grandfather
clauses, poll taxes, and white primaries.[80] It was during this period that
a slow shift of African American support from Republicans to Democrats began. Given the Democratic stranglehold in the South, a few
southern black Democrats were elected to local offices between 1890
and 1915.[81] African American votes would become increasingly important as blacks migrated north by the hundreds of thousands in search
of a better way of life. As a result, they formed large African American communities throughout the North and Midwest with strong, uni-
fied political blocs that were slowly falling under a form of populism
spurred on by the Democratic Party.[82]

A Racial Shift in the New Deal

The Great Depression was a devastating blow to all Americans, but particularly to southerners and African Americans, because they were already on the underside of the economy. From 1929 to 1932, unemployment skyrocketed from 1.6 million to 12.8 million and from 3 percent to 25 percent of laborers.[83] Even in the midst of widespread economic suffering, many southern whites remained opposed to Republicans because of their past support of racial equality. Moreover, with the election of President Herbert Hoover and his commitment to entrepreneurial capitalism, Republicans were seen as pro–big business and not for the common (white) man.[84] In this climate, Hoover overwhelmingly lost his bid for reelection to Franklin D. Roosevelt in 1932.

FDR enacted ambitious projects to improve the economy, particularly through his landmark program, the New Deal. As a result, Democrats became more appealing to black voting blocs.[85] Intentionally appealing to black voters, the Democratic Party seated blacks as full-fledged convention delegates for the first time.[86] Black Americans began to herald the New Deal that provided jobs through programs like the Works Progress Administration.[87] The black shift to the Democratic Party was most recognizable in black votes for FDR's reelection in 1936.[88] Roosevelt formed what is known as the "black cabinet" to address issues relevant to black communities, of which Mary McLeod Bethune was, arguably, its most famous member.[89] While these measures generated the beginnings of a racialized political realignment, FDR was not to go out of his way for racial equality—especially when it might jeopardize other objectives.[90] For example, no civil rights legislation passed during Roosevelt's four terms as president,[91] and NAACP president Roy Wilkins stated, "Mr. Roosevelt was no friend of the Negro. He wasn't an enemy, but he wasn't a friend."[92] Roosevelt seldom directly challenged the powerful southern wing of the Democratic Party on racial issues, but many of his policies had unintended consequences, which inevitably promoted the interests of a more dynamic, entrepreneurial generation of southerners less committed than their predecessors to maintaining tradition.[93]

The Beginnings of the Southern Strategy
and the Dixiecrat Revolution

While FDR and the New Deal cemented blacks to the Democratic
Party, it was Harry S. Truman's commitment to civil rights that further entrenched black support for the Democrats.[94] Truman pushed for
the Fair Employment Practices Act, reached out to black voters, and
made a worldwide radio address to the NAACP.[95] As a consequence, the
1940s saw many a white southerner disgruntled with Democrats; they
doubted the ability and willingness of national Democratic leaders to
uphold the Jim Crow system.[96] By the 1940s and '50s, to combat many
of the policies of Roosevelt, Truman, and Eisenhower, southern Democrats and conservative Republicans formed an alliance called the "Inner
Club."[97] Reaching the breaking point, southern Democrats stormed
out of the 1948 Democratic National Convention after hearing about
Truman's civil rights plan.[98] Resultantly, they formed the States' Rights
Democratic Party, more commonly known as the "Dixiecrats." Led by
Strom Thurmond, the party ran on a platform of segregation and racial
purity. It only won thirty-nine electoral votes, but the 1948 elections signaled a sea change in modern politics—all over the issue of race.[99]

The Dixiecrat movement was principally a revolt of the Black Belt,
heavily shaped by its antebellum plantation and antipopulist past.[100] The
primary motivation for the formation and spread of the movement was
to maintain white supremacy, prevent federal entities from intervening
in their supremacist system, and curtail the growing agitation among
African Americans in their region for racial and economic democracy,
especially coming from returning World War II veterans.[101] Southern
Democratic politicians held a virtually united opposition to organized
labor and high wages for working-class whites. As they strove to shape
public opinion and behavior during the course of a campaign, political
elites constructed appealing narratives and views that mastered the use
of negative images of African Americans and outside agitators to maintain the raced and classed status quo.[102]

African Americans protested at varying levels throughout the reign
of the elites in the South, but they generally met little success until the
middle of the twentieth century.[103] Experiences during and after the
1930s and 1940s increased the militancy and urgency of the demand for

rights among southern blacks.[104] The New Deal and World War II freed blacks from their tie to the land. Union organizers attempted to mobilize southern blacks in the 1930s and 1940s. Supreme Court decisions, executive orders, and other federal measures motivated African Americans as their rights increased.[105] The Supreme Court ruled in the 1944 *Smith v. Allwright* case that the Texas white primary law violated the Fifteenth Amendment. This ruling gradually dismantled all white primaries across the nation.[106] The African American fight for civil rights during World War II led the African American press to call it the "Double V" movement—fighting for democracy at home and abroad.[107]

Democratic southerners from politically peripheral states like Arkansas, Tennessee, Florida, and North Carolina were more hesitant to walk out on the Democratic Party.[108] Historians Earl and Merle Black attest to the fact that there were fewer blacks in those areas, and although racism was still strong among whites in those states, they were less concerned about it given that they felt less confronted by blacks.[109] In fact, two of the peripheral states, Tennessee and North Carolina, already had several Republican representatives in Congress. The Republicans could have had a more effective presence elsewhere in the South, but the party suffered from racial factionalism among the liberal, moderate, and conservative Republicans through the 1940s, 1950s, and 1960s.[110] Mary Brennan attributes the severe factionalism to party members focusing on their differences instead of their similarities.[111] However, the "Southern Strategy" continued to gain momentum in the late 1950s and early 1960s by attracting discontented and racially paranoid southern white voters, who saw race relations as an out-of-control issue that would destroy Western civilization if the federal government continued to "meddle" in local matters.[112]

A Hard Right Turn for the GOP

Conservatives generally disagreed with Republican president Eisenhower's administration (1953–1961) and believed it grew the welfare state for the undeserving segment of the populace.[113] Toward the end of Eisenhower's administration, businessman Robert Welch formed the John Birch Society in 1958.[114] The society was, and still is, a radically conservative group that believes that government should be limited and that clandestine "forces" within the United States wish to institute worldwide communism. They claimed that many American leaders were Communists and thought that even conservative Republicans, like Richard Nixon, were not conservative enough.[115] Many, if not most, conservatives tried to distance themselves from this extremist organization at the edge of the party, and several denounced it.[116]

To many Republicans in the 1960s, groups like the John Birch Society were seen as fringe and atypical elements of the GOP. They failed to see the growth of ultraconservatism in their party and the ultraconservative discontent with the traditional liberal doctrine.[117] Divisions between liberal and conservative Republicans became more apparent during the 1960 presidential campaign of Richard Nixon. Thurston Morton, Republican National Committee chair at the time, complained that the party had "paid too little attention to specific segments of the electorate—such as the Negro vote" and had not fought "hard enough in the centers of mass population."[118] Ray Bliss, state chair of the Republicans in Ohio, encouraged party members to create "special activities" aimed at enticing various ethnic groups, women, blacks, and youth to join the GOP.[119] Yet, GOP leadership largely ignored these appeals.

With the Civil Rights Movement picking up speed in the 1960s due to sit-ins, bus rides, marches, boycotts, lawsuits, and other modes of activism, the progressive agenda of John F. Kennedy carried the Democrats into the White House in 1960. Kennedy was perceived as a huge threat to Republicans, especially conservatives, because of his liberal image. He received large support from various black voting blocs, especially after his brother Robert Kennedy helped get Martin Luther King Jr. released from jail.[120]

After JFK's assassination in 1963, GOP presidential candidate Senator Barry Goldwater emerged to challenge Lyndon Johnson. A Republican senator from Arizona, Goldwater emerged as a strong conservative and staunch advocate of states' rights. While Goldwater avoided directly speaking about race in his campaign, he relied heavily on coded words and racialized topics to unite whites behind a program of racial and economic conservatism,[121] from which he benefited in white support from the South.[122] Goldwater's implicit appeals to race were bookended by other GOP candidates' more overt uses of racial fear mongering. When Strom Thurmond (a 1948 presidential candidate for the "States' Rights

Democratic Party," aka the "Dixiecrats") switched his party allegiance to the Republicans in 1964, he set a precedent for other GOP members to oppose measures to achieve racial equality and to abandon the chase for black votes. Thurmond, like many GOP members, opposed the 1964 Civil Rights Act and helped unify the Republican Party under the banner of staunch conservatism by critiquing Johnson's handling of the disorder and violence of various 1960s protest movements. The GOP actively contended that the Civil Rights Act would only worsen race relations.[123] Conservatives became a dominant force in the 1960s and by 1964 had gained control of the party.[124] Consequently, the riots of the summer of 1964, the Civil Rights Movement, and the growth of Black Power together put Lyndon Johnson in a precarious situation— he had to keep from alienating white voters without losing his black constituency.[125]

President Johnson won the presidential election in 1964 and endorsed the passage of the Voting Rights Act of 1965. Yet, in *The Race Card*, political scientist Tali Mendelberg writes, "Landmark breaks with legal discrimination did not remove race from electoral politics, they enhanced the importance of race in elections."[126] In fact, the 1964 election—and the civil rights revolution with which it was closely linked— pushed the two-party system into alignment along racial lines.[127] By 1964, with the Democratic victory of Lyndon Johnson over Republican candidate Barry Goldwater, the Southern Strategy was said to have been fully implemented and successful. Numerous white voters, formerly loyal Democrats, defected to the Republican Party and many black voters, formerly loyal Republicans, became Democrats after the 1964 elections.[128] By the late 1960s, the GOP had a firm hold on the white and conservative "Solid South"; the Southern Strategy led to a full-scale electoral realignment of southern states to the Republican Party, but at the expense of losing more than 90 percent of black voters to the Democratic Party.[129] Since the advent of the modern Civil Rights Movement, the vast majority of African Americans have uniformly voted for every Democrat who has run for president.[130]

The GOP and the Post–Civil Rights Era

In the contemporary United States, race, class, and religion continue to explicitly divide along party lines. But since there is no longer a "Solid South," both parties are now competitive nationally. In the years prior to the 1960s, the Republicans depended on huge majorities in the North to offset their devastating losses against the Democrats in the South.[131] Small-town and rural Republicans now preach low taxes, anti-union capitalism, and the belief that the United States is a meritocracy, and they hold a strong commitment to family and community.[132] They generally focus on economic and social conservatism and veil any racial rhetoric, unlike the old southern Democrats.[133]

Yet, racial messaging, as in years past, is omnipresent in the post–civil rights era. Politicians convey racial messages when two contradictory conditions hold: "(1) they wish to avoid violating the norm of racial equality, and (2) they face incentives to mobilize racially resentful white voters."[134] These conditions hold for most Republican politicians and for many, if not most, white voters.[135] Yet, both of the major parties have used the aforementioned tactics at different times.[136] White Republicans, particularly in the contemporary South, perpetuate and symbolize the rule of white majorities; they attract substantial white votes. White Democratic victories have rested upon the rule of biracial coalitions.[137] For example, both Bill Clinton and Barack Obama were elected with the help of strong biracial coalitions.[138] They had the solid support of blacks, albeit slightly differing levels of white support.[139] Alternatively, districts with very low black populations had the most potential for receiving large Republican gains.[140] Republican representation of low-black-population districts in the South increased from less than two-fifths in the late 1980s to 46 percent in the 1990s.[141]

Recent Republican approaches toward securing black votes have been criticized. Tali Mendelberg examined how Republicans made some efforts to reach out to African Americans, but concluded that "their efforts show that they are self-deluded about African American voters because they sometimes assume that they can get black votes with token gestures or patronage."[142] Mendelberg goes on to suggest that modern conservatives, particularly southern Republicans, fall victim to the "barbecue syndrome": the belief that barbecues will attract African

Americans and that the substance of Republican positions means nothing to most African Americans. Tali Mendelberg wrote, "Republicans cannot win the votes of significant numbers of African Americans with racially and economically conservative programs. All the barbecues in the world won't change that."[143] Conversely, Republicans have incentives to appeal to white voters' racial resentments and fears over matters and stereotypes that many whites still have about race, crime, and poverty.[144]

In the 2000 Republican National Convention, the GOP presented itself as a more racially inclusive party.[145] In order for this presentation to be believable, the Republican display of diversity had to deviate from voters' existing pictures of the party.[146] In a CBS News monthly poll, taken six months before the 2000 convention, 79 percent of blacks and 49.2 percent of whites believed that the Democratic Party better represented the interests of blacks.[147] Alternatively, only 12.3 percent of whites and 4.2 percent of blacks believed that the Republican Party better represented African Americans.[148] George W. Bush's appointments of Colin Powell and Condoleezza Rice to the position of secretary of state, making them the first African American and first African American woman, respectively, to hold this position could also partially be attributable to an effort to paint an image of the GOP as being more racially inclusive.

The two-party system has undergone many changes since its establishment. Both Democrats and Republicans have radically altered their approach toward racial issues. The party that was racially conservative is now the more racially liberal party, and vice versa.[149] Great strides have been made in both parties, culminating in Michael Steele leading the GOP and President Barack Obama, Democrat, leading the nation. Black grass-roots vigilance and white political allies helped overcome seemingly insurmountable obstacles and transformed the Solid South into a Shifting South. In the chapters that follow, we examine the continued use of race by the GOP and other right-wing elements to undermine and critique Barack Obama and African Americans. Just as race was the crucial factor in the passage of legislation and the recruitment of different demographics for voter support, so, we demonstrate, anti-black rhetoric continues to be used for political mobilization.

2

Unsweet Tea and Labor Pains

The Tea Party, Birthers, and Obama

On December 12, 2011, right-wing commentator and former Fox News host Glenn Beck directed a statement toward the Tea Party Movement (TPM): "[A]sk yourself this, Tea Party: is it about Obama's race? Because that's what it appears to be to me. If you're against him [Barack Obama] but you're for this guy [Newt Gingrich], it must be about race."[1]

When Glenn Beck—one of the nation's most incendiary commentators, a former organizer and defender of the TPM, and a man who attempted to alienate Obama from white voters when he said that the president had a "deep-seated hatred for white people or the white culture"—finds the Tea Party's racism beyond the pale, then such an evaluation certainly serves as a critical barometer of the extremity of racial animus directed at the nation's forty-fourth president. The right-wing backlash against the first black occupant of 1600 Pennsylvania Avenue indicates a visceral form of hostility intimately linked to xenophobic, nativist, authoritarian, and racist rhetoric and iconography that seeks to frame Barack Obama as an out-of-place "other" who does not qualify as a "real American." Such invective exists in a bizarre political world in which race is both explicitly and implicitly evoked and then shunned at what may seem to be the most arbitrary and strangest of times. In fact, the contemporary intersection of race and political discourse recalls the strange world of *Alice in Wonderland* in which the Cheshire Cat said, "We're all mad here," and Alice remarked, "It would be so nice if something made sense for a change."

Many conservative voices shun such characterizations. They claim to represent little more than neutral, mundane, and color-blind support of "limited government," "Constitutional originalism," and laissez-faire individualism. Moreover, some claim—as *New Yorker* essayist Hendrik Hertzberg does—that opposition to Obama stems not so much from race but from "Obama's erudition, his ivy-league-ness, his urbanity, his citizen-of-the-worldness, his foreign-sounding name, his respect for authority of reason and science, his 'aristocratic' 'aloofness.'"[2] In what follows, we directly challenge this diagnosis. While race is not the only variable that is substantively significant in the meaning making over Obama, we show that it is certainly one of the most predictive. Drawing from empirical evidence, social-scientific studies, and media coverage, we demonstrate the integral place of racial animus directed at nonwhites in general, and Obama in particular, within the Birther and Tea Party movements.

The Whiteness of Belonging

Sociologist Evelyn Nakano Glenn wrote that "[c]itizenship is not just a matter of formal legal status; it is a matter of belonging, which requires recognition by other members of the community. Community members participate in drawing the boundaries of citizenship and defining who is entitled to civil, political, and social rights by granting or withholding recognition."[3] The activism from the Birthers and Tea Party Movement members covered later in this chapter reflects the arbitrary white demand that Obama somehow prove his de jure US citizenship and de facto cultural "Americanness." This dynamic invites several considerations.

First, beliefs in nonwhites' (especially blacks') supposed natural or learned inferiority is widespread. The right-wing media is replete with discussions of black cultural and biological pathologies and dysfunctions, and historically, African Americans had to jump through a series of legal hoops to prove their citizenship and belonging. As a consequence, black attempts to attain leadership positions are often directly opposed or subjected to harsher and more virulent critiques than white attempts to lead.[4] The rhetoric of "bad values" and "pathological behavior" reigns as a powerful tool for media discussion of people of color. For example, after the housing market crash of 2006–2007, many blamed African Americans and undocumented Latinos for holding millions of bad mortgages and causing the housing bubble to burst. The problem was—as with blaming Jews for the spread of the fourteenth-century Black Plague—that it was not true.[5]

Second, and piggybacking off the first consideration, this discourse provides a glimpse into not only how nonwhites are discursively "othered" from inclusion in the national project but also how a kind of true and authentic citizenship aligns with a specific and ideal form of whiteness.[6] These narratives reveal the sustained conflation of citizenship with a nativist, xenophobic, Christian, hyper-masculine, white identity that stakes claim to being objective, moral, truth-seeking, and nearly omniscient. The ideal is the default position by which authentic claims to Americanness must be proffered. The racial, religious, and regional othering of Obama makes meaning of his body—and presidency—as "out of place" and illegitimate. Regardless of his policies and positions, Obama cannot attain that ideal type of citizenship because of its (white) racial character. Conservative media discourse can deflect charges of racism or racial bias by claiming that they operate from a principled and color-blind position, while paradoxically denying the resiliency of white-supremacist citizenship by demanding that Obama prove his citizenship, educational attainments, or religious beliefs.

Third, due to a more than 230-year US association of white men with the presidency (not to mention white male providence over full citizenship and civil rights during a majority of that time), political authority, leadership, competence, and—perhaps most importantly—the benefit of the doubt have been effectively defined as characteristics natural to white men. This correlation, and the media narratives that propel it, reveal the relatively accepted entitlement of white people to repeatedly and publicly question the national belonging of people of color. This is apparent, for example, in the repeated media questioning of the legitimacy of Obama's citizenship, patriotism, and dedication with neither fear of repercussion nor embarrassment and shame. These narratives reflect—and even produce—a sense of political legitimacy and quasi-religious calling endemic to the questioning of how someone deemed "alien," "un-American," or simply "black" could subvert the implicit white-supremacist social contract to become president.[7]

Fourth, the small yet important challenges to absolute white political dominance over the past few years have resulted in virulent media attacks on nonwhites for being too sensitive and/or wedded to a politically correct form of antiwhite racism. Whether intentional or not, such a white backlash in the media works as an effective political rallying cry for whites who feel their racial privilege slipping within the context of a changing world. By raising the banner of whiteness-under-assault, even mainstream news accounts of demographic changes were framed in ways that played to whites' racial paranoia, such as occurred on May 17, 2012, when the following three headlines appeared: "Whites Account for under Half of Births in U.S." (the *New York Times*), "Minority Babies Majority in U.S." (the *Washington Post*), and "Minorities Are Now a Majority of Births" (*USA Today*). Pat Buchanan then picked up on these stories to plug his book *Suicide of a Superpower,* by drawing attention to one of its key chapters, "The End of White America," and claiming that the rising tide of nonwhites would unfairly take resources away from hard-working and deserving whites.[8] Bear in mind, these stories were already primed by a rising tide of whites-under-attack stories, like the one that ran on CNN in March of 2011, entitled "Are Whites Racially Oppressed?" The article began,

> They marched on Washington to reclaim civil rights. They complained of voter intimidation at the polls. They called for ethnic studies programs to promote racial pride. They are, some say, the new face of racial oppression in this nation—and their faces are white. . . . A growing number of white Americans are acting like a racially oppressed majority. They are adopting the language and protest tactics of an embattled minority group.[9]

Such language carries racial resonance by painting whites as the quintessential racial victims of our day and age, and by blaming Obama and other nonwhites as outsiders and intruders bent on oppressing whites. The effect is the political and social marginalization of Obama's presidency because of his race, even as his detractors claim that we live in a "post-racial" society. In what follows we demonstrate how the Tea Party Movement and Birthers attempted this marginalization tactic.

Unsweet Tea: "Take It Back, Take Your Country Back"

The Tea Party Movement (TPM) is a loose confederation of various individuals and organizations that purport to have organized to reduce budget deficits, trim or eliminate taxes, and curtail the power, scope,

and size of the federal government. At its core lie six national organizational networks: (1) the FreedomWorks Tea Party, (2) the 1776
Tea Party (more commonly known as "TeaParty.org"), (3) Tea Party
Nation, (4) Tea Party Patriots, (5) ResistNet, and (6) Tea Party Express.
Not only do these various organizations often exceed their stated ideological goals to weigh in, quite heavily, on social issues related to marriage, abortion, and welfare, but they are, pardon the pun, steeped in
strong opinions on race and national identity.[10] As Adele Stan writes
on AlterNet, "While economic insecurity gave the Tea Party movement its *raison d'etre*, its ferocity derives from the complicating factors
of race and culture."[11] The TPM has attracted the likes of former KKK
grand wizard David Duke, TeaParty.org was formed out of the Minutemen (the anti-immigrant and nativist vigilante organization), and both
ResistNet and Tea Party Patriots serve as safe havens for an array of
anti-immigrant racists.[12]

A rallying cry of the TPM is "Take It Back, Take Your Country
Back"—quite an overt nationalist mantra. Undergirding this refrain is
the notion that TPM members and supporters are the "real Americans"
who must take their country back from the usurping, imposter, alien,
and inauthentic Americans who are—in the eyes of many in the TPM—
darker in hue, non-Christian, and left-leaning. Such a sour note may
not resonate with every TPM member or supporter, but on the heels
of Obama's election, it is telling that five of the six TPM factions have
Birthers in their leadership. If the overwhelmingly white and middle-
class movement wants to take *their* country back, the questions remain:
from whom and *toward what*? In *The Black Scholar*, Sundiata K. Cha-Jua
writes,

> A significant percentage of white Americans viewed President Obama's
> election in dystopian terms. They believe the dark rabble had seized
> "their" country. Angry white nationalists, led by the Tea Party, have
> mobilized to "take back their country." Much of the anger generated by
> Obama's election resulted from the dread many whites feel toward the
> electoral coalition that propelled him into the White House. The right
> fears a dark and progressive country. . . . The right does not so much fear
> Obama as they fear that he is the prelude to something far darker and
> more progressive.[13]

To fully answer both *from whom* and *toward what* the TPM wishes to take their country, we next examine the racial elements of TPM nationalism, specifically as they pertain to the backlash over Barack Obama's presidency.

A Brewing Movement

Many point to February 19, 2009, as the official beginnings of the TPM.[14] On the CNBC show entitled *Squawk Box*, stock analyst Rick Santelli voiced a five-minute-long rant from the floor of the Chicago Mercantile Exchange. Yelling "This is America!" and "How many of you people want to pay for your neighbor's mortgage?" Santelli brazenly attacked the home mortgage rescue plan proposed by the Obama administration just one day earlier. Such a plan, Santelli warned, promoted "bad behavior" by bailing out the "losers." In summing up, Santelli called for a "Chicago Tea Party" where capitalists could dump some derivatives in Lake Michigan. Soon Santelli's call to arms was dubbed "the rant heard round the world."[15]

On the heels of Santelli's on-air diatribe, Eric Odom (a Chicago libertarian and developer of an online network of conservative activists) created "officialchicagoteaparty.com."[16] The 1776 Tea Party formed the next day on February 20, 2009, as a Christian organization with the following political platform: "Illegal Aliens Are Here Illegally. Pro-Domestic Employment Is Indispensable. . . . Gun Ownership Is Sacred. Government Must Be Downsized. National Budget Must Be Balanced. Deficit Spending Will End. Bail-out and Stimulus Plans Are Illegal. . . . English As Core Language Is Required. Traditional Family Values Are Encouraged. Common Sense Constitutional Conservative Self-Governance."[17] On February 24, 2009, a local Louisiana ResistNet chapter announced their hosting of a "tea party" in the city of Lafayette.[18] Soon, the FreedomWorks Tea Party announced a nationwide Tea Party Tour:

> From this desperate rallying cry [of Santelli's] FreedomWorks has tapped into the outrage building from within our own membership as well as allied conservative grassroots forces to organize a 25-city Tea Party Tour where taxpayers angry that their hard-earned money is being usurped by the government for irresponsible bailouts, can show President Obama

and Congressional Democrats that their push towards outright social-
ism will not stand.[19]

Shortly thereafter, another group called the Tea Party Patriots was
founded by Jenny Beth Martin, Mark Meckler, and Amy Kremer on
March 10, 2009,[20] while yet another group called the Tea Party Nation
was founded by Judson and Sherry Phillips on April 6, 2009.[21]

It would be simplistic to say that some of these Tea Party organizations came into being because of Santelli's rant. Rather, some of these
organizations were already percolating by the time Santelli took to the
Chicago Mercantile floor. For example, some trace the political roots
and networks of the modern Tea Party back to the 1992 Ross Perot
presidential campaign, which was based on a distrust in government
that draws from the long history of hyper-individualist populism in the
United States.[22] Others point to a December 16, 2007, march from the
Boston State House to Faneuil Hall, led by libertarian Ron Paul. This
march (on the 234th anniversary of the original Boston Tea Party) coincided with a virtual fundraising event called "tea party moneybomb"
that raised campaign funds for his 2008 presidential campaign.[23] Since
then, Paul's Campaign for Liberty (CFL) organization has played a large
role in the growth of the Tea Party movement.

Regardless of the founding impetus, one week after Santelli's rallying cry, several TPM protests were held across the United States.[24]
According to Dick Armey, "Frustrated Americans began taking their
grievances to the streets and the tea party movement was born. Just as
the original Boston Tea Party was a grass-roots rebellion against over-
bearing government, tea party participants are reacting to government
that has grown too large."[25] By April 15, 2009 (federal income tax day),
various TPM groups held over 750 protests across the United States. By
September 12, 2009, the "Taxpayer March on Washington" (organized
by right-wing pundit Glenn Beck) drew thousands of protesters to the
national mall to express their distaste for President Obama's proposals
on health care reform, taxation, and federal spending (particularly along
the lines of the "American Recovery and Reinvestment Act" of 2009).
The tone and timbre of these rallies, marked by a vehement opposition
to Obama and his administration's plans, reflects a "lynch-mob mental-
ity."[26] Frequently, Tea Party members label the very programs trying to

help eradicate racial inequality, such as affirmative action, welfare net services, and desegregation, as "reverse racism" against whites.[27]

As the TPM gained mainstream legitimacy, it simultaneously merged its original fiscal conservativism and laissez-faire individualism ("tea" stood for "taxed enough already") with conservative ideologies such as anti-abortion or anti-immigration stances.[28] While the TPM advocates a smaller centralized power and tax breaks, there are significant gaps in the group's knowledge of current policy today.[29] And while supporters claim that policy issues are their reason for participating and that the initial impetus for the group's formation came from economic concerns, the issue of race often becomes a focus and the group has transformed into a machine through which racist comments are spread. For many TPM members, President Obama represents little more than an anti-patriotic "other" and a socialist foreigner who threatens the country.[30]

By early 2010, FreedomWorks Tea Party focused its activism on the 2010 midterm elections and held "the first leadership summit of the Tea Party era" where they gathered more than sixty leaders from two dozen states in Washington, D.C. "The meeting developed 2010 midterm election plans, and gave FreedomWorks the opportunity to roll out their list of 65 targeted congressional races. A workshop taught effective television techniques and mastering social media. Another session was entitled 'what you can and can't say: how to stay out of jail this year.'"[31] By the November 2010 midterms, TPM-linked candidates won 39 of 129 races (30.2 percent) for the House of Representatives, and five of nine (55.6 percent) candidates won Senate elections.[32] As a consequence, Scott Rasmussen and Doug Schown in *Mad as Hell: How the Tea Party Movement Is Fundamentally Remaking Our Two-Party System*, write that the TPM is "anti-systemic, anti-elite, and crisis driven . . . but unlike movements of the past, it is pervasive and here to stay."[33]

Spiking the Tea: Tea Party Racism

Much like the Birthers, TPM members claim that their movement is a color-blind critique of big government and out-of-control spending. However, a thorough report by the Institute for Research and Education on Human Rights entitled "Tea Party Nationalism" offers a different view of the movement:

Despite the fact that Tea Partiers sometimes dress in the costumes of 18th century Americans, wave the Gadsden flag and claim that the United States Constitution should be the divining rod of all legislative policies, theirs is an American nationalism that does not always include all Americans. It is a nationalism that excludes those deemed not to be "real Americans"; including the native-born children of undocumented immigrants (often despised as "anchor babies"), socialists, Moslems, and those not deemed to fit within a "Christian nation." The "common welfare" of the Constitution's preamble does not complicate their ideas about individual liberty. This form of nationalism harkens back to the America first ideology of Father Coughlin. As the Confederate battle flags, witch doctor caricatures and demeaning discourse suggest, a bright white line of racism threads through this nationalism.[34]

Throughout TPM discourse, Obama has been portrayed as a racial, religious, national, and political threat on posters, signs, and e-mails, and in publications. Examples include the "ObamaCare" posters that featured a dark "witch doctor" with Obama's face photo-shopped to the picture; the "Barack the Barbarian" cartoon that features Obama menacing a scantily clad white woman; TPM rally signs stating "Obama's Plan: White Slavery" and "The American Taxpayers Are the Jews for Obama's Ovens"; a remake of the iconic Shepard Fairey poster in which "R@CIST" replaces the word "HOPE"; a sign that read "The Zoo Has an African Lion and the White House Has a Lyin' African"; or a sign that simply reads "Save White America."[35] Moreover, on March 20, 2010, a Tea Party protest grew ugly as select congressmen walked through the crowd to vote on Obama's health care reform bill. Rep. Barney Frank (D–MA) (the United States' first openly gay member of Congress) was called a "faggot," civil rights icon Rep. John Lewis was called a "nigger," and Rep. Emanuel Cleaver (D–MO) was spat upon. Cleaver later described the name calling as a "chorus."[36]

Consequently, in July 2010, the 101st NAACP National Convention unanimously passed a resolution condemning outspoken racist elements within the Tea Party and called upon Tea Party leaders to repudiate those in their ranks who use white-supremacist language.[37] Despite TPM attempts to quell racism in their ranks and to play up their "Diverse Tea" (a play on "diversity" in which the FreedomWorks

Tea Party tried to emphasize TPM racial heterogeneity), the movement retains formal and informal ties to an array of white supremacists and white nationalists, and continues to direct both implicit and explicit racism toward President Obama.

On February 27, 2009, for example, the 1776 Tea Party founder Dale Robertson (a former naval officer who served with the Marines) attended a Tea Party event in Houston with a sign reading "Congress = Slaveowner, Taxpayer = Niggar [sic]."[38] Robertson also has a history of sending e-mails that depict President Obama as a pimp and has promoted antisemitic views on his *Tea Party Hour* radio show. Robertson also chastised Obama for spending a Memorial Day with "his homies in the Chicago hood . . . shooting hoops, smoking cigarettes."[39] Since these incidents, two leaders of the anti-immigrant and nativist organization the Minutemen have joined the leadership ranks of the 1776 Tea Party.[40]

Many factions of TPM organizations have decidedly white-supremacist and nationalist foundations and coalitions. For example, the Resist-Net Tea Party frequently works with TakeAmericaBack.org, a website launched in April 2009 with the aim of publishing anti-immigrant propaganda. One such article claimed that Obama was "a Kenyan, Communist, son of a terrorist, as our wannabe president, who has not only expressed his hatred of America, but is also an avowed Muslim."[41] So also, the Wood County Tea Party (formerly known as the Winnsboro, Texas, Tea Party) formed in 2009 and was led by Karen Pack, a former subscriber to the *White Patriot* tabloid and "official supporter" of David Duke's Knights of the Ku Klux Klan.[42]

Official white nationalist groups, such as American Third Position or "A3P," have begun emulating the TPM. A3P staged its own Tax Day Tea Party rally on April 16, 2011, in San Juan Capistrano, California.[43] Neo-Nazi groups and other white nationalists have supported Tea Party protests and have evidenced a desire to awaken TPM members to a white nationalist perspective.[44] Devan Burghart and Leonard Zeskind write in "Tea Party Nationalism,"

> The Council of Conservative Citizens, headquartered in St. Louis with its strongest chapters in the South and Mid-South, is the largest white nationalist organization in the country and the group most active in the Tea Parties. A direct lineal descendant of the white Citizens Councils

that fought to defend Jim Crow segregation during the 1950s and 1960s, the Council of Conservative Citizens promotes the idea that the United States is or should be a white Christian nation; and that Barack Obama and black people generally oppress white people. The Council does not itself advance the same kind of bald anti-Semitic conspiracy theories that motivate national socialists like those at Stormfront.org, although there are hard-core anti-Semites throughout its ranks and leadership.[45]

In the wake of congresswoman Gabrielle Gifford's shooting in January of 2011, Anthony Miller, the sole black Republican Party district chairman in Arizona, resigned after citing threats from the Tea Party faction and concerns for his family's safety.[46] And perhaps the most conspicuous of white nationalist–TPM connections remains Billy Joe Roper Jr., a ResistNet Tea Party member and former leader of the National Alliance (one of the nation's most formidable white nationalist organizations, which advocates the creation of an all-white country through the expulsion and/or murder of Jews and people of color). After Roper's connections to the National Alliance were exposed, the ResistNet Tea Party began to shun association with him.[47] These many incidents reveal the white-nationalist and supremacist foundations, coalitions, and implicit appeals of the TPM even as many of its members attempt to portray a color-blind or racially neutral stance. The TPM was a pivotal player in the GOP's bid to reclaim the House of Representatives in the 2010 midterm elections, and their rhetoric has proven how effective implicit racial biases are in creating coalitions with, and building support among, racially paranoid white voters and activists.

Drinking the Tea: What Do Tea Partiers Support
(and Does the Public Support Them)?

In terms of its members, supporters, and loosely tied sympathizers, national polls show TPM to be about 11 to 18 percent of the adult US population.[48] Core supporters are close to 250,000 people spread throughout the United States.[49] They are overwhelmingly white and middle class.[50] "Tea Partiers are more likely than white people generally to believe that 'too much' has been made of the problems facing black people: 52% to 39%."[51] Compared to the general population, TPM members and supporters are overwhelmingly supportive of Sarah Palin and turn to Fox News as their most trusted media source.[52] In general, Tea Partiers have a low regard for immigrants and blacks and oppose abortion.[53] And Tea Partiers continue to hold these views: they seek "deeply religious" elected officials, approve of religious leaders engaging in politics, and want religion brought into political debates. The Tea Party's generals may say that their overriding concern is a smaller government, but this is not the main issue for the party's rank and file, who are more concerned about putting God in government.[54]

Nearly half (47 percent) of TPM members and supporters say they are part of the religious Right or a conservative Christian movement and are socially conservative rather than libertarian on social issues.[55] While TPM officials and followers overtly claim to be motivated by fiscal woes and a desire for smaller government, they are clearly coalesced by the use of religious language and imagery in relation to anti-immigration stances and opposition to racially tinged social issues like welfare and affirmative action. Over 50 percent of Tea Party supporters surveyed by the New York Times believe that the government favors blacks over whites, a percentage five times higher than that in the general public.[56] A study by the University of Washington Institute for the Study of Ethnicity, Race, and Sexuality found that "[o]nly 14 percent of the content from tea party websites focuses on big government or state's rights, issues that are supposedly the ultimate concern of the tea party, [whereas] 19 percent of the content from tea party websites focuses on immigration, the gay community, race and personal attacks on Obama."[57] The study also found that among white TPM members and supporters, less than half considered blacks hard-working (35 percent), intelligent (45 percent), or trustworthy (41 percent).

In a September 2010 survey, 71 percent of self-identified Republicans claimed that they "have a positive opinion" of the Tea Party movement.[58] During the summer of 2010, 46 percent of registered voters in North Carolina and Tennessee felt favorably toward the TPM, which was slightly higher than the national average at the time.[59] By March 2011, a CNN/Opinion Research Corporation survey indicated that 32 percent of the public held a favorable view of the TPM (down from 37 percent in December of 2010). The TPM's unfavorable rating had risen fifteen points since October 2010 among lower-income Americans, compared to only five points among those making more than fifty thousand dollars (roughly 50 percent of all American households have incomes under fifty thousand dollars).[60] Accordingly, every couple of months' time brings a percentage-point decline in TPM approval ratings. In April 2010, a *New York Times/CBS News* survey found that 18 percent of Americans had an unfavorable opinion of the TPM, 21 percent had a favorable opinion, and 46 percent had not heard enough about the party to express an opinion. By August 2011, TPM supporters slipped to 20 percent, while their opponents have more than doubled, to 40 percent.[61] These figures represent the continued salience of race in politics. And while the political popularity of the TPM is currently waning, the use of racialized appeals to attract white voters to conservative political parties—namely, the GOP—is a tried and true tactic. A politicized discourse built on the tropes of black dysfunction, white patriotism, white paternalism, and white victimhood remains a potent device. As we show next, even with the dwindling political support for the TPM, these racial anxieties proved efficacious in propelling an array of right-wing attacks on Obama, his citizenship status, and, consequently, his legitimacy as the forty-fourth president of the United States.

Labor Pains: Born in Sin

The belief that Barack Obama was not born in the United States and/or was not born to US citizens did not simply fall out of the sky in 2008. Rather, these insinuations (and demands that Obama "show his papers") are motivated by the gestation of logic, laws, and normative practices that historically conflate authentic US citizenship with particular forms of white racial identity.[62]

US national belonging was racialized from the outset. For example, ratification of the Constitution allowed only white male property owners and taxpayers to vote; the "three-fifths compromise"—originally discussed at the Philadelphia Convention of 1787—rendered slaves three-fifths of a citizen and person, and the US Naturalization Law of 1790 extended citizenship only to "free white persons" of "good moral character." Before the passage of the Thirteenth Amendment, manumission papers proved essential credentials for those who obtained freedom from slavery. Without possession of such documents, white persons and law officials were empowered by laws such as the Fugitive Slave Law of 1850 to capture any person *suspected* of being a runaway slave. Such manumission documents were invested with more power and vocal agency than their black wielders, as suspected runaway slaves could not request jury trials or testify on their own behalf in court. Moreover, whites' failure to attempt to apprehend any suspected runaway slave could result in a one-thousand-dollar fine. This propelled what sociologist George Lipsitz calls a "possessive investment in whiteness" whereby whites were literally subsidized for their participation in the socio-legal regime of white supremacy and black surveillance.[63]

On the heels of *Dred Scott v. Sandford* (an 1857 decision that both African slaves and their US-born descendants could never be US citizens), the Civil War (1861–1865), and the Reconstruction era (1866–1877), whites, in order to curtail black political power, increasingly demanded that blacks show documentation before engaging in civic participation.[64] Reliance on racial documentation—part and parcel of the cultural logic of these laws (called the "Black Codes")—further quilted the legal marginalization of nonwhites into the social fabric of the nation even as it sewed together whiteness and citizenship. Per the Black Codes, without written documentation, nonwhites were forced to pay poll taxes and/or pass literacy tests in order to vote.[65] Even with documentation or successful passage of tests, many blacks faced charges that documents were forgeries, they were told that more documentation was required, or vigilante groups like the Ku Klux Klan simply intimidated them away from civic and political participation.[66] After the "separate but equal" precedent was enshrined in *Plessy v. Ferguson* (1896) and the Black Codes gave way to the formal practices of Jim Crow segregation (1876 to 1965), blacks and other nonwhites were all but completely eliminated from voter rolls and thus became invisible from formal political participation due to capricious and subjective standards of documentation.

The passage of the 1964 Civil Rights Act and the 1965 Voting Rights Act promised relief for African Americans. However, the laws meant to protect black political and social agency were not adequately followed or enforced by government agencies, making for ugly encounters between people of color and law enforcement. With the violence of the 1964 Freedom Summer, the birth of staunch black power groups like the Black Panthers, and the nationwide race riots in the wake of Martin Luther King Jr's assassination in 1968, racial tensions heightened and the question of full citizenship rights for blacks was anything but settled. Moreover, the 1956 passage of the Immigration and Nationality Act (also known as the Hart-Celler Act) abolished the "National Origins Formula" (a set of quotas based on race and nationality) that had been in place since the Immigration Act of 1924. This led to a steady rise in the influx of nonwhite immigrants into the United States that was coupled with explicit nativist and xenophobic public language and more disruptions between people of color and policing agencies.[67]

Throughout the 1970s, '80s, and '90s, the GOP played to these white anxieties over both blacks' growing political and social power and the rising tide of nonwhite immigrants. Just as the Dixiecrats once used poll taxes and literacy tests to bar blacks from voting, a new crop of GOP activists began using implicit racial code words and fears to disenfranchise blacks and immigrant populations (two groups that, since the political realignment of the 1960s, have voted Democratic). For example, influential conservative activist and cofounder of the Heritage Foundation, Paul Weyrich, told a gathering of evangelical leaders in 1980, "I don't want everybody to vote. . . . [O]ur leverage in the elections quite candidly goes up as the voting populace goes down."[68] That same year, then presidential candidate Ronald Reagan kicked off his general election campaign in Philadelphia, Mississippi—the site of the 1964 murder of civil rights workers James Chaney, Andrew Goodman, and Michael Schwerner by Klansman Edgar Ray Killen. During the speech, Reagan expressed his support for "states' rights"—a tacit appeal to southern white voters and domestic terrorists who used "states' rights" to resist federal attempts to both legislate and enforce civil rights laws. In continuing appeals to white southern racism in the 1980s, Mississippi senator Trent Lott gave a speech to the Sons of Confederate Veterans in which he stated, "The spirit of Jefferson Davis [former president of the Confederacy] lives in the 1984 Republican platform."[69] Of course, Lott denied any formal racist intent, even as he continued to speak to the Council of Conservative Citizens (an anti-immigrant and white-nationalist group), for whose *Citizen's Informer* publication he wrote columns.[70]

In the 1990s, hyper-conservative and libertarian candidates were gaining entrance into the GOP. These candidates built much of their political platforms on implicit appeals to anti-immigrant and antiblack sentiment among whites. For example, in 1997 Ron Paul was elected a US representative for Texas. In years prior to his election, he wrote articles in mainstream papers and his own *Ron Paul Freedom Report* and *Ron Paul Survival Report* in which he made remarks about race that stirred up whites' already entrenched stereotypical fears about blacks: "I think we can safely assume that 95 percent of the black males in that city [Washington, DC] are semi-criminal or entirely criminal. . . . [W]e are constantly told that it is evil to be afraid of black men, [but] it is hardly irrational. Black men commit murders, rapes, robberies, muggings and burglaries all out of proportion to their numbers."[71] By 2004, Paul was making statements from the floor of the US House of Representatives about his refusal to vote for the renewal of the 1964 Civil Rights Act. By 2008, GOP candidates and incumbents, like Virginia congressman Virgil Goode, declared that the greatest threat to America's national security was "anchor babies"—the pejorative term for a child born in the United States to immigrant parents, usually of nonwhite status (Vietnamese "boat people," Haitian refugees, or Mexican immigrants). It is within this context and historical legacy that the public questioning of Barack Obama's citizenship was primed for delivery to racially anxious and frightened white voters.[72] By June 2008, the right-wing *National Review Online* called for Obama to release his birth certificate.[73] Many cite this call as the genesis of "Birtherism."

Birth Announcements

Soon after June 2008, an array of media pundits and authors questioned the legitimacy of Obama's citizenship. Websites, most notably World Net Daily (WND), carried discredited conspiracy theories and stories about Barack Obama and served as clearinghouses for extremists.[74] The WND website became a place where nativist, homophobic, and socially conservative elements of the GOP assembled.[75] At the time, Joseph Farah, editor-in-chief of WND, began to support 2012 presidential hopeful Senator Jim DeMitt (R–SC). DeMitt declared that "openly gay people and unwed mothers should not be allowed to teach in public schools."[76] In editing WND, Farah drew inspiration from former president Ronald Reagan's political mantra that "the government is not the solution to our problem; government is the problem."[77] Farah went on to challenge the place of President Obama's birth at the 2010 Tea Party Convention in Nashville, Tennessee: "There is a lesson in Barack Obama. His nativity story is much less known!"[78] Farah and Birther supporters believed that Obama had a "secret hatred of America and its values," which only seemed to stoke the fires of conspiracy that Obama was not born in Hawaii.[79]

The Birther movement quickly spread to conservative voices like Rush Limbaugh, Sean Hannity, Lou Dobbs, and author Jerome R. Corsim, who wrote the book *Where's the Birth Certificate? The Case That Barack Obama Is Not Eligible to Be President* (published May 2011 by World Net Daily). By 2009, Republicans like Senator Richard Shelby (AL), Senator Roy Blunt (MO), and newly elected governor of Georgia, Nathan Deal, all publicly questioned the legitimacy of Obama's presidency, while several Republican members of Congress signed on to a bill requiring presidential candidates to provide their birth certificates (H.R. 1503).[80] Moreover, the case of Obama's citizenship has seen substantial litigation. Nearly twenty lawsuits have been filed in various US states, and three suits reached the Supreme Court.[81] As of June 2011, several states (Arizona, Connecticut, Georgia, Indiana, Maine, Missouri, Montana, Nebraska, Oklahoma, Tennessee, and Texas) proposed legislation that would require more proof that Barack Obama was born in the United States before his name would be placed on the 2012 ballot for reelection.

Birther leader Orly Taitz, herself born in Soviet-controlled Moldova and a resident of California,[82] stated that she became concerned about President Obama's birth because she hailed from a former communist country and sees parallels between communism and both Obama's governance and radical Islam that would result in an "all-civilian army . . . [including] children dressed in uniforms, saluting Obama and doing drills."[83] Taitz has filed several unsuccessful lawsuits against President Obama. One such instance occurred prior to his January 2009 inauguration and was filed on behalf of failed presidential candidate Republican Alan Keyes.[84] She also filed an "emergency injunction" to the United States Supreme Court on behalf of unsuccessful vice presidential Libertarian candidate Gail Lightfoot, in which she asked the state of California to stop its "certification of the 2008 election results."[85]

The file went without comment from the State Supreme Court chief justice and was dismissed.

There has been an array of other lawsuits and legislation filed over Obama's birth and subsequent citizenship. Although it failed to pass, H.R. 1940 (the "Birthright Citizenship Act of 2007") was introduced in order to eliminate natural-born citizenship via jus soli ("right of the soil" or birth on US or US-controlled territory). In April of 2010, Arizona passed Senate Bill 1070 into law. Akin to the Fugitive Slave Law of 1850, this law gives local and state police broad power to detain anyone *suspected* of illegal status in the United States. The recently introduced H.R. 140 (the "Birthright Citizenship Act of 2011") proposes to summarily end jus soli unless one can supply papers to prove that one's parents were *legally* residing in the United States at the time of one's birth in order to retain or gain citizenship.

Born in the USA

US citizenship is determined by a combination of jus soli or jus sanguinis ("right of the blood"). Specifically, one is automatically a "natural-born citizen" of the United States if born within the borders of the United States or areas controlled by the United States, such as the District of Columbia, Guam, Puerto Rico, and the US Virgin Islands. Also, one is an automatic "natural-born citizen" if born to at least one parent who is already a US citizen, regardless of place of birth.[86] The role of citizenship in relation to the US presidency concerns section 1, article 2 of the US Constitution: "No person except a natural born Citizen, or a Citizen of the United States, at the time of the Adoption of this Constitution, shall be eligible to the Office of President."

Given this background, "birther" claims hinge on two assertions. First, Barack Obama was born in Kenya (rather than Hawaii). Second, Obama's father was Kenyan and not a US citizen. While both claims have been falsified to show both that Obama was born in the United States (August 4, 1961, in Honolulu, Hawaii) and that his mother, Dr. Stanley Ann Dunham, was a US citizen, the Birther conspiracy theories persisted well after Obama proved his American citizenship. Obama and the White House have twice addressed Birther claims with primary evidence of his US birth. On June 12, 2008, Obama posted a scan of his

Certificate of Live Birth, supplied by the Hawaii Department of Health.[87] On April 27, 2011, White House staffers gave members of the press copies of his original birth certificate and posted a scan of the "long form" certificate on the White House website.[88] The website stated, "It shows conclusively that Mr. Obama was born in Honolulu and is signed by state officials and his mother."[89] During the 2008 campaign, two fact-checking groups, Factcheck.org and PolitiFact, both concluded that the certificate of live birth was legitimate. Furthermore, the *Honolulu Advertiser* found "two separate newspaper announcements of the president's birth, one in the *Advertiser* on Aug. 13, 1961, and another in the *Honolulu Star-Bulletin* the next day. Both carried the words "Mr. and Mrs. Barack H. Obama, 6085 Kalanianaole Highway, son, Aug. 4.""[90]

Color-Blind Birthers?

Just after Obama's "long form" birth certificate was released in April 2011, self-appointed Birther leader and entrepreneur Donald Trump (then a presidential hopeful) claimed credit for the form's release to the public. After touting the publication as something "that nobody else has been able to accomplish" he went on to cast doubt on the document's authenticity, Obama's educational validity, and the legitimacy of the Obama presidency that he had previously questioned as possibly "one of the greatest scams in the history of politics."[91] Trump stated,

> Now, we have to look at it [the "long form"]. We have to see. Is it real? Is it proper? What's on it? . . . I'm going to look at it and many other people are going to look at it. You're going to have many people looking at it. And obviously, they're going to have to make a decision. Because, it is rather amazing that all of a sudden it materializes. But, I hope it's the right deal. I'm sure, I hope it's the right deal. We have to look at it. A lot of people have to look at it. Experts will look at it. . . . The word is, according to what I've read, that he was a terrible student when he went to Occidental. He then gets to Columbia. He then gets to Harvard. . . . How do you get into Harvard if you're not a good student? Now, maybe that's right, or maybe it's wrong. But I don't know why he doesn't release his records. Why doesn't he release his Occidental records?[92]

Trump's attack on Obama's presidential and educational accomplishments resonated with the time-tested tradition of right-wing appeals to white fears over an ill-equipped, dysfunctional, and dangerous black man in power. Ironically, it was a black Tea Party supporter named Lloyd Marcus who was one of Trump's loudest defenders. After calling critics of Trump "Black 'race pimps,'" Marcus stated,

> In response to the uppity white boy [Trump], who dared question their king [Obama], a few black celebrities and black bullies disguised as "civil rights" groups are calling Donald Trump a racist, targeting him for destruction. So, are all of the other Americans curious about why Obama was not presenting his birth certificate racist as well? Will somebody please tell these black racist bullies to "stop it and get a life"?[93]

This dynamic represents a quintessential political strategy in which nonwhites and nonwhite political figures are framed as the underachieving beneficiaries of affirmative action and quotas, while their defenders are then framed as the real racists or as overly sensitive people who too liberally play the "race card."[94] Not breaking step, Patrick Buchanan (another GOP presidential hopeful) continued Trump's othering of Obama. Buchanan stated on MSNBC that Obama

> went to Occidental College; then suddenly he shows up at one of the best schools in the country, Columbia. He vaults from there to Harvard Law School; suddenly he's on *Harvard Law Review*; suddenly he's the editor of *Harvard Law Review*. We've never seen any grades of the guy—these are legitimate questions. . . . I think he's affirmative action all the way![95]

These actions and this discourse reflect the fourfold GOP racial framing first mentioned in the introduction. First, blacks and Obama are portrayed as dysfunctional and pathological social pariahs who threaten the foundations of a supposedly white-built Western democratic tradition. Obama's entrance into these schools and the highest political office in the land represents a grave threat to social order, so we are told. Second, even though Trump's and Buchanan's educational and political credentials are suspect, they anoint themselves and other questioning whites as the true and authentic representatives of hard work, success, and authentic patriot-citizenship. Third, whites like Trump and Buchanan—as the defenders of that white-built Western democratic tradition—should be allowed to question black authority as they wish, and these white morality figures are entitled to an immediate and satisfactory answer as the true and rightful paternal representatives of their country. And fourth, whites are framed as under attack from a politically correct society that gives away the keys to both elite universities and the White House to underachieving and undeserving people like Obama, simply because they are black. Here, being white is reframed as a detriment and the white-supremacist social order is mystified as one in which only people of color have a fair shot. These rhetorical dimensions are similar to those of the discourse of hate groups like the KKK. But while the Birthers, Trump, and Buchanan may not be card-carrying members of the KKK, they certainly pander to racial prejudices in a climate where overt advocacy of white supremacy and citizenship is considered taboo.

On December 1 and 3, 2008, various Tea Party groups, like "Resist-Net Tea Party," in conjunction with "We the People Foundation for Constitutional Education, Inc.," took out full-page ads in the *Chicago Tribune*, entitled "An Open Letter to Barack Obama: Are You a Natural Born Citizen of the U.S.? Are You Legally Eligible to Hold the Office of President?" The advertisement went on to assert that if Obama failed to meet the groups' "demands," then they would consider Obama an illegal "usurper" of the presidency who "would be entitled to no allegiance, obedience or support from the People."[96] In 2009, Mark Williams of another group called the Tea Party Express published *It's Not Right versus Left, It's Right versus Wrong; Exposing the Socialist Agenda* (republished in 2010 as *Taking Back America One Tea Party at a Time*). In the book, Williams writes that it's an "open secret that Mr. Obama is improbably a native-born citizen of the United States."[97] After comparing Obama to Hitler and the Nazi Party, Williams went on to defame African Americans as the "unwashed, inarticulate, and brutalish":

> The Chosen One's cult is remarkably unlike their Dear Leader. He—as his running mate Joe Biden so famously said, is a "clean and articulate one." They—unwashed, inarticulate, and brutish, are his future Schutzstaffel, to be used in the continuing Kristallnacht being waged against

independent thought. He pits race against race, class against class, Americans against America. (My use of German is not unintentional.)[98]

Just before the 2008 election, Amy Kremer (who later became an important figure in both the Tea Party Patriots and the Tea Party Express) wrote of Senator John McCain on the blog Southern Belle Politics, "[H]e needs to tell Nobama to bring his authentic birth certificate to the debate. I am so tired of the spin from his spinmeisters! Johnny Mac . . . just go straight to the source!"[99]

Together, these forms of racial othering and thinly veiled "states' rights" secessionist rhetoric both rely upon and reproduce racism. In this sense, the Birther controversy is an abstracted and coded attack on the racial belonging of a US president who breaks with the staunch tradition of white male presidents. However, Birthers and their supporters often claim, adamantly so, that their distrust of Obama's natural-born citizenship (and thus the legitimacy of his presidency) is devoid of racial animus. Even in the face of racist rhetoric, Birthers often claim they hold color-blind views, dismiss such rhetoric as a joke, or insinuate that their critics are oversensitive. Case in point: in April 2011, Marilyn Davenport—an elected Republican official from Orange County, California—distributed a photo of a chimpanzee family with Obama's face photo-shopped over the chimp child. The picture included the text "Now you know why—No birth certificate."[100] After Davenport's e-mail was covered in the media, Davenport responded, "Oh, come on! Everybody who knows me knows that I am not a racist. It was a joke. I have friends who are black. Besides, I only sent it to a few people—mostly people I didn't think would be upset by it."[101]

It is striking, to say the least, that shared photos of Obama as a primate—a well-known and historically embedded racist slur against African Americans—would be dismissed as lacking in racial meaning.[102] In this vein, Michelle Bachmann, GOP representative and one-time Republican presidential candidate, one of the original Birther leaders, and founder of the Tea Party Caucus in Congress, has been one of the most extreme and racially insensitive opponents of Obama and his family. Just before the 2008 election she accused Michelle Obama of being "very anti-American." After the election she stated that Barack Obama operated a "gangster government" whose actions "have not been based on true American values."[103] As Mark Potok of the Southern Poverty Law Center wrote, "The continuing conspiracy theories about Obama—from his country of birth to his religion to his relationships with the radical left—come from people who are essentially motivated by antipathy toward black people."[104] Moreover, research published in the March 2011 issue of the *Journal of Experimental Social Psychology* demonstrated that in comparison with blacks, whites tend to view Obama as less American and as an underperforming president. Additionally, whites with higher levels of prejudice than other whites rated Obama as less American. The authors of the study, social scientists Eric Hehman, Samuel Gaertner, and John Dovidio wrote,

> The influence of racial prejudice in contemporary U.S. society is typically manifested in subtle, indirect forms of bias. Due to prevailing norms of equality, most Whites attempt to avoid appearing biased in their evaluations of Blacks, in part because of a genuine desire to live up to their egalitarian standards, but also because of concern regarding social censure. As a consequence, Whites' prejudice is more likely to be expressed in discriminatory responses when these actions can be justified by other factors.[105]

In another academic study, conducted by one of this book's authors, a random sample culled from 12,539 public comments left on the *New York Times* and the *Wall Street Journal* online news articles about Birthers (from January 1, 2009, to May 31, 2011) found that Obama was constantly derided as an un-American threat.[106] For example:

> If Obama didn't act like an alien, nobody would question his birth place. But he is so unAmerican in words and actions, people look for an explanation. The Birthers are just one group of questioners.

> It is clear that Obama does not meet the "spirit" of the requirement that a president be a natural born citizen. Hawaii is pretty far from mainland US, Kenya is farther still and Indonesia still further.

> I believe these rumors about Barack Obama not being from America are true. I mean, who in this country would name their child Barack Hussane [sic] Obama. Remember Saddam Hussane [sic]. Coincidence?

This study demonstrates the rhetorical mechanisms by which people publicly frame Obama—as an illegitimate imposter because of his race and parental lineage who could never either be a "real American" or attain the success he has because of his intellectual acumen but rather because of unfair and racialized handouts and quotas.

This nuanced study of the mechanisms for racial "othering" reflects large public support for Birther claims. Public belief in Birther claims remained relatively sustained from late 2008 to mid-2011. In October of 2008, approximately one-third of self-identified Republicans surveyed believed that Obama was born outside of the United States.[107] By July of 2009 nearly a quarter of all Americans either thought Obama was born outside of the United States or were unsure as to his birthplace.[108] By August of 2009, nearly 75 percent of southern whites asserted that Obama was not born in the United States or had doubts that he was.[109] By September 2009 a national poll of registered voters revealed that 23 percent of the public thought Obama was born outside the United States, with 42 percent of Republicans saying the president was not American born.[110] This attitude grew by March of 2010, when 25 percent of adults asserted that Barack Obama was "not born in the United States and so is not eligible to be president."[111] Just before the release of the "long form" birth certificate in April 2011, a USA Today/Gallup Poll found that only 38 percent of respondents believed Obama was "definitely" born in the United States.[112] After the release of the "long form," support for Birtherism waned, but only slightly. An April 2011 Washington Post poll showed that almost one-third of the country did not believe Obama was born in Hawaii. As more time elapsed, support for Birtherism declined further.

After the killing of Osama bin Laden in May 2011, Gallup polls found that "birther beliefs were cut roughly in half," with 47 percent of people surveyed believing that President Obama was born in the United States.[113] Paradoxically, some read the drop in Birther support after the Obama administration killed public enemy number one (bin Laden) as reinforcing the very racial and religious fears that motivated the Birther movement in the first place. Michael Eric Dyson stated,

> The reality is that [President Obama] was being questioned as an un-American . . . then, he has to prove he's an American by killing the

Muslim. And by going to the extreme, he proves that he's most American when he's most violent. . . . Obama has been seen as the ultimate "other." And the only way he's included in the larger circle of American privilege and democracy and identity is that he kills the Muslim, and now we may let him in the back door. Why couldn't he be an American when he graduated from Harvard? Why couldn't he be an American when he was the smartest guy in the room? Why couldn't he be an American when he was putting forth policies that had the potential to change America? Why is it only killing the Muslim achieves it?[114]

In that vein, weeks after bin Laden's death, and despite the significant drop in support for Birtherism, 13 percent of all Americans and nearly 25 percent of Republicans continued to say that Obama was either definitely or probably born in a country other than the United States, while one in five Americans said that they didn't know enough about the issue to say where Obama was born.[115]

The Continued Conflation of Whiteness and Authentic Americanness

The origins of whiteness (and its legal, social, economic, political, and religious conflation with US citizenship) hinge on distinguishing one racial group from another—particularly blacks.[116] Whiteness has been continually marked as a highly valued racial identity relative to other racial groups; it represents what is moral, worthy, and right, while blacks have been framed as biologically and/or culturally lacking the capacity to govern.[117] Birther and TPM reactions to the election of Obama certainly have many facets, but at their core resides the implicit conflation of whiteness and citizenship that marginalizes nonwhites. With this framing of Obama as a usurper of US citizenship and the presidency, his status (regardless of actions) is always already framed as wrong and unacceptable. The obsession with Obama's birth and the unprecedented use of implicit and explicit racial rhetoric to oppose Obama reveals that many Birthers and Tea Partiers are motivated by race rather than strict adherence to the Constitution or pure political goals.[118]

In this light, it would be a mistake to dismiss the logic of the Tea Party or "Birtherism" as irrational or driven by conscious racial animus.

Rather, racism is neither the domain of a few irrational people nor is it predicated upon conscious intentions. The proper analysis looks to the ways such a movement relies upon—and reproduces—the use of racist imagery, representations, and symbols (such as apes, watermelons, aliens, etc.) by those who advance this rhetoric under the pretense that it is racially neutral, little more than humor, and/or meaningless banter that others take too seriously.

3

A Fox in the Idiot Box

Right-Wing Talking Heads

In the landmark text *The Black Image in the White Mind*, Robert Ent-man and Andrew Rojecki began with a prescient observation: "Recent studies reveal that racially distinctive images pervade news of Blacks and other minority groups, and that these images can influence Whites' opinions, and political preferences and votes."[1] A decade after these words were penned, and with Barack Obama occupying the White House, does racism in the news continue to structure opinions about nonwhite people? Contemporary research answers this question with a resounding "yes,"[2] but while we know a great deal about the effects of such racism on racial attitudes and voting patterns, we know much less about the landscape of this discourse. In an age marked by what some social scientists call "subtle" or "color-blind" racism, how has racism directed at Obama and nonwhite "others" become more overt and vit-riolic in its tone and timbre? What do these narratives look like? What racial images does color-blind racism rely upon and reproduce? In this chapter, we address these questions by describing some of the major right-wing news commentators and outlining their use of racially coded and explicit language to critique Obama and various communi-ties of color. Together, these conservative voices assemble a rather uni-fied chorus that posits black dysfunction, white patriotism, white pater-nalism, and white victimhood as a dangerous and normal aspect of the contemporary US landscape.

The Advent of Cable News

Television news matters. Even with magazines, newspapers, the radio, and the advent of the Internet, television is the most frequently used source of news for Americans.[3] Moreover, cable news is a significant draw for audiences. In 2012 the Pew Research Center found that 36 percent of Americans regularly get their political news from cable news networks. "That is virtually unchanged from previous campaigns, yet cable news is now the top regular source for campaign news," the report stated.[4] And also by 2012, Fox News marked a decade of dominance as the number one cable news network (In January of 2012 Fox averaged 1.9 million viewers for its full day of coverage compared to 841,000 viewers for CNN and 801,000 for MSNBC.).[5] Once considered a background player, cable news (especially right-wing news) is now center stage. CNN—the first cable news network, first aired on June 1, 1980—garnered little attention in its beginnings. But after a fast-paced and daily-changing Gulf War in 1991, CNN was hailed for its nonstop, sophisticated, and timely coverage.[6] By 1993, 60 percent of Americans regularly watched broadcast news. By 2004, that number declined to 34 percent.[7] Today, nearly 40 percent of those residing in the United States regularly watch cable news networks like CNN, MSNBC, or Fox.[8]

Like its competitors, Fox News billed itself as a no-nonsense, fact-finding organization. Much like CNN, which launched itself on the back of an event like the Gulf War, Fox attached itself to political scandals such as the Clinton-Lewinsky debacle, the 2000 Florida vote recount, and the Gary Condit scandal. When the attacks of September 11, 2001, occurred, Fox News glued itself to the event. After 9/11, Fox began to consistently beat CNN, and especially MSNBC, in the ratings.[9]

Unfair and Imbalanced: Fox News

Roger Ailes—a media consultant for Rudy Giuliani's first mayoral run in 1989 and for Republican presidents Nixon, Reagan, and George H. W. Bush—was hired in 1996 by Keith Rupert Murdoch (CEO of News Corporation, owner of Fox). After Murdoch failed to purchase CNN, Ailes was tasked with developing a new TV network. The newly hired Ailes stated, "We're going to be basically a hard-news network" that will offer "straight, factual information to the American people so that they can make up their own minds, with less 'spin' and less 'face time' for anchors."[10] Despite claims of neutrality, Murdoch and Ailes had a political agenda from the outset. According to an article in *Rolling Stone*, "Like Joseph Coors before him at TVN, Murdoch envisioned his new network as a counterweight to the 'left-wing bias' of CNN."[11] After Ailes was installed as president of Fox News, he embarked on a purge of existing staffers. "There was a litmus test," recalled Joe Peyronnin, whom Ailes displaced as head of the network. "He was going to figure out who was liberal or conservative when he came in, and try to get rid of the liberals."[12] Reporters understood that a right-wing bias was hard-wired into the culture of the Fox newsroom. "All outward appearances were that it was just like any other newsroom," says a former anchor. "But you knew that the way to get ahead was to show your color—and that your color was red."[13]

Ailes also had a long history of race baiting from his days as a Republican strategist. "As media consultant for Richard Nixon's 1968 presidential campaign, Ailes directed televised town hall meetings in which Nixon answered questions from a supportive audience," wrote historian Rick Pearlstein, who added that Ailes suggested Nixon take a question from a "good, mean, Wallaceite cab-driver. Wouldn't that be great? Some guy to sit there and say, 'Awright, Mac, what about these niggers?'"[14] Pearlstein continued, "Nixon then could abhor the uncivility of the words, while endorsing a 'moderate' version of the opinion. Ailes walked up and down a nearby taxi stand until he found a cabbie who fit the bill."[15]

Yet, much of these political and racial dynamics were, at the time, behind the scenes and hidden from the camera. Media scholar Jonathan Morris contends that Fox News' early success can be attributed to three general factors. First, Fox was the first to develop dynamic audio and visual presentations (such as the scrolling "ticker"). Accordingly, the *New York Times* observed,

> As the military buildup continues in the Persian Gulf, another conflict is brewing at home, among MSNBC, CNN and the Fox News Channel. The battle is putting an especially high premium on showmanship and drama. . . . [R]eporters are taking on a hyper charged tone as the cable networks try to persuade viewers ahead of time that they are the ones to watch should war break out. . . . Serving as a backdrop to all this jockeying is the success of the brassy Fox News, now the top cable news outlet in almost every ratings category. Its rapid rise has led CNN and MSNBC to try to match the kinetic Fox production style.[16]

Second, like nearly all cable news channels at the time, Fox has infused entertainment into the reporting of noteworthy events. When important stories break, ratings for cable news channels rise. But the problem for networks is how to attract audiences for everyday and mundane news. The answer came in a blend using high-powered personalities (e.g., Bill O'Reilly and Sean Hannity for Fox in the late 1990s; Keith Olbermann and Rachel Maddow for MSNBC in the late 2000s; Nancy Grace and Glenn Beck for CNN in the late 2000s), flashy graphics and sensationalist headlines, and the concentrated use of the "if it bleeds, it leads" media strategy that sensationalizes the coverage of an isolated violent crime.

Third, and most significant to this book's thesis, is that Fox News appealed to a decisively nationalist and conservative base that held antiblack bias. Morris writes, "During the second Gulf War, Fox News gained notoriety for allegedly covering the initial efforts of the Iraqi invasion from a pro-Bush/prowar perspective. . . . This approach on Fox became evident after September 11, 2001, when the network adopted a heavy tone of American patriotism to its coverage."[17]

To this list of three, we add a fourth. Journalist Tim Dickenson writes,

> In the normal course of business, cable outfits such as Time Warner pay content providers such as CNN or MTV for the right to air their programs. But Murdoch turned the business model on its head. He didn't just give Fox News away—he paid the cable companies to air it. To get Fox News into 25 million homes, Murdoch paid cable companies as much as $20 a subscriber. "Murdoch's offer shocked the industry," writes biographer Neil Chenoweth.[18]

Murdoch paid nearly half a billion dollars to cable companies. In so doing, before Fox News even took to the air, Murdoch had a bought-and-paid-for audience.

Watching Fox

Right-wing political figures have often defended the content of Fox News and other right-leaning media. A common ploy is the insinuation that the "mainstream" news establishment is in fact biased in favor of liberal ideological framings of issues or that it is actually antiwhite. For example, Sarah Palin famously blamed the "leftist lamestream media" for allegedly pressuring Newt Gingrich to soften his critique of Republican congressman Paul Ryan (while in fact the disapproval came from Fox News),[19] and Palin again insinuated charges of political targeting when she decried the media as attacking right-wing figures with their brand of unfair "gotcha journalism."[20] Rush Limbaugh also compared the mainstream press to a "drive by shooter except the microphones are guns."[21] Limbaugh further asserted that the antiright, mainstream media attempts to "destroy people's careers. Then they get in the convertible, head on down the road and do it all over again, while people like you and me are left to clean up the mess with the truth. So I call them the drive-by media."[22]

The Fox News audience is distinct. Numerous studies have found Fox viewers to be less informed about political and current events than viewers of most other broadcast news and cable networks.[23] This could mean either that Fox News performs less effectively in educating viewers or that Fox news attracts less knowledgeable audiences. Other studies have found that individuals who like news with in-depth interviews tend to watch network news and CNN more than Fox, and that individuals who prefer news that aligns with their already-formed opinions are much more likely to watch Fox News (while no such relationship exists for the CNN or network audiences).[24] More research indicates that ABC, CBS, and NBC all favored their own polling numbers and reported "positive" polls for Bill Clinton and "negative" polls for George W. Bush, while Fox appeared to favor exactly the reverse. This would seem to indicate that Fox is simply on the conservative side of media bias. However, while all media outlets have political leanings, Fox News is exceptional in that Fox was especially willing to cite external polling numbers of Clinton if they were damaging—a practice that other news outlets did not perform.[25]

Fox News also appears to cater to ethnocentric assumptions. This discourse has grown with the election of Obama to the White House.[26] In one study, researchers asked panelists where they obtained their televised news about national and international affairs. Roughly one-quarter of respondents indicated that they received their information from Fox News.[27] At the time of the study, questions of Obama's birth were being raised. When asked if they believed Obama was born in the United States, only 21 percent of Fox viewers said that Obama was American born.[28] The authors of the study, Michael Tesler and David O. Sears, wrote, "[T]he reinforcing and/or persuasive role of oppositional media outlets like Fox News and conservative talk radio could make it increasingly difficult to disabuse the sizable minority of individuals disposed to accepting invalid assertions designed to paint Obama as the 'other.'"[29] In the face of such evidence, many Fox apologists, commentators, and guests often defended the views of Birthers and Tea Party activists. While frequent Fox talking head Ann Coulter claimed that that no one on Fox ever mentioned "Birtherism,"[30] research indicates that not only did Fox News mention it; they ramped up coverage of the Birthers leading up to the April 2011 release of the "long form" birth certificate.[31] Moreover, at least 85 percent (forty-four out of fifty-two) of false claims about Obama's birth went unchallenged on Fox News. Fox segments repeated that Obama never produced a birth certificate, that Obama's grandmother said he was born in Kenya, and that Obama spent $2 million in legal funds blocking the release of his birth certificate.[32]

As social scientists Theda Skocpol and Vanessa Williamson make clear in *The Tea Party and the Remaking of Republican Conservatism*, Fox News realized in early 2009 that the Tea Party was a major conservative phenomenon in the making and "moved to become [its] cheerleader-in-chief."[33] Fox began speaking of major Tea Party events weeks in advance and they became more of an advertiser for the Tea Party than a source of news about them. This coverage glorified the future Tea Party events by creating buzz about the expected large crowds and the political and social effect of the rallies. Having just defected from CNN, Glenn Beck traveled to various cities to interview people days before Tea Party rallies even occurred. Skocpol and Williamson contend,

> A week before the first annual April 15th Tea Party rallies in 2009, Fox News promotions kicked into an even higher gear. Glenn Beck told his viewers, "We're getting ready for next week's Tax Day tea parties. All across the country, people coming together to let the politicians know, OK, enough spending." Sean Hannity was even more explicit: "And,

of course, April 15th, our big show coming out of Atlanta. It's Tax Day, our Tax Day tea party show. Don't forget, we're going to have 'Joe the Plumber.'" At times, Fox anchors adopted an almost cajoling tone. On Sean Hannity's show, viewers were told, "Anybody can come, it's free," while Beck fans were warned, "You don't want to miss it." . . . [D]uring the first weeks of the Tea Party, Fox News directly linked the network's brand to these protests and allowed members of the "Fox Nation" to see the Tea Parties as a natural outgrowth of their identity as Fox News viewers.[34]

Simply put, Fox did not simply cover Tea Party events as they transpired, but rather helped to create and sediment support for the fledgling movement in its weakest stages.

With the alignment of Birther and Tea Party movements with GOP and other hard-right-wing candidates, Fox News is shown to have a significant effect on voting patterns. In a study for the National Bureau of Economic Research, Stefano DellaVigna and Ethan Kaplan find that

[t]owns with Fox News have a 0.4 to 0.7 percentage point higher Republican vote share in the 2000 Presidential elections, compared to the 1996 elections. A vote shift of this magnitude is likely to have been decisive in the 2000 elections. We also find an effect on vote share in Senate elections which Fox News does not cover, suggesting that the Fox News impact extends to general political beliefs. Finally, we find evidence that Fox News increased turnout to the polls.[35]

Consistent with evidence of media effects on political beliefs and voting, this recent research indicates that exposure to Fox News may very well induce undecided viewers to vote for Republican candidates. Together, these findings demonstrate the unique character of Fox News, its power to influence voting patterns, and the makeup of its audience.

Lies My Media Told Me

In the opening pages of the popular text *Lies My Teacher Told Me*, sociologist James Loewen cites James Baldwin's astute observation: "What passes for identity in America is a series of myths about one's heroic ancestors."[36] As the following sections will attest, much of the right-wing media appears to long for white-supremacist, nativist, Christian, capitalist heroes of yesteryear. The problem is, this is a past that is not entirely the way the United States ever was. But by evoking a set of mythologies about the way we never were—and anointing Obama as the cause for our present wayward direction—these media structures transform Obama's actions, ipso facto, into proof positive of his supposedly dangerous, dogmatic, and even demonic agenda. In what follows, we present the structural dimensions of this media framing that, regardless of individual commentator or story, served as the mass-mediated method for constructing a decidedly anti-Obama message.

Race Baiting

To frame their stories, much of right-wing media routinely engaged in "race baiting"—the use of racially derisive discourse in order to coerce or frighten white audiences into supporting the GOP. This tactic was often used to oppose, and then racialize, a policy, law, or practice. That is, the issue at hand was either implicitly or explicitly connected to race in ways that seemed to threaten white interests. For example, in making a case to cut entitlement spending, Bill O'Reilly stated, "I don't believe that my money and everybody's money who's worked for a living should be going to people who are on crack. I don't believe that. Yet it continues and continues into trillions of entitlement money that goes right down the rat hole."[37] By specifically targeting crack (a drug habit strongly correlated with inner-city African American communities whereas "cocaine" is associated with whites), he subtly made entitlement spending into a racial issue, while also implying that the typical "entitlement" recipient is African American.

Sometimes the race baiting was more overt. At one point before the 2008 election, O'Reilly stated, "Obama must condemn organizations like MoveOn and the Daily Kos if he truly wants to run without a race component. These are the people that are dividing Americans along racial lines. It is not a stretch to say MoveOn is the new Klan."[38] Such overt race baiting continued with other commentators. Glenn Beck's race baiting in relation to Obama stretched back to before the election, to the Democratic primaries. In 2008, Beck went on CNN to state that "if Hillary Clinton wants to be consistent, I believe, affirmative action, she should give Barack Obama an additional 5 percentage points just for the years of oppression."[39] Here, the dropping of the phrase "affirmative action" in the middle of the sentence, and then the ending of the sentence with "years of oppression" draws upon a reservoir rich in racial meanings. Beck painted affirmative action as a ridiculous set of handouts due only to people of color, specifically African Americans. And finally, Obama was reframed as a candidate who cannot make it on his own without a handout.

After the election, Beck continued his anti-Obama tirades by frequently mentioning slavery and reparations in reference to an Obama administration that would pay back whites for their years of oppression. Beck once stated that Obama was "addicting this country to heroin—the heroin that is government slavery" and that "the government's irresponsible spending is turning us into slaves."[40] Here he ties the progressive movement to slavery (racial injustice), allowing his listeners to feel as if they are on the correct side of race relations and morality. Beck also cast Obama's health care plan as "reparations" when he stated, "These massive programs are Obama brand reparations—or in presidential speak, leveling out the playing field. But, just in case the universalness of the program doesn't somehow or another quench his reparation appetite, he's making sure to do his part to 'pay the debt' in other areas."[41]

Rush Limbaugh also played upon white racial fears regarding Obama in the White House. He stated, "This has been the argument the Reverend [Jesse] Jackson has proffered throughout my life, that it's impossible for minorities to be racist because they don't have any power. Well . . . [chuckling] President of the United States? . . . The days of them not having any power are over, and they are angry. And they want to use their power as a means of retribution."[42] Limbaugh often used his media platform to criticize Obama as "insufficiently humble, insufficiently pious, [and] insufficiently American."[43] He repeatedly stated that Obama was little more than an "affirmative action candidate"[44] and that the United States would have "segregated buses" under "Obama's America."[45] Moreover, Limbaugh has often racialized the policies of the Obama administration as the machinations of a president bent on black payback for white misdeeds of the past. For example, Limbaugh stated, "There's no question that payback is what this administration is all about, presiding over the decline of the United States of America, and doing so happily."[46]

The narrative of Obama as a racial revenge seeker was repeatedly used to paint Obama as an "angry" affirmative action president ready to act out "retribution" against whites and protect other blacks who held antiwhite ideologies. Fox News repeated this trope throughout the spring and summer of 2012, as the GOP geared up for the November election. In his Fox Business show in May 2012, Lou Dobbs suggested that the New Black Panther Party (NBPP), a group the Southern Poverty Law Center designated a hate group, was a core constituency of Obama's political base. Dobbs then quoted NBPP criticisms of Obama and asked, "[W]hat is going on here? This president is starting to get, at the very least, friction, if not outright attacks coming from his base." Dobbs then went on to falsely assert that Obama-appointed Attorney General Eric Holder (also black) claimed that the NBPP "can't be prosecuted for intimidating white voters"—a reference to an incident in which an NBPP member carried a nightstick outside a Philadelphia polling place in 2008 and that Fox News repeatedly called "white voter intimidation." (It was the G. W. Bush administration that decided not to prosecute criminally, but to file a civil case instead.)

Still, Dobbs, and the other Fox correspondents, used this event to continually race bait viewers against Obama. For example, on the Fox segment *America's Newsroom*, cohost Megyn Kelly asked, "[W]hat . . . [do] we know about Eric Holder and his history of prosecuting this kind of case?" to which Fox's Peter Johnson Jr. responded, "[A]t Columbia college, he [Holder] was active in black student association[s] there. . . . [A]t some point, there had been a takeover of the dean's office at Columbia." In other segments on Fox, like the July 15, 2010, edition of *On the Record with Greta Van Susteren*, political consultant Dick Morris stated that Obama's lack of prosecution of the New Black Panther Party meant that Obama was "stereotyping himself as a racial president."[47] And in July 2010, on Fox Business News' *America's Nightly Scoreboard*, host David Asman claimed that Obama was "defending racists in . . . letting the Black Panthers off."[48]

Even Abigail Thernstrom, an outspoken conservative scholar and member of the right-wing think tank the American Enterprise Institute, criticized the media and the Republican-dominated Civil Rights Commission's investigation of the New Black Panther Party case, stating in July 2010 in *Politico* that "[t]his doesn't have to do with the Black Panthers; this has to do with their fantasies about how they could use this issue to topple the [Obama] administration."[49] All in all, the website Media Matters for America reported that by the end of July 2010, Fox News mentioned the "scandal" surrounding the New Black Panther Party more than one hundred times.[50]

The media tactic is clear. Race baiting appeals to latent racial animus in order to generate a new-millennium white backlash akin to the disenfranchisement strategies and attacks that removed newly elected African American legislative officials in the Reconstruction era. While that strategy invalidated the votes of newly freed men and ushered in the Jim Crow entrenchment of racial disparities, the attacks on the Obama administration may generate a similar social world in which conservatives cry foul and may serve as a rationale for rolling back civil rights legislation and human rights gains of the past sixty years.

Constructing Race Baiters on the Left

On the other side of this coin, conservative media often claimed that Obama and his administration engaged in divisive forms of race baiting. For example, Sean Hannity often came to the defense of Sarah Palin's many racially divisive remarks, such as her consistent labeling of Obama as un-American, her claims that he is not a real American, or her accusations that he is someone who "sees America . . . as being so imperfect that he's palling around with terrorists who would target their own country."[51] Hannity defended Palin while simultaneously denying that anyone on the Right plays on racial fears or anxieties. Hannity stated,

> [T]here are some extreme, left-wing Democratic lawmakers accusing her [Palin] of resorting to race tactics on the campaign trail. Why? Palin recently referred to Barack Obama as, quote, "not one of us," prompting New York Congressman Greg Meeks [who is black] to say the following, quote: "They know they can't win on issues, so the last resort they have is race and fear."

Hannity went on to assert, "If it wasn't so ridiculously idiotic and absurd, it'd be funny. But—you know, but this—this sounds a lot like Barack Obama: 'They're going to tell you I have a funny name, and I don't look like those guys on the currency. And they're going to say, "Oh, he's black?"'" Hannity later added, "Nobody in the Republican Party is bringing this up except him and his supporters."[52]

After black and gay members of Congress, particularly John Lewis, Emmanuel Cleaver, and Barney Frank, were spat at and called racial and sexual names as they walked into Congress to vote on health care legislation in March of 2010,[53] Ann Coulter remarked,

> This is what "racism" has come to in America. Democrats are in trouble, so they say "let's call conservatives racists." We always knew it, but the Journolist postings gave us the smoking gun. This explains why we've heard so much about Tea Partiers being "racists" lately. . . . Most sickeningly, the mainstream media continue to spread the despicable lie that someone called civil rights hero Rep. John Lewis the "N-word" 15 times during the anti-ObamaCare rally in Washington. Fifteen times! . . . Democrats did their best to provoke an ugly confrontation by marching a (shockingly undiverse) group of black Democrats right through the middle of the anti–ObamaCare protest. But they didn't get one, so the media just lied and asserted Lewis was called the N-word. (If they wanted to hear the N-word so badly, they should have sent the congressional delegation to a Jay-Z concert.)[54]

Coulter went on to blame "liberal journalists, hundreds of them, chit-chatting about how to protect Obama. You know, they're openly saying, 'We're in trouble, we need to distract from what's going on. Let's just randomly call the conservative racist.' Liberals use this all the time to distract from what's going on."[55]

In July 2010 conservative author Andrew Breitbart appeared on Sean Hannity's show to defend the Tea Party and to refute charges that protesters verbally assaulted congressmen Lewis and Frank. Breitbart stated,

> The provable falsehood that the n-word was hurled by Tea Party people as part of a resolution to condemn the Tea Party. . . . I thought this is

outrageous because the Tea Party Federation sent a letter to the Congressional Black Caucus saying they wanted to investigate it. They do not want to talk about the exculpatory evidence that shows that the n-word did not happen. And so I told Ben Jealous of the NAACP, you want to divide this country on race? You want to keep negatively branding the Tea Party, constantly asking, are they racist, are they racist, are they racist? That is an act of sending a message—negative branding—to the American people and to black people that these are people to be feared.[56]

Breitbart also referenced an e-mail from a "good Samaritan" who supposedly sent him a video of the protest that showed no epithets or spitting occurred.[57]

Glenn Beck's messages often aligned with those of both Breitbart and Coulter; he frequently claimed that the Left unfairly accused the Right of racism in order to distract from substantive issues. In July 2009 Beck stated,

We have demonstrated President Obama's desire for racial justice, but how is he setting out to achieve it? Exactly the way a community organizer would: through intimidation, vilification, bullying, a system, an underground shell game. . . . Look how he has handled different things. [Henry Louis] Gates—he calls the cops stupid and racist before he admits, he says, "I don't know all of the facts." But he jumps to the conclusion that the cops are racist.[58]

Such messages have experienced an increase in recent years; right-wing media has traversed farther to the right since the early 1990s. For example, in a particularly interesting reversal of accusations, in May 2011, Mark Levin (a former advisor to Ronald Reagan's cabinet) went on the offensive against left-leaning media, calling them racist because they have white, and mainly white male, commentators:

NBC News is run by very, very white guys. "Meet the Press" has only had white guys in the anchor chair. "NBC Nightly News"—a white guy. Let's look at their bastard off-child, MSLSD: Chris Matthews—the whitest of the white guys, Joe Scarborough—white, Ed Schultz—fat and white,

Larry O'Donnell—mental patient and white, Rachel, what is her name anyway, Maddow—white. It's so white over there I'm blinded. Isn't it great they're standing up for minorities over there? Where's the EEOC? Oh yes, the EEOC. Why don't they investigate the on-air talent, take a look at their statistics as they're one to do. Are 12, 13, 14 percent of the on-air talent black? No. How about Hispanic? No. Why not? Why not, David Gregory? Why not give up your post, David Gregory, to some-body of color? Racism abounds over there at MSNBC and NBC. I sup-pose, right? Just look at it. Blindingly white.[59]

Levin detracts from the insinuations of racism leveled at the nearly all-white Tea Party and Birther movements by leveling charges of racism at the Left. And without the slightest bit of irony, he ignores the fact that Scarborough is a former Republican congressman. This speaks to the increasingly conservative bent and use of racial discourse by right-wing media.

A prescient example speaks to this tactic. On June 15, 2012, Neil Munro (a reporter for the right-wing website the Daily Caller), contin-ually interrupted a presidential speech on immigration.[60] Shortly after the incident ABC News reporter and anchor Sam Donaldson stated, "[M]any on the political right believe this president ought not to be there—they oppose him not for his policies and political view but for who he is, an African American. . . . These people and perhaps even cer-tain news organizations (certainly the right wing talkers like Limbaugh) encourage disrespect for this president."[61] In defense of Munro, conser-vative commentator Tucker Carlson stated that Donaldson's remarks were "prima facie ludicrous" and continued, "So, you don't like the way our reporter addressed the president and therefore he's racist? You sort of wonder how long that blanket charge can exist before people say, 'You know what? I'm not taking you seriously anymore.' Anyone who charges racism with no evidence is not a serious person, and shouldn't be taken seriously."[62] Yet, the evidence in question was quite blatant: Munro continued to interrupt Obama, even after Obama asked that he hold his questions and even after Obama returned to his questions at the completion of the speech.[63] Second, the questions reeked of nativist ideology: "Favoring jobs for foreigners over American workers?" and "What about American workers who are unemployed while you import foreigners?" Third and finally, Munro yelled that he was an immigrant (he emigrated from Ireland) and walked away from the press pen while shouting, "What about American workers who are unemployed, while you employ foreigners?"[64]

This exchange and defense of Munro's disrespectful and nativist comments demonstrate the depth and breadth of racist apologia and blame that recent right-wing media employs. Unsurprisingly, most white journalists (and right-wing media is overwhelmingly white) resent and push back against accusations of racism against Obama. And when faced with evidence of racist (and previously unseen) disrespect against Obama, the right-wing media resorts to a number of defense strategies. First and foremost is that the right-wing media ignores most of its critics. Second, when it does address critiques, it may affirm its good intentions and present counterevidence ("We've said positive things about Obama."). And with seemingly increasing intensity, it engages in a third strategy of throwing the charge back ("We're not racist, but it's racist of them to say we are."). While we have little interest in branding an individual commentator or even a specific network as "racist," we have outlined the methods by which the right-wing media operates as a structural and ideological property of white group dominance, how it mystifies its racialized attacks on Obama, and how it mitigates any identification of that agenda or strategy.

Dysfunctional Depictions

Right-wing talking heads have consistently described people of color as inherently dysfunctional or pathological in terms of their cultural habits, important values, or inability to defer gratification. For example, in discussing a 2007 dinner with Al Sharpton at the Harlem restaurant Sylvia's, Fox commentator Bill O'Reilly reported that he

> couldn't get over the fact that there was no difference between Sylvia's restaurant and any other restaurant in New York City. I mean, it was exactly the same, even though it's run by blacks, primarily black patronship. . . . There wasn't one person in Sylvia's who was screaming, "M-Fer, I want more iced tea." You know, I mean, everybody was—it was like going into an Italian restaurant in an all-white suburb in the sense of

people were sitting there, and they were ordering and having fun. And there wasn't any kind of craziness at all.[65]

O'Reilly lays bare the belief that black people are crazy and uncouth people who act out in ill-mannered ways. Hence, he is shocked when he fails to witness this behavior and confirm his stereotypical views. These implicit attitudes matter because they work to subtly frame the meanings of race and racial interaction. While some read O'Reilly's comments as complimentary of black people at Sylvia's, we see them as both a specific backhanded compliment and a general indicator of the subtle conflation of blackness with bad values and rude behavior that permeates much of O'Reilly's and Fox News' coverage of African Americans in general.

O'Reilly has a long history of depicting people of color as dysfunctional social pariahs. For example, in August 2006, O'Reilly argued for the "profiling of Muslims" at airports and that "Muslims between the ages of 16 and 45" should be automatically detained for questioning. He implicitly associated Islam with criminality, stating that such detention "isn't racial profiling" but rather "criminal profiling."[66] Furthermore, in the wake of the devastation of Hurricane Katrina in New Orleans, O'Reilly claimed (without providing any evidence),

Ten percent of Americans, and 10 percent of any society, simply are so chaotic for whatever reason that they're never, ever going to be able to fend for themselves and make a living. . . . It's not massive neglect, it's not; it's human nature. . . . They're not going to pay their rent, they're going to spend it on drugs and alcohol. And therefore, they're going to be out on the street with their hand out. Many, many, many of the poor in New Orleans are in that condition. They weren't going to leave no matter what you did. They were drug-addicted. They weren't going to get turned off from their source. They were thugs, whatever.[67]

This type of eugenics-based logic (that the poor are poor because it's "human nature"), coupled with the pathology discourse that the poor are all drug-addicted, is a common way of dismissing empathy and rationalizing a Spencerian or Social Darwinist approach to the poor—let them die out. If they are all "thugs" anyway, then why should we help them, or even care for them as fellow human beings?

The rhetoric of racial dysfunction and pathology continued with other Fox News commentary. For example, during Obama's May 2011 trip to Ireland, Fox's Eric Bolling tweeted, "Obama chugging 40's in IRE while tornadoes ravage MO" ("40's" refers to forty-ounce bottles of malt liquor—stereotypically associated with black consumption).[68] Laura Ingraham then told *Fox and Friends*, "I do think of the disconnect and maybe the tone-deafness, if you will, of that devastation from Missouri . . . heartbreaking pictures and then President Obama lifting a glass of Guinness. There's something about that, that I think hits people in the gut. Maybe the Irish part of the trip could have been put off to another day."[69] Ingraham's comment recalls an earlier statement she made about Reverend Al Sharpton's 2008 visit to George Bush in the White House, in which she said she hoped President Bush "nailed down all the valuables."[70]

So also, when Gabon's president met with Obama in the White House in June 2011, Fox ran the headline "Hoods in the House." During the segment of Fox Business's *Follow the Money* host Eric Bolling stated, "Guess who's coming to dinner? A dictator. Mr. Obama shares a laugh with one of Africa's kleptocrats. It's not the first time he's had a hoodlum in the hizzouse." The show then aired a picture of rapper and poet Common.[71] Regarding Common's visit to the White House—part of a 2011 celebration of American poetry and prose that included writers Elizabeth Alexander, Billy Collins, Rita Dove, Kenneth Goldsmith, Alison Knowles, Aimee Mann, and Jill Scott—right-wing talking heads used the event to bring up more stereotypical aspects of black culture. Of Common, Sarah Palin remarked, "You know, the White House's judgment on inviting someone who would glorify cop killing during Police Memorial Week, of all times, you know, the judgment—it's just so lacking of class and decency and all that's good about America with an invite like this."[72] Sean Hannity stated, "This administration will never learn its lesson . . . not surprisingly. . . . This is not the guy that you invite to the White House for a poetry reading. . . . This is not the guy we want our kids to listen to. . . . [President Obama] goes back to his radical roots again and again and again: Ayers, Wright, Pflager." In his next segment, Hannity invited right-wing analyst Karl Rove to discuss the matter, whereupon Rove called Common a "thug" and said the invitation of Common to the White House was a slap in the face when the country needed to unify in the killing of Osama bin Laden.[73] And just a couple of months later, on the occasion of Obama's fiftieth birthday celebration, Fox News ran the following headline: "Obama's Hip-Hop BBQ Didn't Create Jobs."[74]

The invocation of negative racial stereotypes associated with bad value judgments, poor choices, and below-average intelligence allows for right-wing wielders of that discourse to frame their subjects as dangerous, immoral, and unsuitable leaders, all with the authority of a supposedly "objective" and "neutral" reporter. When attached to Obama, the references to "40's," thugs, hoods, radicalism, and hip-hop together work to associate Obama with a dangerous racial underclass that is bent on waging violence and engaging in depraved behaviors, all with the consequence of bringing down a country already in need of economic and political repair. Bear in mind that these remarks were often couched in a context in which Obama's supposed drinking and partying were distracting from the real needs of the country. Hence, Obama emerges not only as a dysfunctional individual but as an incapable and distracted leader.

Constructing the White Viewer

Fox News and associates constantly constructed the average white viewer as a hard-working American who is, at base, frightened by the unfair and racialized agenda of Obama. Characterizing the white viewer as an American under the assault of a dark and dangerous "other" implies a racial conflict in which the white viewer is an innocent bystander in the racial drama directed by the Obama administration.

For example, in July of 2008 Glenn Beck engaged in a pithy race-based fear-mongering remark on his Fox News show. He stated that Obama "has a deep-seated hatred for white people or the white culture" and that Obama "is, I believe, a racist."[75] After other journalists and activists asked him to specify, rationalize, or retract his remarks, Rupert Murdoch defended Beck's comment. In a November 2009 interview with Australia's *Sky News*, Murdoch said,

On the racist thing, that caused a grilling. But he [Obama] did make a
very racist comment. Ahhh . . . about, you know, blacks and whites and
so on, and which he said in his campaign he would be completely above.
And um, that was something which perhaps shouldn't have been said
about the President, but if you actually assess what he was talking about,
he was right.[76]

Moreover, Sean Hannity joined Murdoch in defending Beck's assertion that Obama is a "racist." In discussing Beck's comment, Hannity
stated, "But wait a minute. Wait, hang on a second. When the president hangs out with Jeremiah Wright for 20 years, I'm—can one
conclude that there are issues with the president, black liberation
theology?"[77]

Right-wing pundit Mark Levin went so far as to frame Obama as a
cult-like figure whom whites should reasonably fear as heralding the
opening stages of a fascist social order:

There is a cult-like atmosphere around Barack Obama, which his campaign has carefully and successfully fabricated, which concerns me. The
messiah complex. Fainting audience members at rallies. Special Obama
flags and an Obama presidential seal. A graphic with the portrayal of the
globe and Obama's name on it, which adorns everything from Obama's
plane to his street literature. Young school children singing songs prais-
ing Obama. Teenagers wearing camouflage outfits and marching in military order chanting Obama's name and the professions he is going to
open to them. An Obama world tour, culminating in a speech in Berlin
where Obama proclaims we are all citizens of the world. I dare say, this
is ominous stuff.[78]

During an October 2008 broadcast of his nationally syndicated radio
show, Michael Savage stated,

I fear that Obama will stir up a race war. You want to ask me what I fear?
I think Obama will empower the racists in this country and stir up a
race war in order to seize absolute power. I believe that's what he will do.
It will not be as overt as you may think, but it'll be a subtle race war on
every level imaginable.

As the show went on, Savage took an online caller, who stated,

> I absolutely agree with you as far as the race war goes. I think the great-
> est thing that concerns me about Obama is his resentment toward this
> country. I feel that him and his wife feel that they have fought very hard
> against whites, and that everything that they have, they are entitled to
> versus being thankful and feeling privileged for living in this country,
> and what this country has provided in terms of opportunities.

To this Savage replied, "Correct. And affirmative action helped both of
them, there's no question about it."[79]

White viewers of Fox were constantly framed as people who should
be frightened and apprehensive about issues pertaining to race. In
February 2007 Glenn Beck stated that he doesn't "have a lot of African-American friends [because] . . . I'm afraid that I would be in an
open conversation, and I would say something that somebody would
take wrong, and then it would be a nightmare."[80] In this same vein,
Bill O'Reilly stated, "Instead of black and white Americans coming
together, white Americans are terrified. They're terrified. Now we can't
even say you're articulate? We can't even give you guys compliments
because they may be taken as condescension?"[81] In this way, Fox commentators played up racial fears and anxieties, while painting whites
as victims of overly sensitive nonwhites, race-baiters, and political
correctness.

Seizing upon this fear, Fox News and right-wing commentators
anointed themselves as the real civil rights activists of today's "antiwhite" era. Glenn Beck stated that his Restoring Honor rally was to
"reclaim the civil rights movement."[82] So also, in 2007, Michael Savage
stated,

> [B]asically, if you're talking about a day like today, Martin Luther King
> Junior Day, and you're gonna understand what civil rights has become,
> the con it's become in this country. It's a whole industry; it's a racket. It'
> s a racket that is used to exploit primarily heterosexual, Christian, white
> males' birthright and steal from them what is their birthright and give
> it to people who didn't qualify for it. Take a guess out of whose hide all
> of these rights are coming. They're not coming out of women's hides.

Are they? No, there's only one group that's targeted, and that group are white, heterosexual males. They are the new witches being hunted by the illiberal left using the guise of civil rights and fairness to women and whatnot.[83]

By stoking racial fears and framing themselves as the true heirs of the Civil Rights Movement, conservative commentators can effectively advance a pro-white agenda that seeks to roll back some of the progressive gains toward equality of the past half-century while mystifying any such overt claim or color-conscious agenda.

These examples illustrate that the white-as-victim narrative both is widely shared and carries resonance across the right-wing media airwaves. Indeed, the story of white victimization is, in our supposedly "post-racial era," a dominant feature of the media's obsession with race. The right-wing media calls out to its viewers to identify as racialized white victims. And in competing for audience viewership, networks like Fox attract white viewership by telling them they deserve both social sympathy and a (white) badge of courage for the battle wounds they have received for simply being white. The white audience's righteous indignation is constructed through a media narrative that tells them they should feel displeasure with the legal initiatives (for example, affirmative action) that are not redressing past discrimination but enacting it upon them in the present. This makes the political quite personal. Such right-wing media discourse reinterprets historical and current patterns into personal attacks in which a black bogey man (today incarnated in the personage of Obama) hates them only because they are white. Importantly, these media messages attempt a paradoxical recovery of white political domination through the discourse of personal white victimization.

"Race-Obsessed" Obama

While a significant talking point of right-wing commentators is that race is declining in significance, this course was frequently reversed when they discussed Obama. That is, Obama was often framed as a racially obsessed man, driven to institute draconian measures that would drive the country into a race war or that would, at least, cause a bevy of unfortunate racial interactions. For example, Glenn Beck has constantly framed Obama's policies and statements as evidence of a secret plan for black reparations. In July of 2009 Beck stated, "This guy [Obama] is not who he says he is. None of his bills, none of his proposals are about what he says they're about. The health care bill is reparations. It's the beginning of reparations. He's going to give—if you want to go into medical school, the medical schools will get more federal dollars if they have proven that they are putting minorities ahead."[84] The very next day, Beck returned to the theme:

> Everything getting pushed through Congress—including this health care bill—is transforming America. And it's all driven by President Obama's thinking on one idea: reparations. "Oh Glenn, you are crazy! President Obama is against reparations. He said so himself." Yes, he did say that. What the media conveniently ignores is the reason why he is against them. As I warned before the election, he doesn't think they go far enough: "I fear that reparations would be an excuse for some to say, 'We've paid our debt' and to avoid the much harder work." I had forgotten about Obama's position on reparations until a couple of days ago. It ties everything together. What is that "harder work"?[85]

The notion that Obama would put racial identity politics above the good of the entire country continued to be expressed in right-wing media outlets. Months later on November 5, 2009, a tragic shooting at the Fort Hood military base outside of Killeen, Texas, took place. Obama addressed the nation from a Tribal Nations Conference that was hosted by the Department of the Interior. He began his remarks by acknowledging the US government's commitment to ensuring that "the first Americans get the best possible chances in life in a way that is consistent with your extraordinary traditions, and culture and values." Obama then went on to address the "tragic shooting in Fort Hood army base in Texas. . . . My immediate thoughts and prayers are with the wounded and with the families of the fallen and with those that live and serve at Fort Hood."[86]

In response to Obama's remarks, Glenn Beck stated on Fox News, "When the president was sitting there, or standing there, and he was talking about Native American rights in the middle of a tragedy, Fort

Hood, it didn't feel right. And it seemed, maybe to me, that he was even promising reparations."[87]

Beck was not alone in painting Obama as a president obsessed with race. In June 2009, Rush Limbaugh opined,

> They want reparations. What they don't know is that Obama's entire economic program is reparations! If I were Sharpton, if I'd been guest hosting Sharpton's show and I got a call like that, somebody complaining, I'd say, "Shhhh. Shhhh. Shhhh. Let me tell you the truth here. Everything in the stimulus plan, every plan he's got is reparations. He gonna take from the rich. He's going to take from the rich and he's going to give it to you. It just can't happen overnight. Be patient." It's redistribution of wealth, reparations, "returning the nation's wealth to its rightful owners," whatever you want to call it. It's reparations.[88]

If not framed as a reparations-obsessed president, Obama has often been painted as either a candidate or a politician pandering to racial interests. In January of 2007 Rush Limbaugh stated, "Hey Barack Obama has picked up another endorsement: 'Halfrican-American' actress Halle Berry. As a 'Halfrican American' I am honored to have Ms. Berry's support as well as the support of other 'Halfrican Americans.'"[89] In February 2008 Ann Coulter said in utter simplicity, "You're electing a black guy and he only cares about African Americans."[90]

Obama was also characterized as a racial hypocrite who would exacerbate racial tensions due to his unfair bias toward blacks. In July 2010 Fox Business News' *America's Nightly Scoreboard* host David Asman stated that Obama "is defending racists in . . . letting the Black Panthers off."[91] Conservative radio host, author, and political commentator Laura Ingraham stated in July 2010 on *The O'Reilly Factor* that "I believe much of what's been done in this administration unfortunately has set back race relations in this country, perhaps a generation. I predicted that would happen a year ago on my radio show. And I stand by that today."[92]

The attacks on Obama and his administration reached a fever pitch in July 2010 when conservative blogger Andrew Breitbart falsely suggested (via a doctored video) that Shirley Sherrod—in her former position with the USDA—had racially discriminated against white farmers.[93] The video was hosted on Breitbart's website and broadcast on *The O'Reilly Factor*, after which Bill O'Reilly called for Sherrod's resignation.[94] Tea Party organizer Dana Loesch also appeared on *Larry King Live* to frame Sherrod as antiwhite and the Obama administration as soft on black racists.[95] In particular, conservative commentators referenced Sherrod in relation to the Obama administration's earlier decision to scale back prosecution of allegations that the New Black Panther Party had engaged in voter intimidation.[96] Such comparisons were used to label the Obama administration as racially hypocritical and antiwhite.[97] In the wake of these accusations, Sherrod received numerous demands from government officials to submit her resignation.[98] Days later it was revealed that Breitbart had doctored the video in order to racially defame Sherrod and the Obama administration.[99] In such a racially hostile climate, *Washington Post* writer Jonathan Capehart suggested that the Obama administration fired Sherrod in order to avoid conservative claims that it was racist.[100] Toward that end, Capehart said that Sherrod was Obama's "sacrificial lamb."[101] Princeton professor Imani Perry wrote that the entire spectacle was a conservative manipulation of latent white fears that Obama—and black officials in his administration—would discriminate against whites: "I think many white Americans are fearful that with Obama in the White House, and the diversity in his appointments, that the racial balance of power is shifting. And that's frightening both because people always are afraid to give up privilege, and because of the prospect of a black-and-brown backlash against a very ugly history."[102]

Othering Obama

If not engaging in discourse that framed Obama as a man obsessed with racial reparations or with giving black people the upper hand against whites, conservative media pundits caricatured Obama. Through religious, economic, political, nationalist, and racial themes and symbolism, Obama was implicitly and explicitly "othered" as out of place and unbelonging in the United States. For example, in April 2008 Ann Coulter published an article about Obama's autobiography, *Dreams from My Father*. Her essay, entitled "Obama's Dimestore 'Mein Kampf,'" stated, "Has anybody read this book? Inasmuch as the book reveals

Obama to be a flabbergasting lunatic, I gather the answer is no. Obama is about to be our next president: You might want to take a peek. If only people had read 'Mein Kampf.'"[103] Here, Obama is painted as a National Socialist and compared to Adolph Hitler. Yet, later that year, in October, Michael Savage framed Obama as a "communist," an "Afro-Leninist," and a "noncitizen":

> We're getting ready for the communist takeover of America with a non-citizen at the helm—I love it. He won't even produce a birth certificate. Don't you love that? Something as basic as Obama's birth certificate now is an issue. I mean, if he's got nothing to hide, show it to me. Doesn't exist. It does not exist, they can't find it in the Hawaii government. It's never been produced. The one that was produced is a forgery. Go to my website, read the story.[104]

Continuing in the trend of othering, Glenn Beck framed Obama as a non-Western other who would seek US destruction through foreign policy choices. Specifically, Beck stated that Obama's policy would lead to "the destruction of Israel and . . . the end of the Western way of life, period."[105]

Sean Hannity took the othering discourse even farther when he explained how Obama would destroy nearly every supposedly cherished aspect of Western culture. In his book *Conservative Victory: Defeating Obama's Radical Agenda*, Hannity wrote, "Obama and his party stand for America's economic bankruptcy, virtual surrender in the war on terror, and a culture of death, from abortion to embryonic stem cell research to healthcare rationing tantamount to death panels."[106] Obama is constantly reconstructed as the quintessential anti-American. Ann Coulter (in dialogue with liberal commentator Alan Colmes) stated in 2007, "I do think anyone named B. Hussein Obama should avoid using 'hijack' and 'religion' in the same sentence." Colmes replied, "I see. So, in other words, you want to paint him as a terrorist by continuing to use—to highlight that his middle name is Hussein?" Coulter responded, "Just avoid those two together."[107]

Similarly, in February 2010, Glenn Beck stated, "He chose to use his name, Barack, for a reason. To identify not with America—you don't take the name Barack to identify with America. You take the name

Barack to identify, with what? Your heritage? The heritage, maybe, of your father in Kenya, who is a radical?"[108] Here Beck denies the melting-pot theory and the diversity of America and insinuates that Obama's first name is a valid window into the soul of a radical Kenyan who refuses to identify with the United States. Moreover, Ann Coulter stated simply, "He has a middle name that sounds like a 'terrorist' therefore he's 'soft' on terror and national defense."[109] The right-wing tactic of drawing audience attention to Obama's full name as evidence of his quintessential otherness has been continually deployed to the effect of it becoming a slur. As Nathan Thornburgh of *Time* magazine wrote of Obama's middle name "Hussein," "So maybe the H-word is more like the N-word: you can say it, but only if you are an initiate. Blacks can use the N-word; Obama supporters can use the H-word."[110]

Bill O'Reilly brought the point home in March 2008 in his description of Obama's supposed hatred for the United States: "How can you be close to a man who hates America that much?"[111] His rhetorical question asks voters how they could in good conscience support, or vote for, Obama, thereby reconstructing the public image of Obama as an evil man, fueled by his hatred of America and bent on destroying the United States. Mark Levin expanded on this trope of hate in terms of Obama's foreignness in an explicit way in July 2009:

> The President, you know, they just put Bernie Madoff away for life; the President's policies are Bernie Madoff times a thousand. He is taking a wrecking ball to this society. The American people love this country. They love its institutions; they revere the Constitution and the Declaration of Independence. What the President is peddling is something utterly foreign.[112]

By reshaping the president's image into that of a thief (akin to Bernie Madoff) bent on stealing money from the US public, coupled with the portrayal of his tax plan (in which the rich pay more than the current tax rate) as utterly foreign, Levin presents xenophobic messages as objective news.

These examples indicate how right-wing news marries Obama to the already hyper-reactionary Islamophobia and nativism that began anew in the post-9/11 United States. That widespread fear of the "others" in our midst (even the White House) drives public support for not only the GOP but also repressive national security policies, any policy that the Republicans can deem "socialist," and a juggernaut industrial-military complex, while it also engenders an organized, grass-roots backlash in the form of hyper-conservative Christian groups and anti-immigrant, vigilante, white-supremacist, and nationalist organizations.

In addition to being labeled non-Western, noncitizen, foreign, US-hating, Nazi, Communist, and "Afro-Leninist," Obama has been consistently constructed as an "affirmative action president." Right-wing commentators continually tell their audiences that Obama did not achieve any of his successes on his own merit and that his inferior candidacy is thus being forced down their throats. A key talking head in this strategy has been Rush Limbaugh. For example, in May of 2008, Limbaugh stated, "Barack Obama is an affirmative action candidate";[113] and "[i] If Barack Obama were Caucasian, they would have taken this guy out on the basis of pure ignorance long ago."[114] Later, in June 2008, Limbaugh stated that the Democratic Party was "go[ing] with a veritable rookie [then Senator Obama] whose only chance of winning is that he's black."[115] Returning to this theme in July 2010 Limbaugh stated,

> [Obama] wouldn't have been voted president if he weren't black. Somebody asked me over the weekend why does somebody earn a lot of money have a lot of money, because she's black. It was Oprah. No, it can't be. Yes, it is. There's a lot of guilt out there, show we're not racists, we'll make this person wealthy and big and famous and so forth. . . . If Obama weren't black he'd be a tour guide in Honolulu or he'd be teaching Saul Alinsky constitutional law or lecturing on it in Chicago.[116]

The tactic of deriding black accomplishment as due to white handouts works to both negate black meritocratic actions and paint the white majority as a group from which resources are being stolen.

Conclusion: The Right-Wing Media as an Interpretive Community

The media is an essential piece of the racialized social order. Commentators' public and authoritative interpretations and employers' hiring practices, which determine who is behind the camera, in the "bullpen," among the writers, and in charge of final cut decisions, structure white dominance in news making, and audiences generally seek out news sources that align with their already politicized and ideological worldviews. So also, the mere exposure to negative representations of certain categories may bias individuals.[117] For example, in a series of experiments, primed subjects were exposed to violent and misogynistic rap music, while control subjects were exposed to popular music. In the first experiment, violent and misogynistic rap music increased the automatic associations underlying evaluative racial stereotypes in both high- and low-prejudiced subjects. Explicit stereotyping, however, was dependent on priming and subjects' prejudice level. In the second experiment, the priming manipulation was followed by what seemed to be an unrelated person-perception task in which subjects rated black or white targets. Primed subjects judged a black target less favorably than a white target. Control subjects, however, rated black and white targets similarly. Subjects' prejudice levels did not moderate these findings, suggesting the robustness of priming effects on implicit attitudes.[118]

In another study, researchers explored how local news crime scripts might create ingrained heuristics for understanding crime and race. Subjects were presented with fictitious news stories. One was a mundane news story, one was a news story about crime without a mug shot, and another was a news story with a mug shot. For those stories with the mug shot, the researchers varied the darkness of the person in the picture. While the picture appeared for only five seconds in a ten-minute newscast, the effect was significant. When whites viewed a darker person in the mug shot, they showed 6 percent more support for punitive remedies than did the control group, which saw no crime story. When they were instead exposed to a lighter person in the mug shot, their support for punitive remedies increased by only 1 percent.[119] Such studies underscore how racial media representations, whether visual or rhetorical, influence and attract those who hold specific and unconscious racial attitudes.

In this chapter, we focused on the various linguistic manners and rhetorical strategies by which the right-wing media—as an institutional norm—uses the tropes of black dysfunction, white patriotism, white paternalism, and white victimhood to cover Obama's candidacy and presidency. In short, the right-wing media builds an easily consumable public discourse based on what the late historian Ronald Takaki called "virtuous republicanism"—concentrated repositories of the Protestant ethic that frame whites as innocent and superior in relation to the supposed impurity and imperfections of racialized "others." While these tropes were not always in play, our intention was to accentuate the repeated, if not ritualistic, features of conservative news. This, in turn, demonstrates the presence of an interpretive community rather than a disconnected group of journalists who rely on their personal journalistic skills or artistic judgments.

In bringing attention to the interpretive-community dynamics of Fox and its ilk, we do not intend to paint this institution as a monolith. Much of the coverage of Obama is complex and multidimensional; interwoven in the tapestry of white-supremacist rhetoric are threads that contest the stories of black dysfunction and white victimization. Yet, these voices are frayed and often cut short. In this vein, we should approach the right-wing media as hijacking the national conversation on race. That is, the interpretive community of right-wing voices on race and Obama affords a space—albeit a narrow one—in which to speak of racial matters in between the rock of a racially fatigued public enamored with "post-racialism" (the discourse that race no longer matters) and the hard place of "racist America" (the reality that race stratifies our lives and life chances). It has found a way to speak directly to a white conservative America weary of race: race doesn't matter except when the black guy hurts you.

4

Political Party, Campaign Strategy, and Racial Messaging

When it comes to race and politics, there is a familiar theatrical dance. Since the political realignment of the 1960s, Democrats have charged Republicans with trying to suppress the voting blocs of blacks, given their decidedly Democratic leaning. In response, Republicans vigorously deny such actions and decry the accusations as an underhanded play of the "race card"—exploiting progressive or antiracist attitudes by accusing others of racism. And so the finger pointing generally goes.[1]

The drama unraveled in May of 2012 when the former Florida Republican Party chairman Jim Greer unloaded a 630-page deposition in which he outlined a systematic effort by the "whack-a-do, right-wing crazies" in the GOP to suppress the black vote. Of a 2009 meeting with GOP officials, Greer stated, "I was upset because the political consultants and staff were talking about voter suppression and keeping blacks from voting"[2] and were saying that "minority outreach programs were not fit for the Republican Party."[3]

Greer's comments came within the context of a new Republican strategy to combat "voter fraud" by introducing the requirement for more and harder-to-obtain state-issued identification in states across the nation. In September of 2011, thirty US states required either photo ID or some other form of ID in order for a person to vote. And by 2012, Republicans had introduced more stringent voter ID legislation in thirty-two states.[4] Critics claim, first, that such laws are unnecessary as there is no evidence of widespread voter fraud.[5] Second, many say that such legislation is racist in either intent and/or effect because it targets a black population already economically marginalized that, on average, fails to possess the disposable income to obtain various proofs of identification. Hence, such legislation may equate to a form of poll tax—a tax historically used in the United States to disenfranchise poor people, blacks, Native Americans, and newly naturalized immigrants (and since 1964 made illegal by the Twenty-fourth Amendment to the US Constitution).

While the introduction of voter ID legislation might appear racially neutral, such measures are efficacious for the political Right because they appeal to a white constituency with preexisting antiblack biases and racial anxieties about a black underclass stealing votes and political power. For example, in February of 2012, the conservative group Minnesota Majority launched an Internet image of an African American male dressed in a black-and-white-striped prison suit and a person dressed in a blue mariachi costume standing in line to vote. A caption at the bottom of the image read, "Voter Fraud: Watch How Easy It Is to Cheat in Minnesota's Elections."[6] Such implicit racial imagery plays upon white voter fears and divisions in order to garner support for Republican legislation. And this tactic works not just in Minnesota but across the nation. A July 2012 study from the University of Delaware's Center for Political Communication demonstrated that support for voter identification is strongest among those who harbor negative opinions toward African Americans:

> To assess attitudes toward African Americans, all non–African American respondents in the poll were asked a series of questions. Responses to these questions were combined to form a measure of "racial resentment." Researchers found that support for voter ID laws is highest among those with the highest levels of "racial resentment."[7]

In this chapter, we continue our excavation of how African Americans as a group (and Barack Obama the individual) are represented as dysfunctional; how whites are assumed to be the standard, normal, and natural representatives of American citizenship; how whites often express control and paternalism over the US political sphere when nonwhite voices enter the political fray; and how white people then frame themselves as the beleaguered victims of nonwhite political and social forces, which have undermined the proper and correct culture and rules of American society. Specifically, we explore these four dimensions by examining the roots and evolution of the GOP's use of proposed legislation and campaign messaging to court white voters by activating, or playing to, whites' racial fears. We argue that, without question, the GOP's playing of the "race card" has proved an effective tool in shaping political attitudes and voting patterns.

Politics and Racial Messaging in the 1800s

The rise of racial appeals coincided with the emergence of the American two-party system in 1860. With the emergence of the party system came the quick alignment of those parties on the issue of race. At this time, the Democrats positioned themselves to the right of the center, while the Republicans moved to the left. In growing opposition to the prospect of emancipation, the Democratic Party decided not to rely solely on the basis of states' rights but also to use direct, explicit, and derogatory racial messages. Instead of arguing their stance in terms of equality and humanitarianism, Republicans also chose to use explicit racial rhetoric to their advantage while mainly playing on the growing antisouthern sentiment among their supporters.[8]

These appeals and rhetorical strategies were based around the societal norm of white supremacy. Due to the widespread belief in racial inequality, Democrats were able to campaign on direct attacks on blacks' supposed inferior biological and cultural traits to justify their stance against granting rights to African Americans, while Republicans had to justify their support for granting rights to blacks without violating the norm of inequality. Republican explicit racial appeals were used to reinforce the belief in white superiority over minorities and were often embedded in important stances toward taxes, immigration, labor, and voting.[9]

A party's rhetorical strategy is formed around that party's stance on a given issue and the societal norms in existence. Societal norms are reflections of the political and social trends surrounding the election period. During the nineteenth century, the widespread use of slavery in the South created the norm of racial inequality to which parties had to conform in order to achieve electoral success. However, with the passage of the Fourteenth and Fifteenth amendments, there was a brief period in which the short-lived norm of racial equality allowed limited political equality between races. During this time, Democrats were restrained from making explicit appeals on the issue of race. The widespread use of slavery in the American colonies led to the deeply rooted racial dispositions of the country. Due to the racial hierarchy established by the institution of slavery, a national assumption of black inferiority emerged. Abolitionists and their opponents both agreed on the inadequacy of blacks, but the groups did not agree on what they believed the cause to be. Abolitionists believed that with the aid of the government, this racial shortfall could be treated in order to liberate slaves from servitude. Many of these advocates, however, paired this idea with the need for segregation of the races due to African Americans' inability to qualify for full equality.[10]

Specifically, distinctions were drawn between whites and blacks on the issues of sexuality, violence, and work ethic. Fears of interracial sex, barbaric violence and crime, and the poor work ethic of blacks were widespread and either exaggerated or completely fabricated. In terms of sexuality, Americans feared the rapes of white women and girls caused by black men's reputations for lacking sexual control and the fear of racial mixing through reproduction. From the colonial period of the United States, prohibitions on interracial sexual relations were enforced to prevent these fears from becoming reality.

Along with their supposed uncontrollable sex drives, blacks were also believed to have an increased tendency to commit crimes and violent acts. This stereotype was a concern to both the northern and the southern states, and gained strength as the population of free slaves increased. Northern states implemented restrictions on voting and on immigration in order to protect themselves from the migrations of freed slaves into their region.[11] Some studies even suggest that the fear of racial violence was so great that the secession of the South from the union was to prevent a "race war" from being declared. Criminal and violent acts were believed to be rooted in blacks' inherent laziness. In the eyes of both advocates of slavery and abolitionists, once slavery was eliminated, crime and violence among blacks would increase due to their poor work ethic.[12]

During the 1860 election, Democratic rhetoric played on the nation's fear of racial equality. Due to the norm of social inequality, the Democrats were able to alter the Republicans' desire for abolition and convince the public that full racial equality was their opponents' main goal. The Democratic Party published a pamphlet that described the

Republicans' desire to fully integrate blacks into society so they could "sit at your table and marry your daughter." In this way the public was convinced that its fear of racial amalgamation could become a reality. Many people were also made to believe that the Republicans were willing to make concessions to blacks at any cost to white society. In addition to the publishing of anti-Republican pamphlets, partisan papers also aimed to exaggerate or even fabricate stories about black violence. Most stories that were originally seen as minor incidents were framed to strike outrage in the hearts of the American people, while others were drawn from around the world and displayed graphic violence involving blacks. As the Emancipation Proclamation drew closer, more explicit appeals were designed to give the public exaggerated images of the country's condition after the liberation of the slaves.[13]

Republican use of explicit racial appeals in the 1860 election was designed mainly to defend their reputation against the Democrats' claims.[14] The Republican campaign of 1860 focused mainly on the idea of "free white soil for free white men." By using this slogan, candidates and party members tried to distance themselves from their image as being allies to the black demographic. While Republicans united on their stance against the institution of slavery, the motive was not to mandate equal rights for the newly freed slaves. Many Republicans felt that slavery should be outlawed because it required the interaction between whites and blacks, because slaves occupied areas of land that could be owned by whites, and because black labor provided undesirable competition for whites. Republicans believed they were no more sympathetic than the Democrats because full equality was not up for consideration under their proposal. In response to the claims that they were pro-amalgamation, Republicans turned the argument against the accusers. For example, Republicans also accused Democrats of fearing that their wives would give in to relations with black men if they were not outlawed.

During Reconstruction, Republicans gained more political support by targeting the issue of sectionalism instead of the issue of racism.[15] While the latter was extremely important in regard to the implementation of policies during this time, the fear of the South rising again was far more concerning to many voters. Southern secession from the union was seen as unpatriotic and traitorous, and concerns about southern autonomy were more of a threat than the newly freed slaves. The language of the Fourteenth Amendment also places more emphasis on the Confederates in three out of the four sections than on race. Although their strategy failed, the Democrats ran on explicitly paternalistic racial appeals that tried to portray the Emancipation Proclamation as being potentially harmful to blacks by removing them from their accepted inferior role in society. Democrats also continued to speak out against interracial sexual relations and blacks' inherent stereotypical flaws.

By the 1880s, the progressive gains of the Reconstruction period began to slow. Republicans began losing support due to the declining importance of antisouthern and racial appeals during elections.[16] During the intersession election of 1867, the proposal to extend state suffrage to blacks signaled a direct challenge to the norm of inequality. These proposals were not only widely rejected in the South, but eight out of the eleven proposals were also rejected in northern states. This policy, coupled with proposed minority aid, caused the Republican Party's representational majorities to shrink by three quarters. By the 1868 presidential election, Republicans' direct appeals to blacks' civil rights waned. But in order to mobilize the black demographic in the South, party members began promising "racially neutral" resources and civic privileges such as schools, voting rights, political positions (although not highly public offices), and legal justice. While Ulysses S. Grant held the presidency for two terms, the political dynamics were once again on the brink of change.

By the beginning of the 1870s, a number of formal government actions shifted the norm from the use of explicit racial appeals to the use of implicit racial appeals.[17] After the ratification of the Fourteenth and Fifteenth amendments, the Democratic Party had to appear to conform to the legislations to avoid federal intervention in the South. The rise of black suffrage also guided the Democrats to appeal to the new voting demographic. Most appeals to the black community included events such as barbecues and picnics, along with the general trend of false promises. Due to the complicated history between southerners and racial tensions, southern Democrats only needed to give the appearance of recruiting black supporters because only a small minority would be willing to align with the party.

This shift forced parties to either use implicit racial appeals or avoid the issue of race altogether. One of the earliest implicit appeals was the

Democratic Party's plea for a laissez-faire system of government. Due to the heavy federal involvement in southern state affairs during Reconstruction, racial conservatives wanted to prevent further intervention in their attempts at segregation. The party used the cover of high taxes and restrictive budgets for government programs, instead of race, to justify their opposition to centralized power. Unfortunately, the other option of racial silence did not signal the end to racial discrimination. Violence still stood as a barrier between newly enfranchised blacks and their ability to exercise this right.

The end of the 1870s signaled the diminishing role of explicit racial appeals in campaigns and the beginning of the party reimaging and realignment that continued for a century—into the 1960s. Liberal Republicans, who emerged during the 1872 election, promoted a hyper-individualistic stance on racial inequality. They preached the message that it was not the government's responsibility to cure racism by fixing the ills of society. Instead the government should provide the rights and protection necessary for equality and individual success, but blacks must survive on their own. This strategy effectively disregarded structural disadvantages and pinned the quest for equality on black bootstrapping. During this election period, party lines began to blur along ideological lines, forming the "Republicrat" and "Demican" parties. After this election, Reconstruction and race disappeared from the national agenda, signaling another rise for the norm of inequality. Without the national anti-South sentiment, the government had no ability to protect black rights and the national government began to back away from the issue of race.[18]

By 1876 the party divide on race died away.[19] While racist actions were in some ways limited by the existence of the Fourteenth and Fifteenth amendments, racial conservatives found ways to exploit the black population. This period was built around segregation into "separate but equal" facilities, state-sponsored studies to prove a "natural" racial hierarchy, and political efforts to deny black rights. Without the feature of race on the national agenda, there no longer existed a formal institution to protect black human or civil rights.

Racial appeals were briefly reintroduced with the emergence of the southern Populists.[20] As a reaction to the economic crisis, southern Populists rallied around the farmer and laborer. In order to recruit black support, the party supported the protection of rights, biracial ballots, and antilynching laws. To defend their position on race, party leaders also framed the Democrats as being sympathetic toward blacks by highlighting Grover Cleveland's White House dinner party with Frederick Douglass and his white wife.

The anti-Populist response aimed to ruin the Populist Party by any means necessary. Besides the normal reactions of violence, fraud, and derogatory racist rhetoric, a number of formal measures were taken to prevent the mobilization of black voters. Many states used state amendments on voting rights to disenfranchise blacks once again. The long-residency-period, poll-tax, and crime-conviction measures were created with racial undertones to limit voting rights to whites. These measures were justified by the criminality stereotype, which also was used to justify the increased number of violent acts being perpetrated against blacks.

Politics and Racial Messaging: The Early
to Mid-Twentieth Century

The political reawakening of African Americans in the early twentieth century helped expand the movement against the norm of social inequality. By 1930 the Great Migration had shifted 21 percent of African Americans into the northern states. This cohesive relocation allowed minority leaders to mobilize voters and create powerful minority political groups such as the NAACP. The NAACP was active in protesting Judge John J. Parker's nomination to the Supreme Court on the basis of his racial biases, which correlated with his affiliation with the lily-white Republicans. This organization also challenged racial rhetoric and derogatory acts of speech and put public pressure on rural towns associated with lynching.[21]

During the 1948 election, the NAACP pressured Truman to take formal actions to protect African American citizens and their civil rights. During his presidency, legislation was passed to outlaw lynching, remove the poll tax, and desegregate the armed forces. Truman's pro-equality actions caused the Democratic Party to once again divide along the issue of race in what was called the Dixiecrat Rebellion. The States Right Democratic Party focused on the implicitly racial issue of states' rights, but its limited explicit outbursts violated the norm of equality, which many people were not willing to publicly defy. At the 1948 Democratic National Convention, for example, southern Democrats came determined to oppose the party's civil rights plank.[22]

In general, mass media and public endorsements for equality indicated a shift not only in African American mobilization but also in the mobilization of the country at large. For the first time, racist images and derogatory rhetoric in the media were replaced with positive representations of blacks' achievements and characteristics and condemnations of the norm of white supremacy. One specific endorsement by the media was its support of the *Brown v. Board of Education* decision.[23] A number of public endorsements for racial equality were given by presidents. Even presidents' wives called for an end to racism. Common racial misperceptions were also corrected by scientists who abandoned the theory of hereditarianism, which had previously supported the notion that intelligence and moral values were inherited and varied chiefly by racial groups.[24]

From the 1940s to the 1960s the National Opinion Research Center (NORC) conducted surveys about various racialized issues, and the results show the growing egalitarianism of the white demographic. From 1942 to 1946, majority northern white opinion reversed on the issue of racial inferiority with the belief that blacks and whites were on the same intellectual level. It was not until the mid-1950s that white southerners also subscribed to this idea. By 1963 survey responses indicated the desire for the integration of public facilities and schools and for equal career opportunities for African Americans.[25]

With the shift of popular opinion toward racial equality, southerners had to reshape their rhetorical approach to include implicit racial appeals in order to prevent segregation without violating the new norm.[26] Southerners stopped warning about the dangers of "beastly black rapists" and began making paternalistic arguments about the well-being of African Americans, with congressmen such as Senator John Bell Williams assuring the nation that "our Negroes know that we have their interests at heart."[27] Although southern party members gave up the ideology of white supremacy, segregation was defended by new methods. Southerners recast segregation as necessary to protect whites from African Americans' supposed inherent violence. By coupling a stereotype with a seemingly moral motive, party members attempted to hide their belief that minorities were overprotected at the expense of the white community. As the civil rights movement gained momentum and pushed the Civil Rights Act of 1964 into debate, the rhetorical strategy of the South once again changed course. Congressional members avoided explicit racial appeals in their own speeches but did not feel the need to limit them when drawing from outside sources. For example, Mississippi senator John Stennis read from a newspaper that "Negroes might start killing the white people in Mississippi pretty soon."[28] The number of explicit appeals made in these references to secondary sources was double the amount used in speeches made by members from the Deep South and quadruple the amount from outer southern states. Party members believed this tactic of quoting racist comments made by others showed adherence to the antiracism norm and avoided punishment of its members.

After the Supreme Court's decision in *Brown v. Board of Education*, southern defenses of racial inequality disappeared at the national level and made only limited appearances elsewhere. Southern party members appealed to the Constitution to defend segregation and removed overtly racial rhetoric from their speeches. Instead of referring to whites, white supremacists referred to the "majority community," and rather than discussing racial minorities, they discussed the "liberal political power structure."[29] It was hoped that this argument would appeal to the more tolerant majorities by removing the argument of race altogether from their defense. Even organizations designed to fight the desegregation efforts, such as the Citizens' Councils, shifted to implicit arguments with the exception of local reassurance of protection for the majority in the wake of racial change.

Politics and Racial Messaging: From the Mid-Twentieth Century to Today

The political Right has used a variety of racial discursive strategies. One approach is to raise an issue full force. A classic example of this is the voter identification laws that proliferated across the United States, particularly after the 2008 election of President Obama. According to the Brennan Center for Justice,

In [the 2012] legislative session, at least 37 states are considering or have considered voter ID and/or proof of citizenship legislation. Those states are: Alabama, Alaska, Arizona, Arkansas, California, Colorado, Connecticut, Hawaii, Idaho, Illinois, Iowa, Kansas, Maine, Maryland, Massachusetts, Minnesota, Mississippi, Missouri, Montana, Nebraska, Nevada, New Hampshire, New Mexico, New Jersey, New York, North Carolina, Ohio, Oregon, Pennsylvania, Rhode Island, South Carolina, Tennessee, Texas, Virginia, Washington, West Virginia, and Wisconsin.[30]

The Lawyers' Committee for Civil Rights Under Law reported that thirteen states—Florida, Georgia, Hawaii, Idaho, Indiana, Kansas, Louisiana, Michigan, South Carolina, South Dakota, Tennessee, Texas, and Wisconsin—passed laws that mandated or requested that voters produce an identification card with their photograph in order to vote.[31]

While these voter identification laws may have appeared benign, a 2006 study by the Brennan Center for Justice "showed that millions of American citizens do not have government-issued photo identification, such as a driver's license or passport. . . . [T]he survey demonstrated that certain groups—primarily poor, elderly, [younger citizens] and minority citizens—are less likely to possess these forms of documentation than the general population."[32] The study further demonstrated that "[t]wenty-five percent of African-American voting-age citizens have no current government-issued photo ID, compared to eight percent of white voting-age citizens,"[33] amounting to more than five million African Americans with no photo ID.

Given the many decades of black voter support for the Democratic Party, it is no surprise that supporters of photo identification laws are generally Republicans while opponents of such laws tend to be Democrats.[34] In fact, during the 2012 presidential election, Pennsylvania House Republican leader Mike Turzai stated that the state's voter identification law was "going to allow Gov. [Mitt] Romney to win the state of Pennsylvania."[35]

Another discursive strategy that Republicans have used is to defend an issue by defending a particular group; here, often that group is white Americans. For example, one perspective on the demise of affirmative action is that it was undermined between the late 1970s and the early 1990s. According to this view, the assault on affirmative action came from three sources—all from the right side of the political spectrum. First, federal courts stacked with conservative Republican judges rendered unfavorable decisions. Second, Republican lawmakers, generally, and Ronald Reagan and George H. W. Bush, specifically, were hostile toward affirmative action. Third, conservative entrepreneurs organized legal and political campaigns against the policy. The mantra among "color-blind" activists was that affirmative action was "reverse discrimination" against a new victim—whites.[36]

A third discursive approach used by those on the political Right is to support an issue but distance themselves from the broader controversy surrounding it. An example of this is the way the GOP benefits from the emotional energy of Birtherism but either explicitly or implicitly distances itself from the inanity of that movement. On August 34, 2012, during the height of the presidential campaign, candidate Mitt Romney learned "a lesson often reserved for small-time candidates and very conservative Republicans. . . . The first rule of birtherism is you don't talk about birtherism unless you want to be labeled a birther."[37] Romney thought it would be humorous to tell a crowd of supporters, "Ann was born at Henry Ford Hospital; I was born at Harper Hospital. . . . No one's ever asked to see my birth certificate. They know that this is the place that we were born and raised."[38]

The "joke" was a not-so-veiled reference to the Birther claim that Obama was not born in the United States. While getting the benefit of the comment—possibly a wink and a nod to Birthers—Romney's campaign quickly distanced him and it from the Birther movement. Romney adviser Kevin Madden contended that "[t]he governor has always said, and has repeatedly said, he believes the president was born here in the United States. He was only referencing that Michigan, where he is campaigning today, is the state where he himself was born and raised."[39]

A fourth, and maybe the most frequent discursive approach has been the clear use of implicit racial appeals. The shift of the social norm of racial equality to the national level pushed suppression of racism into implicit appeals in both the deep and outer southern states. "Nonsegregationist" politicians were endorsed throughout the South, but this group included candidates who simply refrained from using their policy position within their campaigns. Most of the time this label was used to cover racial conservatism in order to increase voters' support.

For instance, noted segregationist George Wallace toned down his racial rhetoric for his 1966 gubernatorial campaign.[40] In sharp contrast to his previous cry of "segregation today, segregation forever," Wallace used more subtle and generalized language in his campaign promise to "awaken the nation to the liberal-Socialistic-Communist design to destroy local government in America."[41] Not only did politicians have to appeal to white voters who supported the shift in the racial norm, but they also had to appeal to the newly enfranchised black demographic in their districts. These changes in party rhetoric, however, were minimal and mainly symbolic and were intended to conceal the lingering negative perceptions of African Americans.[42]

Nixon's campaign in the 1968 election showed the power of implicit racial appeals in capturing the majority vote. During this campaign, Nixon closely aligned himself with southern politicians and aimed to slow desegregation efforts. In order to cover this election stance, the party marketed its determinations as an effort to bring the "new south" to "new blacks." One specific implicit appeal was the demand for law and order to cure social unrest. From a racial standpoint, this appeal was meant to address the violent riots of the Civil Rights Movement, many of which were attributed to the stereotype of blacks as violent.[43]

Nixon's efforts reached beyond the South and also addressed the negative views of African Americans that had reached the North. The enforcement of civil rights legislation outside the South was never accepted by northern voters since many believed that racism did not cause widespread corruption and violence in those northern states. In short, civil rights legislation was thought unnecessary. Although African Americans were ostensibly not viewed as inferior, the threat to the northern status quo stirred up negative feelings.[44] Richard Nixon's 1968 campaign captured some of the mood among white voters in his promise to enforce "law and order"—code for cracking down on black militants.[45]

As implicit appeals began to gain popularity, both Democrats and Republicans engineered racial appeals that were subtle enough to work while not violating the social norm of equality.[46] Specifically for the Democrats, the avoidance of racial appeal in elections was no longer an option. While finding a more salient issue than racial appeals is one factor in defending a party against the opposition's use of them, a direct counterresponse is also needed for success. Particularly, ignoring the opposition's racial appeal may not diminish the support of African American voters, but it might diminish the support of the split white demographic, which is key to the Democratic Party's electoral success. Republicans began appealing to middle-class, conservative African Americans in the 1980s and 1990s. GOP strategists theorized that a gain of 20 percent of African American votes would give Republicans a large advantage over their opponents. Events such as barbecues and parades held in predominantly African American towns and neighborhoods were created to recruit voters, but the GOP was fighting its own image and largely failed to recruit blacks to the party.[47] It was widely known that only limited recruitment was possible given the party's conservative stance on race and social issues known to disproportionally impact blacks.

Because of the failed Republican strategy to recruit blacks, the GOP turned full-scale to abstract and implicit racial messaging. In 1981, former Republican Party strategist Lee Atwater gave an interview discussing the racialized political strategy of the GOP:

> You start out in 1954 by saying, "Nigger, nigger, nigger." By 1968 you can't say "nigger"—that hurts you. Backfires. So you say stuff like forced busing, states' rights and all that stuff. You're getting so abstract now [that] you're talking about cutting taxes, and all these things you're talking about are totally economic things and a byproduct of them is [that] blacks get hurt worse than whites. And subconsciously maybe that is part of it. I'm not saying that. But I'm saying that if it is getting that abstract, and that coded, that we are doing away with the racial problem one way or the other. You follow me—because obviously sitting around saying, "We want to cut this," is much more abstract than even the busing thing, and a hell of a lot more abstract than "Nigger, nigger."[48]

When Ronald Reagan spoke of supposed "welfare queens" gaming the system, voters knew what he meant.[49] This latter imagery melded the Republicans' focus on lower taxes and smaller government with whites' racial animosity. The message to whites was implicit, but clear: your taxes are high because Lyndon Johnson's programs are funneling your money to undeserving black women. These seemingly race-neutral campaign themes, welfare and crime, have demonstrably racially loaded undertones.[50] Nixon's effort was sufficiently successful at galvanizing white support that it survived an election in which a third-party candidate (George Wallace) ran on overtly racist themes. Republican candidates Nixon and Reagan ultimately won the support of a majority of white voters, having used racial themes to begin the process of converting southern and blue-collar whites from their traditional affiliation with the Democratic Party.

As more overt racism has become increasingly taboo, white politicians have begun to appeal to white voters' race concerns through subtle overtures.[51] In 1988, a group that supported George H. W. Bush's presidential campaign, with the apparent approval of his campaign, ran a highly controversial ad that baited white fears about young black male violence. The ads featured a menacing image of Willie Horton, a black escapee from Massachusetts who fled to Maryland and broke into a white couple's home. There, Horton stabbed the husband and raped the wife. The ads showed Horton's menacing, scowling headshot. In addition to highlighting Horton's crimes, the ads also attacked Democratic presidential candidate Michael Dukakis—then governor of Massachusetts—for the weekend release program under which Horton had fled the state.[52] Republican political operatives knew that the Horton ad would use continuing racism as a way to win white support.[53] In response to this ad, Dukakis's campaign manager, Susan Estrich, stated, "[I]f you were going to run a campaign of fear and smear and add appeal to racial hatred you could not have picked a better case to use than this one."[54] Since the election, some consensus has formed around the idea that "the Bush campaign trafficked in racially loaded stereotypes" in its use of the furlough issue.[55]

Nixon's and Reagan's more subtle race baiting was matched by the overt racism of other candidates in the late 1980s and 1990s, such as David Duke and Jesse Helms. In his 1989 bid for a Louisiana US Senate seat and 1991 bid for Louisiana governorship, Republican and former Ku Klux Klan leader David Duke made explicit racial appeals. He directly mentioned nonwhite racial groups—especially African Americans—as composing a "welfare underclass" that encouraged "illegitimate births," and stated that the system involved taking white money in taxes to set aside to "promote the incompetent." Duke lost both races but received

44 percent of the overall vote and 60 percent of the white vote in his 1991 Senate bid.[56] Arguably, Duke's unapologetic relationship with the Klan and his emphasis on racially loaded themes was clear notice to Louisiana voters that his position on race was no different than that of the former Governor Wallace when he demanded "segregation today, segregation tomorrow, segregation forever."[57]

When Jesse Helms, a white senator from North Carolina, faced a black challenger, Harvey Gantt, in 1990, few were surprised that race played a role in Helms's ultimate victory. In the race, Helms brought up several issues tied to race, including his allegation that Gantt favored racial quotas that would benefit blacks.[58] One of Helms's advertisements showed the hands of a white person crumbling a rejection letter. "You needed that job," the announcer said, "and you were the best-qualified. But they had to give it to a minority because of a racial quota. Is that really fair?"[59] The ad was broadcast just a few days shy of the election and boosted Helms to victory in an election that surveys had predicted would be a dead heat.[60]

Another ad aired by Helms attacked Gantt for using "racial ads" on black radio stations. Helms's commercial accused Gantt of running a "secret campaign," asking, "Why doesn't Harvey Gantt run his ad on all radio stations, so everyone can hear it instead of just on black stations? Doesn't Harvey Gantt want everyone to vote?" Surprisingly, this Senate race was unlike others, in that Gantt had a large campaign fund and was able to advertise widely before the election, giving Helms the opportunity to attack him for his supposedly exclusive radio ads.[61]

Such explicit appeals also worked between white candidates, which suggests the continued centrality of antiblack bias in politics. For example, during the 2000 presidential primaries, strategist Karl Rove masterminded a much-needed victory for George W. Bush during his South Carolina primary with a campaign that featured a quiet racial attack. Rove strategically used racial innuendos like the rumor that John McCain had fathered a black child out of wedlock.[62] People in some areas of South Carolina received "push polling" phone calls—wherein the caller attempts to influence or alter the view of respondents under the guise of conducting an objective poll. The self-described pollsters would ask, "Would you be more likely or less likely to vote for John McCain for president if you knew he had fathered an illegitimate black child?"[63] These rumors were based on a reference to Bridget McCain, a darker-skinned Bangladeshi baby adopted by the McCains in 1991.[64] At the time, Richard Hand, a professor at evangelical Christian college Bob Jones University, also sent an e-mail message to "fellow South Carolinians" that told its recipients that John McCain had "chosen to sire children without marriage."[65]

These explicit appeals worked in the context of a recession that hit working-class whites hard, in states with high concentrations of white working-class evangelicals who would be swayed by moral and racial issues such as out-of-wedlock children sired across the color line, and in states (e.g., Louisiana, South Carolina, and North Carolina) where white voters held already-entrenched racial and federal animosities. That is, blacks were easily scapegoated for taking "white jobs," and federal measures to protect black civil rights and promote equality were reframed as unfair government intervention that trod too heavily upon "states' rights." However, these explicit appeals were risky. With the growth of politically correct multiculturalism and more and more people heralding the benefits of "diversity" in the culture wars, explicit racial appeals nearly disappeared in the 1990s. By the 2000s, even races in the southern states were based more on implicit racial appeals so as not to offend against the rising tide of the norm of equality.

For example, in the 2006 US Senate race, Tennesseans witnessed attempts at subtle racial appeals in a high-profile election. In a tight race between Bob Corker (white) and Congressman Harold Ford (black), the Republican National Committee played the "race card." A television ad, funded by the Republican National Convention (RNC), insinuated a relationship between Ford and a white woman.[66] The ad's hardest-hitting jab came from the mouth of a scantily clad white woman. "I met Harold at the Playboy Club," she said, casting a flirtatious look into the camera. Then as the ad drew to an end, the woman said, "Harold, call me." That dig was meant to remind people that Ford attended a 2005 Super Bowl party sponsored by Playboy. But it was also meant to suggest that the black congressman had become too familiar with a white woman.

During this election, Ford made an effort to exert a "normalizing effect" by focusing on critical and supposedly race-neutral policy issues such as gay marriage and illegal immigration. Ford's support of a ban on gay marriage and harsh criticism of illegal immigration sought to mobilize the white conservative voters in Tennessee. Also, after showing no signs of prior orthodox Christian beliefs, he made numerous religious references during the campaign that appealed to the Bible Belt culture and white evangelical voters. However, the RNC racialized what had been a deracialized campaign when it aired the Playboy ad, generally referred to as the "Bimbo" ad. The advertisement was made to convince white voters that Ford had violated the southern traditionalism and etiquette that forbade black men from associating with white women. In addition to this ad, a Republican Party pamphlet circulated at the time that urged voters to "preserve your way of life" was also a subtle way to racialize the political contest.[67]

The 2012 Republican Primaries: A Field of Nightmares?

By February of 2012, the GOP had finalized its list of presidential candidates to four: Ron Paul, Rick Santorum, Mitt Romney, and Newt Gingrich. Herman Cain, an African American, had been brought down by the scandals of alleged marital infidelity and sexual harassment with white and light-skinned women, while Rick Perry dropped from the field after serious verbal gaffes in debates and his inability to adequately explain his family's lease of a Texas hunting camp then called "Niggerhead" (now "North Camp Pasture").[68] However, these four candidates have also doled out racist and racially controversial comments of their own.

During the Republican primary in Iowa in December of 2011, Rick Santorum said to a crowd of mostly white faces, "I don't want to make black people's lives better by giving them somebody else's money. I want to give them the opportunity to go out and earn money."[69] When questioned about his statement, Santorum stated that his views were influenced by the movie *Waiting for Superman*. He stated, "Yesterday I talked for example about a movie called, um, what was it? 'Waiting for Superman,' which was about black children and so I don't know whether it was in response and I was talking about that."[70] Yet, when asked about the comment later, Santorum backtracked to state, "[I] didn't recall using that particular word. . . . It was probably a tongue-tied moment. . . . In fact, I'm pretty confident I didn't say, 'black.' I sort of started to say a word and sort of mumbled it and changed my thought. I don't recall saying black. No one in the audience heard me say that."[71]

Ron Paul helped form the Ron Paul & Associates corporation in 1984, for which he served as president. Under his tenure, the corporation published several newsletters, including *Ron Paul's Freedom Report*, *Ron Paul Survival Report*, *Ron Paul Political Report*, and *Ron Paul Investment Letter*, in which some have noted a "consistent ideological line" of racist paranoia.[72] In his book *White Party, White Government*, Joe Feagin cites comments like the following: "opinion polls consistently show only about 5% of blacks have sensible political opinions"; "if you have ever been robbed by a black teen-aged male, you know how unbelievably fleet-footed [sic] they can be"; and a statement that black representative Barbara Jordan is "the archetypical half-educated victimologist" whose "race and sex protect her from criticism." Feagin comments,

> They were published under a banner containing Paul's name. . . . What they reveal are decades worth of obsession with conspiracies, sympathy for the right-wing militia movement, and deeply held bigotry against blacks, Jews, and gays. In short, they suggest that Ron Paul is not the plain-speaking antiwar activist his supporters believe they are backing— but rather a member in good standing of some of the oldest and ugliest traditions in American politics.[73]

For example, a June 1992 newsletter (a special issue of the *Ron Paul Political Report*) purported to explain the Los Angeles riots of that year. The issue stated, "Order was only restored in L.A. when it came time for the blacks to pick up their welfare checks three days after rioting began."[74] The newsletter went on to say that the "looting" was allowed by police and government, and was another example of government indulgence of "'civil rights,' quotas, mandated hiring preferences, set-asides for government contracts, gerrymandered voting districts, black bureaucracies, black mayors, black curricula in schools, black tv shows, black tv anchors, hate crime laws, and public humiliation for anyone who dares question the black agenda."[75]

After statements in Paul's newsletter that praised former Klansman David Duke, critiqued Martin Luther King Jr., supported the

Confederacy, and justified black rates of poverty due to blacks' supposedly inherent bad values and predilection for violence, all went public in 2011, Paul changed his story. In 1996, Paul stated that the comments on race and crime in his report could be taken as arguments from other data and not necessarily his own beliefs.[76] In 2001, the *Texas Monthly* reported that Paul claimed his campaign staff told him not to tell others he had written the report because it was "too confusing" to explain to the public.[77] However, by 2012, Paul completely denied writing these reports.[78] In fact, Paul has become so obstructionist about his connection to these newsletters that he has, at times, refused to entertain questions about them. After being questioned about the newsletters by CNN's Gloria Borger, Paul stated,

> Why don't you go back and look at what I said yesterday on CNN and what I've said for 20 something years. 22 years ago? I didn't write them, I disavow them, that's it. . . . I never read that stuff . . . I was probably aware of it 10 years after it was written. . . . You know what the answer is? I didn't read or write them. I didn't read them at the time. And I disavow them. That is the answer.[79]

Borger then responded, "[T]hese things are pretty incendiary" to which Paul replied, "Because of people like you."[80] Shortly thereafter Paul abruptly ended the interview by taking off his microphone.

Despite this sordid past, Paul redefended his views on race during a Republican debate in early January 2012, when he claimed that blacks are victims of a racist social order rather than social pariahs upon the social landscape. He stated,

> I'm the only one up here and the only one in the Democratic Party that understands true racism in this country. It's in the judicial system. And it has to do with enforcing the drug laws. The percentage of people who use drugs are about the same with blacks and whites, and yet the blacks are arrested way disproportionately. They're prosecuted, imprisoned, way disproportionately. They get the death penalty way disproportionately. How many times have you seen a white rich person get the electric chair or get execution? But poor minorities have an injustice. And they have an injustice in war as well. Because minorities suffer more. Even

with the draft, they suffered definitely more. Without a draft, they're suffering disproportionately. If we truly want to be concerned about racism, you ought to look at a few of those issues and look at the drug laws which are being so unfairly enforced.[81]

Paul's retort unsettled many among the Right, especially those already uncomfortable with his libertarian policies, which conflict with socially conservative issues.

Newt Gingrich has used an array of implicit racial messaging strategies to appeal to conservative white voters. For example, during the 2011 Republican primaries, Gingrich courted southern conservatives with racial rhetoric concerning federal aid dependency within the black community by calling President Obama a "food stamp president"[82] and going on to make implicit links among people of color, poverty, and laziness.[83] Gingrich even announced plans to deliver a speech to the NAACP about "why the African-American community should demand paychecks and not be satisfied with food stamps," but later denied that he was targeting the black community specifically.[84] Gingrich also stated to a predominantly white Iowa audience, "Really poor children, in really poor neighborhoods have no habits of working, and have nobody around them who works. So they literally have no habit of showing up on Monday. . . . They have no habit of 'I do this and you give me cash,' unless it's illegal."[85]

At another Republican debate in January of 2012, black commentator Juan Williams asked Gingrich about his prior comments. "Can't you see this is viewed at a minimum insulting to all Americans, but particularly to African Americans?" "No, I don't see that," Gingrich replied, following up with an anecdote about his daughter doing janitorial work as her first job.[86] The covert racial language employed by Gingrich, such as referring to Obama as the "food stamp president," coupled with this refusal to admit a racial bias or agenda, demonstrates a return to implicit racial tactics used in Reagan's campaign (e.g., "welfare queens"). Just days after the debate, Gingrich told a crowd that "the idea of work" seemed "to be a strange, distant concept" to Juan Williams.[87] Such discursive sleight of hand implicitly references the social welfare language of "housing projects" and "food stamps" that evoke images of lazy people of color who receive free and unearned handouts that they do not need or do not deserve, which have all been paid for by generous white tax dollars. Despite much in Gingrich's past that has butted heads with the Republican establishment, many GOP faithful seem drawn to him because of his implicit appeal to a white working class thought to be victimized by a decidedly un-American, elitist, and racially "other" Barack Obama.

Such othering language has also been used by Mitt Romney. Romney has often employed thinly veiled race-baiting language, such as his reference to an "entitlement society"[88] or his claim that Obama wishes to transform the United States into a "European-style welfare state."[89] Romney has also been quite overt in a few cases. For example, Romney has promised to veto the Dream Act (a modest immigration reform that provides an avenue for children of immigrants to go to college).[90] And of course, many have already critiqued Romney for his membership in the Mormon Church (which did not allow black membership until 1978).

The GOP came to decide on Romney as the 2012 Republican candidate after a series of twists and turns. After briefly leading in the polls by September of 2011, Herman Cain suspended his presidential campaign on December 3 amid multiple allegations of sexual misconduct.[91] Rick Perry, another candidate who surged after entering the race, repeatedly stumbled during debates[92] and dropped out of the race soon after finishing fifth in the Iowa caucuses.[93] Their exits then left four viable candidates to contend for the Republican nomination: Newt Gingrich, Rick Santorum, Ron Paul, and Mitt Romney.

Gingrich pursued a classic Southern Strategy throughout his campaign, referring to President Obama as the "food stamp president" and accusing the media of "liberal bias" when faced with criticism.[94] Though Gingrich won South Carolina and Georgia, his vitriol-filled rhetoric, characterized by simply too much overtly racist discourse, coupled with his past political failures, together conspired to make him an easy target for opponents. After failing to win a primary for two months and accumulating more than $3 million in campaign debts, Gingrich suspended his campaign on April 28, 2012.[95]

Rick Santorum began the Republican primary race with a surprising win over Mitt Romney in the Iowa caucuses by a mere thirty-four votes.[96] Realizing early on that he did not possess the money or the organizational structure to directly confront the Romney campaign, Santorum courted the smaller states and hoped to parlay victories there into momentum for campaigns in larger states such as Ohio and Michigan.[97] While Santorum's strategy initially paid off with a sweep of Minnesota, Colorado, and Missouri on February 7,[98] the victories did not translate into larger success.[99] By April 10, 2012, Santorum suspended his campaign.[100]

From the outset, Ron Paul's strategy was to collect delegates for the Republican National Convention rather than outright primary victories.[101] Though Paul failed to win a single primary, he maintained a presence among state delegations and swept up many of the delegates left over from other candidates who dropped out of the race.[102] By August 22, 2012 (just days before the Republican National Convention), GOP officials and the Romney campaign cut a deal with Paul's campaign to allow some of Paul's delegates from Louisiana and Massachusetts to be seated at the RNC in order to avert a public clash with Paul supporters.[103]

While the beginning of Romney's run was tepid at best (many GOP supporters began an "Anybody but Romney" campaign),[104] many still considered him the field favorite. Romney received far more endorsements from noteworthy Republican Party members than the rest of the field ($56 million in 2011), a strong indication of establishment support.[105] The primaries and caucuses of March 6, 2012 (so-called Super Tuesday) cemented Romney's position as the presumptive Republican nominee for president. Romney won six of ten contests held that day, including the coveted Ohio primary.[106] Some of the victories were more attributable to opponent gaffes than Romney's campaign. Romney cruised through the rest of the primary season and, we argue, injected implicit racial messaging into the campaign both before and after the field was settled.

For example, in December of 2011, Mitt Romney's son Matt responded to a question over whether his father would release his tax returns. Drawing from the then-settled Birther controversy and anti–affirmative action angst over Obama's citizenship and educational accomplishments, Matt Romney stated, "I heard someone suggest the other day that as soon as President Obama releases his grades and birth certificate, and sort of a long list of things, then maybe he'd do it."[107] The subtle race baiting continued in the months that followed.

Even after Romney appeared before the NAACP (an appearance that could be used to explicitly defend himself against charges of racism: "How could I be racist? Would a racist attend an NAACP meeting?"), he courted white apathy toward and distaste for black identity politics and organizations when he stated that he knew he could be booed by the NAACP but went anyway.[108] Such a statement sends a clear message to racially fatigued whites: Romney is the candidate that the NAACP does not want, so white America should want Romney. And weeks later he followed up this racial divisiveness by deflecting his own race baiting onto his opponent, stating that Obama should take his "campaign of division and anger and hate back to Chicago."[109]

By July 2012, Romney stood in Jerusalem and spoke to a group of donors at the King David Hotel.[110] In courting their support, Romney played to the dominant ideology of anti-Muslim and racial xenophobia in the US context: simply put, Jews are often considered white and Muslims nonwhite.[111] Romney appealed to the dominant conflation of whiteness with a superior and victorious culture, compared to non-whites' supposed cultural pathologies that lead to their relative lack of success compared to whites. Romney stated, "Culture makes all the difference. . . . And as I come here and I look out over this city and consider the accomplishments of the people of this nation, I recognize the power of at least culture and a few other things."[112] In exploiting the Israeli-Palestinian divide qua white-nonwhite divide, Romney deftly expressed a subtle racial notion that the GOP expects will resonate with white voters in the United States. Given that Jews voted in large part for Obama in 2008 and 2012, the statement does not attempt to court Jewish votes but rather taps an underlying current of white resentment, superiority, and patriotism.

By August of 2012, the Romney campaign began running a TV advertisement that falsely claimed Obama had eliminated the work requirement for welfare recipients.[113] A complete fiction, the advertisement plays to the classic racial code word of "welfare." Such a strategy conjures images of people of color as indolent and nonindustrious, while Romney's plan would then require working for welfare in order to stimulate job creation. Simply put, such messages are interpreted by a large proportion of the white middle class as a presidential plan to take and redistribute the fruits of their labor to a lazy underclass. In fact, our assertion is backed up by a recent survey of a thousand people by YouGov that was analyzed by political scientist Michael Tesler.[114] The survey began by measuring levels of racial resentment toward blacks. Then five hundred respondents viewed Romney's welfare advertisement (the experiment), while five hundred respondents did not see it (the control). All respondents then answered a series of questions about how well either Mitt Romney's or Barack Obama's policies would benefit different groups like the poor, the middle class, the wealthy, African Americans, and white Americans. Their answers were coded to range from zero ("hurt them a great deal") to one hundred ("help them a great deal"). For those who saw the TV commercial, their racial resentment affected their opinions on Romney's help of the poor, the middle class, and African Americans. Importantly, seeing these advertisement did not influence or activate other attitudes, such as political party or political ideology; the advertisement only primed racial resentment.[115]

And recalling his son's December 2011 comments about Obama's birth certificate and educational credentials, on August 24, 2012, Romney told a nearly all-white Michigan crowd, "I love being home in this place where Ann and I were raised, where both of us were born. Ann was born in Henry Ford Hospital. I was born in Harper Hospital. No one's ever asked to see my birth certificate. They know that this is the place that we were born and raised."[116]

These examples and experiments simply highlight the long-standing problem of race baiting from conservative political parties and candidates. Accordingly, in *White Party, White Government*, sociologist Joe Feagin writes,

> Examining U.S. politics and system racism means going well beyond examining a few modest political flaws, contemporary rightward shifts in party politics, or eccentric racist candidates. . . . An accurate understanding requires going back deeply into U.S. political, economic, and social history to examine the central and ongoing social structural and institutional realities relevant to these issues.[117]

Indeed, Romney's campaign strategy well reflects how a structurally patterned and institutionally sanctioned construction of race undergirds political messaging: blacks are dysfunctional, and whites are hard-working, patriotic, and ideal citizens; blacks are ungrateful political agents leading the country astray, and whites are unfairly victimized for trying to "take their country back."

The Strength of Implicit Campaign Messaging

Since the middle of the twentieth century, the racialization of politics has declined; however, racial priming persists as a powerful tool in political campaigns. In brief, racial priming is the technique in which racialized images and discourse can activate whites' negative racial predispositions with consequences for their preferences about policy and candidates.[118] Political scientists Vincent Hutchings and Ashley Jardina indicate that although "racially egalitarian norms have become dominant and whites have become more racially tolerant . . . many continue to embrace negative, albeit less crude, views about black Americans."[119] The theory of racial priming often questions the legitimacy of "black demands for racial justice" and states that racial appeals that are implicit make "latent racial attitudes more accessible in memory."[120] The premise of racial priming includes references characterized by persuasive and visual images that "avoid the use of racial nouns or adjectives."[121] For instance, Hutchings and Jardina state that racially explicit appeals reinforce "negative stereotypes about African-Americans."[122]

In a campaign advertisement for presidential candidate George W. Bush, the standard Republican mores were applied in a fairly neutral message. The advertisement did not include any racial cues or obvious implicit racial appeals. However, the "'undeserving blacks' version of the ad showed African-Americans when the narrator mentioned 'wasteful government programs.'"[123] The subtle images connecting black Americans with negative references to governmental policies were juxtaposed to more positive images of whites when "hard-working Americans" were referenced.[124] As expected, this ad generated a huge effect; the most negative images of black Americans gave nearly fifty percentage points to the Republican candidate. In addition, "direct verbal references to racial group policy disputes might also succeed in priming whites' racial attitudes."[125]

The take-away points are that appeals to race work to generate partisan political support, these appeals work unconsciously, and they work best when they are implicit so as not to disrupt the now-dominant and supposedly color-blind norms of individual meritocracy and social equality.[126] Race—through appeals to black dysfunction, white patriotism, white paternalism, and white victimhood—continues to be one of the most salient dynamics that influences voter attitudes and behavior. All the more shocking, these dynamics exist within a white voting populace that increasingly refuses to accept the central role of race and refuses to believe that racial inequality is a central issue today. This begs an important question to be explored in the next chapter: What are the social-psychological mechanisms that generate and maintain this racial bias that has become a regular part of American politics?

5

The Social Science of Political Ideology and Racial Attitudes

In 1985, the national Democratic Party backed a series of focus groups to ascertain why working-class whites had abandoned their traditional support for the party. Pollster Stanley Greenberg attributed politicized white flight to dissatisfaction with the Democratic Party's increasing association with black voters. These defectors expressed an intense distaste for issues salient to black voters and even for black voters themselves. Whites' racial animus influenced much of their thinking about, and attitudes toward, government and political issues. Blacks became an easy scapegoat for what whites perceived to be wrong in their lives; blacks were a "serious obstacle to their personal advancement."[1] "Being black" then became a perceived social advantage. Conversely, their whiteness supposedly relegated them to lower-class status. Personal decisions to segregate themselves from blacks influenced their belief that white neighborhoods were safe and decent places. And just as these whites moved to the suburbs to flee increasing integration in urban public schools, so too they shunned the increasingly integrated Democratic Party and its support for "hot button" racial topics like affirmative action. Arguably, these former Democrats found a new home in the Republican Party. In this chapter, we explore possible reasons for racial-political beliefs and decision making, in particular the notion that automatic, if not unconscious, racial biases may direct political orientation.

In recent years, social scientists have measured the distinction between liberal and conservative racial attitudes. Some researchers suggest that personality and disposition serve to influence and guide racial prejudice and acts of discrimination. Throughout the 1950s and '60s, social scientists argued that some individuals harbored a generalized bias against out-groups. This "authoritarian personality disorder" was marked by a robust sense of conventionalism, aggression, toughness, and power.[2] However, by the 1990s, researchers found that right-wing authoritarians—individuals who strongly endorse traditional values—are inclined to act aggressively toward out-group members, including blacks, while acting kindly toward other members of their in-groups.[3] Soon, researchers centered their attention on more than aggression, addressing the "Big Five" personality traits (i.e., openness, conscientiousness, extraversion, agreeableness, and neuroticism). Psychologists Bo Ekehammar and Nazar Akrami's review of studies on the relationship between personality and racial attitudes found that "Openness to Experience" seems to have a stronger relationship with measures of prejudice and interracial attitudes.[4] In a 2005 study, social psychologist Francis Flynn found that among whites Openness to Experience was inversely related to racial attitudes and positively related to impressions of a fictitious black person. Moreover, Openness was also inversely related to impressions of black interviewees after they observed informal interviews of white and black targets.[5] Accordingly, Openness to Experience is a key personality trait negatively correlated with right-wing political ideologies.[6] In fact, psychologist Paul Trapnell noted that although most scholars "do not equate Openness to liberalism, they have on occasion identified liberal values with this facet."[7]

Other scholars have focused on "symbolic racism." As sociologists Michael Tesler and David O. Sears write, the presence of symbolic racism is marked by four beliefs: (1) that discrimination against blacks has largely declined; (2) that black disadvantage is the fault of blacks' supposedly poor work ethic; (3) that blacks demand too many resources; and (4) that blacks have received more than they deserve. Hence, social scientists argue that symbolic racism has replaced Jim Crow–style overt racism and can be thought of in three ways. First, virulent and overt forms of racism fell out of social favor in the United States—save in the Deep South—and thus could not influence politics writ large. Second, full-scale opposition to black political candidates and liberal, racially targeted policies was less about real or perceived racial threats to whites' interests than it was the result of beliefs in abstract moral principles such as obedience, egalitarianism, and meritocracy. Third, symbolic racism emerged from "early socialized negative feelings about Blacks" and conservative values.[8] It is this latter point that has caused a considerable backlash among academics and the lay public.[9] The variety of theories that capture the relationship between political ideology and racial attitudes, though rich in their description and supported by a robust body of empirical social science, tend not to directly address the extent to which such attitudes may be automatic, if not subconscious. Implicit-bias research over the past couple of decades, however, has helped elucidate this relationship.

Unconscious Race Bias 101

People are complex. One's stated attitudes and beliefs often fail to align with one's actual thoughts and feelings. In experimental settings, for example, social desirability—the tendency of research study partici-pants to reply in a manner that they believe will be viewed favorably by the experimenter—may serve as a motivating factor behind lack of candor.[10] In social settings, impression management, particularly saving face, may be a driving force.[11] For example, some people may lie on a written job application but have difficulty conforming to job require-ments in a face-to-face interview.[12] Given that race remains such a contentious social issue, it serves as a catalyst for impression manage-ment—with whites seeking self- and other-perceptions that they are "not a racist." Instead, they attempt to cultivate a shared sense of self that is color-blind, or even nonprejudiced in disposition or political proclivity—even more so than nonwhite racial groups do.[13] This desire is expected given widely shared beliefs that whites are racially preju-diced.[14] We contend that white presentations of self rest not necessar-ily on an effort to intentionally deceive others but rather on their lack of adequate appreciation for how deeply entrenched and collectively shared pro-white worldviews are.

The assumption that human thoughts are entirely accessible to con-scious awareness, and that human behavior is largely governed by con-scious agency, has been severely undermined in recent years. People's express reports of their cognitive processes are often inconsistent with their actual judgments. Hence, shared cultural logics and psychological influences on judgment seem to operate wholly above people's heads and outside of people's conscious awareness,[15] so much so that social psychologists now contend that people rely on two distinct systems of judgment. One system is rapid, intuitive, unconscious, and error prone.

Another is slow, deductive, and deliberative, but much more accurate.[16] The two systems may operate simultaneously but produce contradictory responses.[17] Moreover, the intuitive system can often dictate choice, while the deductive system may fall behind to search for rationales that align with accessible memories and understandings.[18] As a result, individuals may be unaware (1) of the existence of a significant stimulus that influenced a response, (2) of the existence of the response, and (3) that the stimulus affected the response.[19]

Putting this dual system to a test, social psychologists Timothy Wilson and Richard Nisbett required participants to rate four identical pair of stockings. Forty percent selected the stocking in the right-most display position, while 31 percent selected the stocking just to the left of the most selected stocking.[20] In essence, there was a position effect. Out of the fifty-two participants, eighty spontaneous responses were given for why they made their selection. None mentioned the position of the stocking as the reason for the selection. When the subjects were directly asked whether the order of the stockings might have influenced their decision, only one indicated that reason as a possibility. That participant noted that she was currently taking multiple psychology classes and knew a great deal about order effects. But she, nonetheless, did not display a bias for stockings further to the right on the display. In fact, she chose the stocking in the second position.[21]

Conventional wisdom and even "naïve" psychological conceptions of human thought and social behavior[22] may place heavy influence on select thoughts and conscious intentions as the primary cause of beliefs and behavior.[23] The challenge to such an assessment is that it has long been known that social influences within interview and research settings can lead individuals to inaccurately describe their explicit beliefs.[24] Furthermore, people's explanations as to their behavior often consist of irrational groping for answers, and thus they produce answers that are highly improbable, if not impossible.[25] Hence, when politically conservative voters, activists, commentators, or politicians are asked about what appears to be overly harsh or even racially motivated speech or actions, many defend themselves with the certainty that they know themselves not to be "racist." That is, in our culture, we define the "racists" as hood-wearing and swastika-bearing ignoramuses. They can't be "racist," so they think, because they do not conform to the image of such a racist and they do not actively "hate" people of color. Once racism is conceived as a conscious and overt stereotypical thought or action, one too easily divides the world into those who are "sick" with the disease of prejudice and those who are "healthy" anti- or nonracists.

Thus, a growing body of research on implicit social cognition destabilizes the notion that human thoughts and behaviors are purely accessible and volitional. This body of research suggests that individuals lack absolute awareness of their own thoughts and the ability to control behaviors resulting from those thoughts. Since the 1980s, research on implicit memory has opened the door for the development of measures of other implicit and socially shared mental phenomena. Chief among these advancements were several measures for implicit attitudes.[26] By "attitude" we mean a hypothetical construct that represents the degree to which an individual likes or dislikes, or acts favorably or unfavorably toward, someone or something.[27] By using the term "implicit," we follow psychologists Anthony Greenwald and Mahzarin Banaji, who define implicit attitudes as "introspectively unidentified (or inaccurately identified) traces of past experience that mediate favorable or unfavorable feelings toward an attitude object."[28] So also, people can evidence ambivalence toward select persons, groups, or objects, such that they are imbued with both positive and negative attitudes toward the subject in question. Yet, implicit attitudes are of greatest interest when they differ from explicit attitudes about the same category of individuals or things. Such discrepancies, referred to as dissociations,[29] are often observed in attitudes toward stigmatized groups—e.g., blacks.[30]

Biases certainly reflect preferences for particular groups or individuals. Accordingly, within biases, there are opposite sides to the same coin—favorable and unfavorable categorizations of comparative groups. For example, in-group bias designates favoritism toward one's own group.[31] Such preferences may result in discriminatory biases. These biases are called implicit biases, which may diverge from an individual's expressed beliefs and result in behavior inconsistent with individuals' intended behavior. Accordingly, these implicit attitudes and biases on race might very well shape opinions in other realms, such as politics. To measure such an effect, social scientists would need to develop a strategy that avoided self-reporting. While self-reports of explicit attitudes have served as the social and behavioral sciences' typical method of attitude measurement, the drawback is that respondents may be unwilling or unable to report their attitudes in an unbiased or accurate manner.[32] Moreover, research respondents' answers are dependent on social desirability and interviewer effects—e.g., who asks, how they ask, and what the context of their asking is.[33] These concerns gave rise to measures that would indirectly gauge attitude. It is presumed that research participants are unaware of the relationship between these measures and the attitudes they are employed to ascertain. Indirect measures thus seem to minimize respondents' strategic responses to incentives.[34]

Such indirect measures were realized when social scientists applied subliminal priming techniques to measure implicit attitudes.[35] First, one uses a priming procedure to establish the degree to which the presentation of an object would influence study participants' positive or negative indication of a subsequently presented target. In one study, researchers found greater facilitation "when positively valued primes were followed by positive targets and when negatively valued primes were followed by negative targets than when the prime-target pairs were incongruent in valence."[36] That is, objects that evoked negative attitudes caused subsequent evaluations of other, even nonrelated objects, to be negative. Nearly a decade later, researchers used African American and white faces as primes and then employed adjectives with positive or negative connotations. Participants pushed keys labeled either "good" or "bad" as quickly as possible. White study participants' reaction times to the good words were faster following presentation of white faces. Their reaction times to the bad words were quicker when those words followed the presentation of black faces.[37] This work was monumental in that it gave direct, empirical support for the long-theorized hypothesis that within the context of a historically white-dominated society, blackness reproduced negative dispositions compared to whiteness.

Building upon this work, the Implicit Association Test (IAT) became the dominant attitude measure. Today, it is employed to circumvent strategic responding. IAT-related research has found people to harbor a wide range of implicit attitudes concerning many aspects of social life, some of which people had previously thought rather mundane. For example, the research indicates that people hold implicit attitudes about such everyday aspects of life as yogurt brands, fast food restaurants, and soft drinks.[38] While these implicit attitudes may predict behavior thought inconsequential,[39] the effect of implicit attitudes toward group identities—whether racial or political—engenders a heightened level of concern.

Research on implicit racial attitudes and bias—particularly research focused on blacks—stands as the most robust area of current research. As previously indicated, people's explicit and implicit attitudes are not completely concordant. Such discordance is most evident when it comes to the sensitive topic of race. Research suggests that Latinos demonstrate a limited explicit preference for whites (25.3 percent favor) over blacks (15.0 percent favor), with most showing no preference (59.7 percent). At the implicit level, however, Latinos show a substantial preference for whites (60.5 percent favor) over blacks (10.2 percent favor), with far fewer showing preferential neutrality (29.2 percent) in comparison to their explicit preferences. In comparison to Latinos, Asians and Pacific Islanders show more of an explicit preference for whites (32.9 percent favor) over blacks (9.6 percent favor), with only slightly fewer showing preferential neutrality (57.5 percent). At the implicit level, however, Asians and Pacific Islanders demonstrate a substantial preference for whites (67.5 percent favor) over blacks (7.7 percent favor), with far fewer showing preferential neutrality (24.8 percent) in comparison to their explicit preferences. Whites show much more of an explicit preference for whites (40.7 percent favor) than blacks (3.4 percent favor), especially when compared to other racial groups, but still more than half (56.0 percent) show no preference. At the implicit level, however, whites show a robust preference for whites (71.5 percent favor) over blacks (6.8 percent favor), with only 21.7 percent showing no preference.[40] And in a recent study, data extends the evidence that whites hold a great deal of implicit and explicit in-group and out-group bias;[41] whites express more in-group favoritism on implicit measures (78.4 percent) than on explicit measures (51.1 percent).[42]

Without question, race matters. And racial categories influence the way people perceive and judge phenomena. This process occurs whether people are conscious of it or not. Such findings point toward the necessity to move past discussions of whether or not people are "racist" or not based on their self-appraisals—which is clearly methodologically flawed if not an obvious conflict of interest. The use of such research is particularly important in the context of a rising Republican and hyper-conservative backlash against the first nonwhite, and Democratic, president of the United States.

Political Ideology and Unconscious Race Bias

The theory of "principled conservativism" suggests that white opposition to policies like affirmative action is largely derived from race-neutral political ideologies and value systems (e.g., self-reliance and a desire for small government), rather than racist or racialized ideologies or opinion.[43] The principled conservativism perspective emerged from the dominant discourse of perceived American post-racialism[44]—a widely shared perspective and narrative that racism and dominance-oriented motives no longer undergird white attitudes toward race-targeted policies.[45] Proponents of principled conservativism contend that political values—not racism—provide the dominant framework for understanding race-based policies.[46] Accordingly, those who subscribe to the principled conservative model believe that once the effects of ideology (i.e., conservativism) and race-neutral political values are accounted for, racism and dominance-oriented attitudes should hold no predictive power in whites' opposition to race-based policies such as affirmative action.[47] This theory has found some support in studies that indicate (1) that antiblack affect is weakly related to conservatism and opposition to race-targeted policies[48] and (2) that conservatives are not more likely to hold a double standard with regard to blacks in the allocation of aid vis-à-vis disadvantaged members of other groups.[49] These are points we aim to upend.

To be clear, the principled-conservatism model does not suggest that opposition to race-targeted policies is free from racism, but rather that the opposition-racism relationship is more likely to be found among the poorly educated.[50] Theoretically, then, since some individuals supposedly lack the intellectual sophistication to understand both the explicitly egalitarian ethos of American political culture and abstract ideas, their attitudes toward race-based policies and politics are driven by racial animus.[51] In contrast, well-educated, principled conservatives will base their policy positions on abstract principles and articulate them in light of express racial egalitarian norms, thus attenuating the influence of racism and in-group preference.[52]

However, scholars have long argued that right-wing political conservatism hinges on the embrace of social inequality and resistance to change.[53] Other studies of large datasets (ranging from n = 28,816 to 732,881) found that at the explicit level, conservatives, when compared to liberals, generally favor higher-status groups to lower-status groups (e.g., others to Arabs-Muslims, others to Jews, straight people to gays, whites to blacks, light-skinned to dark-skinned people, and white to black children).[54] We believe that such research destabilizes the contention that education, to the exclusion of political orientation, is the key variable for determining explicit racial bias. But what about implicit racial bias? The same pattern occurs. For example, at the implicit level, research suggests that conservatives, when compared to liberals, favor higher-status groups to lower-status groups (e.g., thin people to overweight people, others to Arabs-Muslims, others to Jews, others to the disabled, straight people to gays, whites to blacks, light-skinned to dark-skinned people, and white to black children).[55] The notion that liberals hold more egalitarian implicit attitudes than conservatives has found support in an array of studies.[56] Importantly, for whites and blacks both, the more conservative they are, the more they prefer whites over blacks.[57]

This robust correlation certainly poses a chicken-or-egg problem: Does being conservative make you more likely to harbor racial biases, or does the possession of racial biases make conservative ideological paradigms more attractive? While we make no claims regarding which it could be, we are confident that the "principled-conservatism" retort often evidenced is both intellectually bankrupt and morally deficient. In consideration of the former, the evidence simply fails to uphold the mantra of principled conservatism. In regard to the latter, the repeated refusal to admit that racial meanings might play a role in conservative ideology only drives home the point that the banner of "post-racialism" is devoid of ethical currency.

The Root Differences between Liberals' and Conservatives' Unconscious Race Biases

From where do racial biases stem? Consider that the mild distinction between liberals and conservatives in implicit racial biases may reflect differential exposures to antiblack sentiments, even very early in life. In an IAT assessment of white American six-year-olds, ten-year-olds, and adults, even the youngest group showed implicit pro-white/anti-black bias (self-reports also aligned with this finding). The ten-year-olds and adults showed the same magnitude of implicit race bias, but self-reported racial attitudes became substantially less biased in older children and vanished entirely in adults.[58] Though this research does not indicate where such implicit biases originate, it does underscore that individuals both learn biases early on and learn how to hide such biases through an overt comportment with socially desirable answers and egalitarian norms.

Another study underscores these findings. Children's implicit racial attitudes may develop from exposure to antiblack socializing agents. Fourth- and fifth-grade children were asked to complete measures of implicit and explicit racial attitudes, as well as a survey assessing the degree to which the children identified with their parents. Parents completed a survey that measured their attitudes toward blacks. Results reveal a greater correspondence between parents' prejudice and children's prejudice among those children who were highly identified with their parents vis-à-vis those who were less identified with their parents.[59] Similarly, another study indicated that mothers' (but not fathers') implicit racial attitudes predict racial preferences among three- to six-year-olds. Parents' explicit racial attitudes, however, did not predict their children's preferences.[60]

These findings suggest that early life experiences greatly shape how individuals become oriented toward liberal or conservative political ideologies. Given this research, one can imagine a household that explicitly espouses the ideals of racial equality and recounts the horrors of American slavery, the virtues of the Civil Rights Movement, and the value of racial egalitarian policies like affirmative action. Comparatively, imagine a household where parents bemoan blacks' acquisition of "unearned" advances and rights, complain about blacks on welfare, and describe blacks' supposed biologically or culturally rooted dysfunctions. One would reasonably expect children growing up in these environments to cultivate vastly different racial dispositions, especially toward blacks. Accordingly, if we consider the still-racialized social institutions of the nation, from racially segregated schools to houses of worship, neighborhoods, media, and workplaces, we face a possibly static, if not worsening, political-racial divide in coming generations.

Conclusion

It is of little surprise that those on the political Right are offended when confronted or critiqued about the racially tinged elements of some of their opposition or obstruction vis-à-vis President Obama. There is a strong argument that they are aware of the societal proscription against being "racist," and hence, they are likely to possess a conscious and strong incentive to deny such attitudes. This is particularly the case when such words or deeds are not so patently racist that the typical individual would not believe the argument that they come from an egalitarian and principled place. Just as there is a strong argument that such right-leaning critics of President Obama may be lying about their racial attitudes and the way those attitudes motivate their evaluative judgments of and actions toward President Obama, there is an alternative and equally strong argument. Those critics could be wholly unaware of the fact that their assessment of President Obama is clouded by their racial attitudes, given the automatic and subconscious nature of racial attitudes. And their articulations of their feelings about President Obama are a mere reflection of what they "think" they feel about him based on what they believe their racial attitudes are. As we discuss in the following chapter, these automatic attitudes have significant behavioral implications with respect to President Obama.

6

Unconscious Race Bias and the Right

Its Meaning for Law in the Age of Obama

We have attempted to demonstrate that for some decades the political Right has harbored an aversion toward, fear of, and dislike concerning nonwhites—particularly African Americans. Such animus has become nowhere more evident than in the rising right-wing racial angst since the 2008 election of Barack Obama as the forty-fourth president of the United States. As we noted in chapter 5, for those on the Right who harbor some racial bias against President Obama, that bias is likely to reside outside of their conscious awareness. Nonetheless, despite the fact that those biases may be unconscious, they are quite consequential. In this chapter, we analyze the ways in which unconscious race bias on the Right may be consequential to President Obama with respect to law and policy.

First, we indicate that unconscious bias that associates "white" with "American" and "black" with "other" motivates Birther legislation and litigation. That is, unconscious racial bias (stimulated by implicit racial messages and priming) helps to fuel the agendas of the hyper-conservative Right. Second, we note that the proliferation of dehumanizing symbolism (e.g., primate imagery) associated with President Obama may serve to dehumanize him among witnesses of these images. Such dehumanization makes it easier for would-be assassins to view him as a potential target, thus implicating the extent to which President Obama should be provided long-term Secret Service protection. Third, we state that right-wing, including Tea Party, opposition to President Obama's policies—and the impact that their opposition has on members of Congress—may have as much to do with race as it does with actual policy preferences. Fourth and lastly, we note that President Obama's election could have a surprising effect on the Voting Rights Act provision for majority-minority districts, especially among those who believe that his election signifies that such legislation is no longer necessary. Over-estimation of racial progress could lead to an erosion of the majority-minority jurisdiction provision, thus undermining the chances of black congressional candidates to be elected in the future.

Soul (Br)Other Number One: The Rise of Birther Legislation and Lawsuits

The status of President Obama's citizenship has been a popular issue among the ultraconservative fringe of the GOP since 2008.[1] As we outlined in chapter 2, the Birther movement has doggedly questioned whether Obama is a natural-born citizen, and therefore eligible to hold office as president of the United States.[2] The United States Constitution requires that presidential candidates be "natural born" US citizens, at least thirty-five years old, and residents of the United States for at least fourteen years.[3] In response to calls for proof of his birthplace, Obama released his short-form birth certificate before the 2008 election to quell the controversy. The form reflected that he was, in fact, born on August 4, 1961, in Honolulu, Hawaii.[4] However, some were not persuaded. In April 2011, President Obama sought to defuse the controversy once and for all by procuring a copy of his long-form birth certificate, which was signed by his mother, the local registrar, and the delivery doctor.[5] The certificate was shown live by George Stephanopoulos on *Good Morning America*.[6] Even so, some on the Right continued to pursue legal action in the form of state-level legislation or lawsuits.

A favorite tactic for conservative activists has been to propose legis-lation, aptly called "Birther bills," which require presidential candidates to present proof of citizenship and birthplace in order to be placed on state ballots. One such bill was proposed in 2009 at the federal level by six Texas congressmen and would require presidential candidates to provide birth certificates in 2012 and thereafter.[7] Congressman Ted Poe, a Republican behind the proposal, refrained from alleging that Obama had actually been born outside the United States, and instead compared the legislation to requirements in place at a benign organi-zation like Little League baseball, which requires birth certificates to be presented at the time of registration. Rep. Louie Gohmert, R-Tyler, went so far as to justify the bill on the grounds that it would "avoid unnecessary controversies and conspiracy theories."[8] Rep. Sheila Jackson Lee, D-Houston, took a very different viewpoint, pointing out that this is the first time anyone has ever questioned the birthplace of a sitting president. The proposal, she said, represents an attempt to impeach Obama's birthright as the first black president.[9]

Many more bills have swirled at the state level. In the New Hampshire House of Representatives in March 2011, Republicans were split in support of a proposed bill that would require candidates to file their birth certificates to be eligible to run for president starting in 2013.[10] According to David Bates, R-Windham, the effective date on the bill was pushed back to 2013 to avoid the appearance that it intended to erect barriers to President Obama's reelection bid in 2012. Other GOP members, however, remained strongly opposed to the amendment, as they believed it detracted from work on more important business, like the economy, or could harm New Hampshire's image.

A similar bill was introduced in Pennsylvania, but faced familiar opposition from Democrats and moderate Republicans, despite being "red meat" for many conservatives.[11] Representative Daryl Metcalfe, an ultraconservative Republican member of the Pennsylvania House, proposed the bill in 2010 but was rejected. After electoral gains, he reproposed the legislation in 2011 in hopes of gaining traction. The bill enjoyed local Tea Party support from Roberta Pfeiffer Gick, legal adviser to the Pittsburgh Tea Party. She e-mailed members urging them to contact lawmakers in support of the bill, but insisted it was not aimed at President Obama. Instead, she claimed it was intended to make sure candidates adhered to the US Constitution. The bill itself never mentioned President Obama.

Birthers came close to success in Arizona, where Republican governor Jan Brewer vetoed a bill in April 2011 that would have required President Obama and other candidates to prove their US citizenship before their names could appear on the state's ballot in November.[12] The legislation would have required candidates and political parties to hand in affidavits stating a candidate's citizenship and age, a birth certificate, and a sworn statement saying where the candidate had lived for the preceding fourteen years.[13] Arizona would have been the first state to pass such a requirement. If there was no copy of a birth certificate available, candidates could use baptismal certificates, or, hilariously, circumcision documentation as a failsafe. If the documents were inconclusive, the Arizona secretary of state would set up a committee to determine the eligibility of the candidate. Governor Brewer stated that she was troubled that the bill empowered a single person, the secretary of state, to judge the qualifications of all candidates. Bill sponsor Carl Seel, R-Phoenix, countered that the bill would have helped maintain the integrity of elections and was not intended as a swipe against President Obama.

As of April 2011, "Birther bills" had failed in five states but were debated in at least a half-dozen more.[14] At the time (just before President Obama produced his long-form birth certificate), a *New York Times* poll found that 57 percent of adults believed he was born in the United States, while 25 percent believed he was born elsewhere. Among Republicans, just 33 percent believed Obama was born in the United States, while 45 percent of Republicans believed he was born out of the country. Majorities in all regions believed the president was born in the United States, but those majorities were smaller in the South and Midwest. The poll was nationwide and had a 3 percent margin of error.

Even after the production of the long-form birth certificate, "Birther bills" continued marching forward. In Oklahoma, Senate Bill 91 passed with overwhelming and even bipartisan support, with Governor Mary Fallin (R) expected to eventually sign it into law.[15] Oklahoma Democrats were divided on the matter. An assistant Democratic floor leader in the House, Al McAffrey, called the bill an embarrassment.

In Louisiana, Republicans continued to press forward with a bill in the weeks following the long-form certificate's debut.[16] Shreveport state representative Alan Seabaugh, Republican, offered a particularly creative justification for the bill, saying that he had no doubt Obama was a US-born citizen and that his intention was merely to pass the bill to put to rest the many lawsuits swirling around the matter.[17] Governor Bobby Jindal stated that he would sign the bill into law if given the opportunity.[18]

In Connecticut, Michael McClachlan, R-Danbury, introduced a "Birther bill" in the state senate in January 2011.[19] Democrats immediately pounced on the Republican for wasting the legislature's time on frivolous matters when it should be focusing on jobs instead.

McClachlan fired back that those who oppose his bill are "probably *Huffington Post* readers."[20]

Montana's "Birther bill" gained special notoriety when Representative Bob Wagner made waves on *Anderson Cooper* in February 2011.[21] United States laws do not, of course, consider where a candidate's parents were born for eligibility purposes. This did not stop Wagner from erroneously explaining, while defending his state's proposed legislation, that natural-born citizens were limited to those who are the son or daughter of two parents born as citizens of the United States. Wagner's bill had been tabled by the time the interview actually aired.

Indiana's Republicans gave an especially half-hearted attempt at passing a "Birther bill" in April 2011. The legislation never proceeded because of an inability to obtain a quorum in the state senate.[22] Even the bill's sponsor, Mike Delph, failed to attend the hearing where the bill was discussed. This was consistent with a common strategy among Republican lawmakers, called "Birther-curious," in which they pretend to care about the issue in order to appeal to right-wing supporters energized by the anti-Obama activism in the legislature.

We contend that the legislative maneuvering by Republican and Tea Party congressional representatives, governors, and other elected officials together appeal most to those with both explicit and unconscious racial biases against African Americans. For those with explicit racial animus, the attempt to legislate Obama out of office symbolizes a potent white-nationalist defense of the Anglo-Saxon heritage of the United States. Some of the legislation's wording, and the rhetoric of its supporters, is vicious and overt enough in its "othering" strategy to attract hard-line supporters willing to believe the myths that Obama is really a Kenyan or Malaysian unfairly usurping a white person's job in the White House. Those holding implicit levels of bias, such as those who introduced "Birther bills," may easily hide behind supposed "color-blind" reasons for the legislation—from upholding the "integrity" of elections to strict and patriotic adherence to the Constitution. Because such attacks on Obama are couched in such supposedly "race-neutral" terms, those holding implicit racial biases may be unconsciously drawn to the GOP and induced to support many of its social and political issues not directly related to race. In either case, such political tactics are only appealing in the first place because they rely on the already established cultural logic of the United States that has historically "othered" nonwhites from full inclusion in the national project and aligns authentic citizenship with a specific and ideal form of whiteness.[23]

Those questioning President Obama's citizenship have also resorted to lawsuits. Wiley Drake and Alan Keyes, who ran together on the American Independent Ticket, filed a lawsuit in 2008 in California asking California secretary of state Debra Bowen not to certify the state's election results until President Obama provided more concrete evidence of his eligibility for office.[24] Drake and his attorneys claimed to have an audiotape of Obama's grandmother recalling how she witnessed his birth in Kenya. The short-form birth certificate (Obama did not obtain the long form until 2011) was insufficient, according to the complaint, because it failed to list a doctor or hospital. The trial court sustained demurrers by Bowen and Obama, holding that the petition failed to identify a ministerial duty on the part of the candidate (to supply information), nor did it identify a ministerial duty on behalf of the secretary of state to demand documentary proof of birthplace from presidential candidates.[25] Therefore, there was no cause of action stated in the petition. The court also noted that it lacked jurisdiction over the action because election procedures and means for challenges to presidential elections are the territory of federal law. On appeal, the California Third District Court of Appeal affirmed the trial court decision.[26]

Also in 2008, Leo Donofrio filed a suit against New Jersey secretary of state Nina Mitchell Wells.[27] The Donofrio lawsuit alleged that neither Obama nor McCain was natural born and eligible to run for office.[28] The suit echoed the sentiment of Representative Bob Wagner of *Anderson Cooper* fame, asserting that even if Obama was born in Hawaii, he would not be natural born because his father was from Kenya. The lawsuit was rejected by state judges in New Jersey on November 6, 2008 (the courts did not hand down any major rulings), and Donofrio immediately filed an application for an emergency stay with Justices Thomas and Souter.[29] Thomas rejected the application without elaboration on December 8, 2008.

Perhaps the most unusual suit was filed by Orly Taitz, a noted leader of the Birther movement. In September 2009, US district court judge Clay Land shut down a suit filed by Taitz on behalf of US Army captain Connie Rhodes, wherein Rhodes attempted to avoid deployment to Iraq under President Obama's authority as commander-in-chief because he was not eligible to hold office.[30] Judge Land noted that Rhodes's third and fourth years of medical school (as well as her residency) had been funded by taxpayers in exchange for a promise by Rhodes to serve two years' active service in the army. She began her term of service in July 2008 and had no problem serving under Obama as commander-in-chief until she was ordered to deploy in September 2009. Because the complaint did not seek a discharge but rather an injunction halting her deployment, Rhodes was presumably okay with serving under Obama, just as long as she was able to do so on the comfort of US soil. Judge Land did not buy the logic of Rhodes's argument.

The suit featured some entertaining legal finagling by Taitz. She cited "the general opinion of the rest of the world" that "Barack Hussein Obama has, in essence, slipped through the guardrails to become President."[31] Additionally, Taitz cited an AOL poll saying that 85 percent of Americans believed Obama had not been vetted and needed to be. The main crux of her argument, however, was that documentation of Obama's birth could not be verified and should be presumed fraudulent. This argument fruitlessly attempted to shift the burden of proof onto President Obama to prove his natural-born status.

In response to losing the suit, Taitz vowed to continue fighting for Rhodes if her client wanted her to, and even went so far as to compare Rhodes's situation to the plight of Nelson Mandela.[32] Additionally, Taitz said, "Somebody should consider trying [the judge] for treason and aiding and abetting this massive fraud known as Barack Hussein Obama. Judge [Clay] Land is a typical puppet of the regime—just like in the Soviet Union."[33] Land warned in the dismissal that the pleadings were frivolous, sanctionable, and contemptuous.

Rather than heeding the judge's warning, Taitz turned around and immediately filed a motion for reconsideration, reasserting outrageous political allegations and again accusing Judge Land of treason.[34] Additionally, Taitz requested that Land recuse himself from the case because of a (fabricated) friendship with Eric Holder and supposed conflicts of interest stemming from ownership of Microsoft and Comcast stock. Land responded by socking Taitz with twenty thousand dollars in sanctions and gave her thirty days to pay up. Further, plaintiff Connie Rhodes wrote to the judge saying that Taitz was acting without her permission in filing the motion to further attempt to block her deployment. Rhodes said she was filing a complaint against Taitz with the California bar.

To call Birthers—even those who have gone to the lengths of passing legislation or filing lawsuits—"conspiracy theorists" is to evade parsimony. A simpler, and possibly more accurate, explanation for their concerns is racism. In our supposedly "post-racial" era, the ease by which such fantastically outrageous and dishonest legislation and lawsuits are filed is likely rooted in the ease with which people automatically associate Americanness with whiteness. In fact, whites have long held racial minority status to be at odds with being American or committed to America. For example, during World War II, being Japanese was synonymous with being disloyal.[35] During the Gulf Wars (and particularly in the aftermath of 9/11), those identifying as either Arab or Middle Eastern were subject to attacks from individuals and groups identifying as patriotic and right-wing defenders of the American homeland.[36] And as recently as twenty years ago, a poll indicated that more than 50 percent of nonblacks believed that blacks are less patriotic than other racial groups.[37]

Such attitudes may be more pervasive at the unconscious level. Recent research indicates that most people make no overt distinctions between blacks and whites on explicit measures of "Americanness." Yet, when implicit measures are employed, people more easily pair American symbols with white faces than with black faces. So also, when people viewed photos of eight black and eight white US track and field athletes who participated in the 2000 Olympics, participants both were more familiar with black than with white athletes and, when they were asked to self-report, reported a stronger association between black athletes and Americanness than between white athletes and Americanness. Again, when implicit measures were used, the reverse was found, with participants more strongly associating the white athletes with the category "American" than the black athletes.[38]

Research on Americanness, and the extent to which it has been associated with Barack Obama, began to emerge during the 2008 presidential campaign. In a study conducted during the 2008 election season, it was found that people more automatically associate all-American symbols with white politicians—whether those politicians are American

(Hillary Clinton) or even European (Tony Blair)—than with Obama. In fact, the difference in the degree to which Americanness was automatically associated with Clinton versus Obama was greater when their race difference was made salient than when their gender difference was made salient.[39] Furthermore, another study discovered that when whites and Asians are primed with the American flag, their attitudes toward blacks become more negative. Moreover, when they are primed with images of the American flag, their attitudes toward Democrats were not altered, but their attitude toward blacks generally, and then Senator Obama specifically, become more negative.[40]

This research is striking. It is not simply the case that people, especially some on the Right, more easily associate whiteness with Americanness than blackness. That is, it is more than a matter of degree when it comes to the racialization of Americanness and national belonging. Rather, there seems to be something racially pernicious about this association that drives conservatives to oppose and resent political measures when African Americans are involved—even to the extent of wasteful and harmful legislative and legal maneuvering.[41]

Principled Opposition to Obama Policies?

President Obama has received strong legislative opposition, not only from the Birthers but from the Tea Party as well. As Lee Harris wrote, "[T]he Tea Party movement is not about ideas. It is all about attitude."[42] We contend that it is a party of racial resentment and political frustration. The Tea Party could also be described as a revolt against an elite that has "increasingly solidified its monopoly over the manufacture and distribution of opinion."[43] Emerging in early 2009 and typically consisting of older, white, middle-class conservatives disenchanted with the establishment, the Tea Party revitalized right-wing activism in their lead-up to the 2010 midterm elections.[44] In those midterms, Republicans gained sixty-three seats, forty-two of which were associated with the Tea Party.[45] Underlying policy beliefs of the Tea Party are based on "resentment of perceived federal government 'handouts' to 'undeserving' groups, the definition of which seems heavily influenced by racial and ethnic stereotypes."[46] However, these beliefs are contrasted with their support of federal institutions like Social Security and Medicare, programs from which many Tea Partiers receive benefits. Their fundamental problem, therefore, seems to be with the racial group that receives the benefits of such entitlement programs.

Leaders in the movement frequently espouse extraordinarily radical suggestions such as the abolition of Social Security or the return to the gold standard, to name just a couple. Yet, many have gained considerable ground in the political world. The midterm elections of 2010 demonstrated to mainstream conservatives the power of the Tea Party in energizing the conservative base. Meanwhile, two of the former forerunners in the 2012 Republican race, Michele Bachmann (the Tea Party darling) and Rick Perry (former Tea Party darling), helped to drive debates farther to the right. Despite many notable conservative intellectuals decrying the movement's lack of "intellectual respectability,"[47] their opposition does not seem to weaken the movement's appeal among the conservative base. This effectively means that the Republican Party is slowly being pushed farther to the right, thanks to the Tea Party. The GOP is now in a position in which party leaders seem to fear alienating their base if they do not take the Tea Party, and many of their candidates, seriously. As Lee Harris wrote in "The Tea Party vs. the Intellectuals," "the nature of American politics has been revolutionized by the Tea Party's ability to politicize people who were once apolitical."[48]

The number one priority in the far Right's opposition to President Obama's policies has not been to guide the country in the way it sees fit, but rather to ensure that he did not return for a second term. And while the Tea Party seems increasingly at odds with the conservative mainstream when it comes to central conservative issues, its anti-Obama influence has still infiltrated much of the GOP, in what one reporter called its "obscene genuflection" to the group.[49] As Senator Mitch McConnell, R-KY, the minority leader, stated in 2011, "The single most important thing we want to achieve is for President Obama to be a one-term president."[50] Congresswoman Carolyn Maloney highlighted this stubborn, at times unreasonable, opposition to the president with this observation: "If Obama came up with a cure for the common cold or cancer, these guys would say no."[51]

This kind of personal invective has defined the ongoing Republican campaigns, with more moderate candidates, like those who voted for the debt deal (for example, Jon Huntsman), seeing their numbers

steadily drop in the polls. This is another effect of the Tea Party movement on the GOP. Instead of materializing as a true third party to desta-
bilize two-party-system hegemony, the Tea Party has emerged within
the context of mainstream conservatism, thereby allowing a "rebrand-
ing" of the core Republican image.[52] The Tea Party's effect on elected
Republicans is nowhere better seen than in the 2011 debt talks in which
the GOP threatened to force a national default.[53]

One of the most successful rallying points for the Tea Party has been
opposition to Obama's health care plan. The main point of contention to
Obama's proposed reform was its perceived government intrusion and
"takeover of the healthcare system."[54] During the development of the
health care bill, thousands of protesters participated in anti–health care
reform rallies near at least one hundred congressional district offices.
Some of these protests made headlines with their use of overt racist and
homophobic language. For example, members of the Congressional
Black Caucus, including Representatives John Lewis and Andre Car-
son, accused Tea Party groups of "hurling the N-word at them 15 times
at a 'Code Red' protest in the run-up to the health care reform vote on
March 20."[55] At this same protest, one protester spat on Representative
Emanuel Cleaver of the Congressional Black Caucus.[56] Representative
Barney Frank was "heckled with anti-gay chants," while House majority
whip James Clyburn stated, "I have heard things today that I have not
heard since March 15, 1960, when I was marching to get off the back of
the bus."[57]

The health care fight saw a large alignment of mainstream Republicans with the Tea Party. In an interview held in early 2010, chairman of the Republican National Committee Michael Steele referred to
himself as a "a Tea-Partier, a town-haller, a grass-rooter" and spoke on
the phone to Dick Armey, "head of FreedomWorks, an umbrella for
Tea Party groups, to talk about how they would fight together against
healthcare legislation."[58] During the health care battle, mainstream
GOP members often aligned themselves with the Tea Party, in order
to uphold party unity and avoid factionalization. Many were quick to
point out that the Tea Party's opposition to Obama's health care plan
was less reflective of racism than the fact that "white workers . . . have
seen their plight worsen at dramatic rates."[59] "[O]pposition to healthcare reform from the tea party is not based on racism but self-interest,"

wrote Juan Williams in the *Wall Street Journal.* Yet, the older and whiter segments of the American populace stood at the core of opposition to the president's health care proposal, even though they were likely to benefit from it.[60]

Repealing "Obamacare" has become a priority of the far Right. After Michele Bachmann's win in the Iowa straw poll, she proclaimed her support for repealing the health care plan.[61] Additionally, in Ohio activists submitted a ballot initiative to weaken health care reform; then Missouri voters supported a "referendum against mandating health coverage," and this was soon followed by Arizona and Oklahoma.[62] In a memo distributed to all incoming House Republican lawmakers, Dick Armey, a former Republican majority leader who is chairman of the conservative group FreedomWorks, and Matt Kibbe, its president, wrote, "Politically speaking, your only choice is to get on offense and start moving boldly ahead to repeal, replace and defund Obamacare in 2011, or risk rejection by the voters in 2012."[63]

Implicit social cognition research has demonstrated how unconscious racial biases may influence attitudes about policies and laws like health care. One study found that a stereotype Implicit Association Test (IAT)—measuring the degree to which people associate minority group members with negative attributes and majority group members with positive attributes—predicted participants' recommended funding for religious and racial minority and majority student organizations. Participants who had implicit minority-negative and majority-positive stereotypes were more likely to recommend budget cuts for target minority student organizations. That is, among this group, Jewish (versus Christian), Asian (versus white), and black (versus white) student organizations were recommended to receive less money. They similarly found that an attitude IAT—measuring the degree to which people associate pleasant and unpleasant words with blacks and whites—predicted participants' recommended funding for racial-minority and -majority student organizations. Participants who had implicit pro-white associations were more likely to recommend budget cuts for Asian (versus white) and black (versus white) student organizations.[64]

With an eye toward national policy, another study surveyed whites in order to gauge their support for allocating funds to prisons "to lock up violent criminals." Half the time, the researchers inserted "inner-city" between "violent" and "criminals." The researchers presumed that the racialized connotation of the prime phrase ("inner-city") occurred outside of conscious awareness for participants. Results showed that insertion of the prime phrase made whites with negative attitudes toward blacks more likely to support prison funding; that is, explicit racial attitudes predicted policy support only when the racialized code word was used.[65] In another study on implicit attitudes and US immigration policy, participants more easily associated positive words with whites and negative words with Latinos. More importantly, these implicit racial associations predict attitudes about immigration policy, above and beyond political ideology, socioeconomic concerns, and measures of intolerance toward immigrants—e.g., authoritarianism and ethnocentrism.[66] Simply put, playing the (implicit) race card through code words can engineer support for policies not directly related to race.

Even where legislation and policy have nothing explicitly to do with race, individuals may still associate them with certain politicians in a racialized manner. The extent to which individuals harbor implicit biases against politicians may influence how they view legislation and policy endorsed by those politicians. In one study, implicit racial associations were found to predict attitudes about legislative proposals that, themselves, have nothing to do with race. For example, researchers collected data on participants' implicit racial associations from October 28 to 30, 2008. Then, from November 1 to 3, 2008, researchers assessed participants' attitudes about Barack Obama on a Likert scale, assessing the degree to which they considered him "American," "patriotic," "presidential," and "trustworthy" versus "elitist," "uppity," and "radical." Then, from November 19 to 21, 2008, they asked participants to report their vote for the general election. Finally, between October 1 and 3, 2009, they divided participants into two groups. One group completed a questionnaire that solicited ratings for Obama's health care reform plan. The second group participated in an experiment designed to test any possible relationship between implicit racial associations and support for Obama's health reform policies. The researchers found that participants' implicit racial associations and their support for Obama's health care plan were mediated by negative attitudes about Obama. Moreover, increased implicit prejudice was associated with concerns over Obama's health care policy implications. That being said, those with higher levels of implicit pro-white associations took greater issue with a proposed health care plan when the plan was represented as Obama's than when it was represented as Bill Clinton's plan.[67]

While implicit racial biases may influence opposition toward Obama's policies among some politicians on the right, we remind the reader that modern politics is the business of getting reelected. Accordingly, elected politicians are beholden to their constituencies. No matter how racially egalitarian a politician is, to the extent that his or her constituents harbor conscious or unconscious anti-egalitarian attitudes, the politician will probably kowtow to those biases. For example, to the extent that far right opposition to President Obama's policies is influenced by unconscious racial bias against Obama the person, ultraconservative voters will exert pressure on their representatives to oppose nearly everything Obama does—i.e., to be the party of "no." As articulated by Theda Skocpol and Vanessa Williamson in their book *The Tea Party and the Remaking of Republican Conservatism,*

> For the Republican Party, the Tea Party cuts both ways. Certainly, its enthusiasm and resources fuel the GOP. But the story is more complex because the Tea Party is not just a booster organization for Any-Old-Republicans. Tea Party activists at the grass roots and the right-wing advocates roving the national landscape with billionaire backing have designs on the Republican Party. They want to make it into a much more uncompromising and ideologically principled force. As Tea Party forces make headway in achieving this ideological purification, they spur movement of the Republican Party ever further toward the right, and align the party with a label that principally appeals to older, very conservative white voters.[68]

In fact, as indicated by Geoffrey Kabaservice in his book *Rule and Ruin: The Downfall of Moderation and the Destruction of the Republican Party: From Eisenhower to the Tea Party,* "[T]he Tea Party movement brought far-right ideas that even conservatives had once resisted into the Republican mainstream."[69] While politicians like President Ronald Reagan kept the most extreme elements of the Republican Party at arm's length, the current crop of GOP politicians seem pressured to embrace the ideas of their brethren on the fringe. Ultimately, GOP politicians may be unable to resist their base, even if they want to.[70]

Primate Imagery, Dehumanization, and Assassination Threat

Another attack on Obama, though often couched as humor or just "good fun," has been the attempt to associate him with various forms of animals, specifically primates. The proliferation of imagery comparing the president to primates has escalated throughout his political ascension and has often been at the hands of those who are presumably rightward leaning. One of the first instances, featured prominently on YouTube, took place at a Pennsylvania Republican Rally during the 2008 presidential election.[71] In the video, an attendee marches toward the camera holding a Curious George doll, repeatedly stating with a smile that "This is Little Hussein," referring to Barack Obama's middle name.[72] Racism and bigotry were common at such rallies, where people were heard to yell "terrorist," "kill him," "off with his head," and other blatantly offensive statements.[73] Similarly, in May 2008 a white Georgia restaurant owner began selling T-shirts adorned with an image of Curious George and the text, "Obama in '08."[74] In June, a Utah company manufactured a sock doll of Obama in the image of a monkey.[75]

Shortly after winning the presidential election, President Obama was depicted in a *New York Post* cartoon showing two police officers who had just shot a chimp.[76] In the cartoon, the police officers state, "They'll have to find someone else to write the next stimulus plan."[77] Sean Delonas, the cartoonist who published the image in Murdoch's newspaper (Murdoch owns the *Post*), is known for "his vile cartoons, particularly anti-gay cartoons."[78] In addition to conjuring images of a potential presidential assassination, the cartoon serves to provide an additional level of humoristic pleasure to those who enjoy racial stereotypes of black people as beasts. The display of a chimp symbolizing a black author further recalls stories like those of Sean Bell, Amadou Diallo, and Oscar Grant—black men recently gunned down by law enforcement.[79]

In addition, Obama's image was placed on "Obama Bucks" (a bill for food stamps), in which his head was superimposed over that of a donkey. The creator of the image, Diane Fidele (president of the Chafey

Community Republican Women), explained that she "wasn't thinking in racist terms" when she designed "Obama Bucks."[80] Although she made clear she had no racist intent, the production of the imagery reveals a gap between Obama and the white presidents who came before him. Given that white presidents have their place on dollar bills, Obama's placement on a food stamp implies the racialized connection of state welfare, blacks, and unearned handouts, reflecting the assumption that Obama "will only represent the interest of poor blacks and will turn the U.S. into a 'welfare state.'"[81]

Also in February 2009, a Coral Gables Barnes & Noble bookstore was the scene of what its corporate headquarters described as a "malicious and despicable act" and a hate crime.[82] On February 17, a customer alerted the store management that a book about monkeys had been added to a window display of books about the recently elected president. Although the store immediately removed the book, the damage was already done—someone photographed the display and circulated the image through e-mail. A corporate spokesperson suggested that the perpetrator was probably a customer, possibly the same person who circulated the e-mail. The backlash against the store was severe. Its staff fielded about two hundred calls per day about the display, some from as far away as New Jersey and Arkansas. The e-mail drew prompt criticism from the NAACP, spurring demand for a boycott. Barnes & Noble employee Julissa Carvahal tried to distance the store from the event, saying, "Obviously we wouldn't do that," and claimed that the act was a terrible joke.[83]

In Clarkston, Michigan, Pastor Peter Peters regularly aired a show called *Scriptures for America* on public access television from his church in Colorado.[84] However, in April 2011, the show was yanked off the air after Peters referred to President Obama as "monkey boy" both on the air and in his church newsletter. Peters regularly threw out racist remarks about Jews and blacks during his ninety-minute sermons, according to viewer Jay Clark, who complained about the incident. Some speculated that the program fueled racism within the Michigan community.

Another particularly disturbing incident took place in Orange County, where Marilyn Davenport, a Tea Party activist and elected member of the Orange County GOP Central Committee, sent out an e-mail with an image imitating a family portrait with chimpanzee parents and a child.[85] President Obama's face had been superimposed on that of one of the chimps, accompanied with the text, "Now you know why no birth certificate."[86] Davenport was eventually censured by the county's Executive Committee by a 12-2 vote in May 2011 because "she knew the email was controversial."[87] Orange County GOP chairman Scott Baugh stated that the e-mail "drips with racism" and sends a despicable message.[88] Similarly, Mike Schroeder, former chairman of the California GOP, said he'd never seen anything so offensive sent out by an elected official.

Davenport eventually offered several back-handed apologies for the racist e-mail. In her April 16 e-mail "apology," she stated, "We all know a double standard applies regarding this President. I received plenty of emails about George Bush that I didn't particularly like, yet there was no 'cry' in the media about them."[89] Four days later during a news conference in her driveway, Davenport read the apology e-mail and subsequently questioned whether Obama had actually been born in the United States, despite the release of his Hawaii birth certificate a week earlier. She continued to dig a deeper hole, saying, "I'm sorry if my email offended anyone, I simply found it amusing regarding the character of Obama and the questions surrounding the origin of his birth. In no way did I even consider the fact that he's half-black when I sent out the email."[90] Davenport concluded, "Again for those select few who might be truly offended by viewing a copy of an email I sent to a select list of friends and acquaintances, unlike the liberal left when they do the same, I offer my sincere apologies to you. The email was not meant for you."[91] Unsurprisingly, many on the Left did not buy the sincerity of her apologies as the California NAACP and Orange County Democratic Party called for an apology and her resignation, which she refused to tender.[92]

Such primate-Obama correlations recall a deep-seated history directly related to the enslavement and political disenfranchisement of blacks. Today, we wonder if the continued use of this racist trope will not only politically marginalize Obama but dehumanize him and his family to the point of engendering violent attack. Such a theory is not beyond the pale, given recent allusions to Obama's untimely death.

For example, in January 2012, Kansas House speaker Mike O'Neal (R-Hutchinson) sent his Republican colleagues an e-mail entitled "Pray for Obama. Psalm 109:8." The prayer, far from being a theologically based plea for assistance, was a call for the untimely death of the president. The Bible passages state, "Let his days be few; and let another take his office. May his children be fatherless and his wife a widow." In the e-mail message, O'Neal wrote, "At last—I can honestly voice a Biblical prayer for our president! Look it up—it is word for word! Let us all bow our heads and pray. Brothers and Sisters, can I get an AMEN? AMEN!!!!!!" The incident recalled a 2009 event in which a Florida corrections officer was suspended after highlighting the passage and referring to it as the "Obama prayer." According to the *Sarasota Herald-Tribune*, a guard attached a handwritten note (entitled "The Obama Prayer") to a coworker's jail-issued book of passages from the New Testament, Psalms, and Proverbs and highlighted the verse in Psalms 109:8.[93] Just after the 2012 e-mail from the House speaker, O'Neil refused to apologize in the face of a petition drive that called for his resignation.[94]

Throughout various political campaigns and criticisms of candidates and other figures, the Internet has been a major media outlet for political messages. In "Imagining Obama: Reading Overtly and Inferentially Racist Images of our 44th President, 2007–2008," Ralina L. Joseph argues that Internet images of Obama can be divided into two general categories. The first is a clear form of prejudice, including images of "Obama as an ape, thug, or terrorist."[95] The other form of racism is inferential and occurs when Obama "is figured as a messiah . . . or a mythical creature."[96] While blatantly prejudicial images of Obama as a primate can be denounced as harsh or insensitive, "inferential racism is harder to read as racist because of the possible good intentions behind such iconography."[97] For example, frequent Internet postings of Obama as "my Black best friend" portray him as nonthreatening compared to "real-life African Americans," which further gives the impression that "no actual Black people are needed to fulfill White desire for Blackness."[98]

In comparison, one of this book's authors and English professor Danielle Heard explored the legal significance of Obama's association with primate imagery in an article entitled "'Assassinate the Nigger

Ape': Obama, Implicit Imagery, and the Dire Consequences of Racist Jokes." In their work, they provided a historical context to understanding the racial meaning of the ape-black association. Primate imagery has long been used to lambast and degrade blacks, dating from the beginning of European exploration on the African continent in the sixteenth century. Explorers began to associate Africans and anthropoids, comparing their virility and facial features and contributing to the myth of the "preference of the hulking primates for fair-haired white women."[99] During early scientific efforts to delineate taxonomic hierarchies among different species, Africans were considered the "missing links in the evolution of ape to man."[100]

Advances in science during the nineteenth century placed even more emphasis on blacks' close association with primates. This belief was particularly espoused by the eugenics movement, which elaborated ad nauseam "the results of comparative anatomy, which indicates that the negro is an ape."[101] Various anatomists made efforts to point out the physical similarities between the two—exaggerated lips, long arms, receding chins, and flat noses, to name a few.

The idea that "the Negro is an ape" also became embedded in nineteenth-century popular culture. African slaves like Ota Benga were captured in Africa and became part of traveling exhibitions. Shows like these helped to dehumanize blacks and create fear of them as a separate species, which later served as the justification for Jim Crow segregation laws and deliberate acts of violence.[102] Fears of miscegenation "based upon the premise that Africans were primates" fueled these laws and acts of violence.[103] Images and myths of blacks as a hyper-sexualized, primal species that desired white women fed paranoia that served to support an institutionalized system of racism.

These stereotypes were not limited to the Deep South, however. They found their way into mainstream culture in both the North and the South, particularly in the form of Hollywood blockbusters like D. W. Griffith's *Birth of a Nation*. This movie rationalized the establishment of the Ku Klux Klan as a righteous, just group dedicated to defending the honor and safety of their women from the savage and oversexed black man with a "tendency toward committing rape."[104] The black man was transformed into a brute in such films, often tagged with "epithets like . . . 'that ape-nigger' and a 'creature of the jungles.'"[105]

This is all to say that "the stereotype associating blacks with apes and monkeys has been deeply ingrained in the 'political unconscious.'"[106] Despite considerable advances in the Civil Rights Movement, these associations continue to conflate blacks and savage brutes. This pattern has been only exacerbated by Barack Obama's run for the presidency and subsequent win. Both he and his wife, Michelle, have been negatively compared with apes and monkeys.

Implicit race bias research also puts the black-primate association into context, generally, and with particular regard to President Obama. One study subliminally showed images of black faces, white faces, or neutral images. Participants were then shown fuzzy images of animals (apes and nonapes), which gradually became clearer. Participants were then instructed to indicate the point at which they could identify the image.[107] The researchers found that individuals more easily identified ape images when primed with black male faces than when not so primed. Moreover, individuals found it more difficult to identify ape images when primed with white male faces.

In a second study, individuals were first subliminally shown images of ape line drawings or jumbled line drawings. Then they were given a facial interference task designed to gauge how distracted they would become when presented with faces prior to a test measuring their attentional bias to black and white faces.[108] Results indicated that priming individuals with images of apes resulted in more attentional bias toward black faces. In yet another study, white males took either a race IAT or a "dehumanization IAT" that included ape words (e.g., "ape," "monkey," "baboon") and big cat words (e.g., "lion," "tiger," "panther"). Subjects then completed a stereotype knowledge questionnaire. Among the questions, one focused on whether participants were aware of the stereotype that African Americans are likened to apes. On the personalized IAT, participants demonstrated a pro-white/antiblack bias. On the dehumanization IAT, participants more easily categorized words in the black-ape condition than they did in the black-big cat condition. Implicit antiblack bias was found not to be responsible for the black-ape association. Furthermore, given the low numbers of participants who reported awareness of the historical representation of blacks as primates, the results suggested that the black-primate association operates outside of explicit cultural knowledge of the association.

Importantly, implicit antiblack bias predicts whites' justification of violence against blacks. In one significant study, researchers subliminally primed individuals with images of apes or big cats. They then asked these individuals to view a videotape of police officers beating a suspect who individuals were led to believe was black or white.[109] Individuals who believed the suspect was white perceived the police as being no more justified when primed with apes vis-à-vis big cats. Individuals who believed the suspect was black perceived the police as being more justified when primed with apes vis-à-vis big cats. Moreover, individuals who were primed with big cats did not think the police were more justified in beating the white or black suspect. In contrast, individuals who were primed with apes thought the police were more justified in beating the black, as opposed to the white, suspect. Another study on 153 capital punishment cases between 1979 and 1999 found that black, as opposed to white, capital defendants were more likely to be portrayed as apelike in news coverage, and this portrayal was associated with higher levels of state-sponsored executions.

Dehumanization, broadly defined as the denial of human characteristics to another, is a social-psychological tool that can lead to increased aggression and violence toward those being dehumanized.[110] The process of dehumanization is often an important precursor to violence and aggression against targeted groups and individuals because it reduces the learned social inhibits to violence.[111] When victims are stripped of essential human traits, empathy is constricted, and people are more enabled to commit acts of violence.[112] This process of excluding a group from moral consideration, called "moral disengagement," can lead not just to the infliction of harm on groups but also to greater degrees of harm.[113] As dehumanization increases, the potential for aggressive behavior increases.[114]

One form of dehumanization, which has gained traction in modern times, is "infrahumanization," wherein an individual or group is denied just some human characteristics, making them distinctively less human.[115] This approach is more palatable to many because Western society has embraced increasingly antiracist norms, which may make it more difficult to advocate more aggressive approaches. Infrahumanization is often accomplished through denial of the existence of secondary emotions within a group, such as love, guilt, and hope.

Scientific studies support the argument that dehumanization is a relatively powerful way to enhance aggressiveness.[116] People who are reduced to being thought of as base creatures are viewed as insensitive to abuse, and as a result, more aggressive and primitive methods are utilized to influence their behavior.[117] Because inflicting harm on people viewed as subhuman is less likely to arouse self-reproach, dehumanization serves as an effective means for reducing self-punishment for cruelty.[118] Additionally, if people feel that their aggression is sanctioned by a legitimate authority, they are more likely to act in ways that they normally would not.[119]

One particularly effective means of denying human characteristics is animalistic dehumanization, wherein people are compared to or portrayed as beasts rather than humans.[120] This strategy of evoking images of lower life forms for certain groups has been deployed in horrific genocides such as that of the Jews during the Holocaust and the Bosnians during the Balkan Wars.[121] Some researchers have documented the role of this kind of dehumanization as a justification for these sanctioned acts of mass violence.[122] According to Primo Levi, a Nazi concentration camp survivor, the operators of the camps needed to view the Jews as subhuman in order to avoid being overwhelmed by distress from the atrocities they were committing.[123] Wars have often featured full dehumanization of enemies, depicting them in propaganda as bestial, subhuman species.[124] Accordingly, while attempts to dehumanize President Obama have not constituted a concerted and coordinated effort by his critics and detractors—especially those on the political Right—they may, nonetheless, be fateful. For example, in February of 2010, Johnny Logan Jr. of Louisville, Kentucky, was arrested and charged with making threats against the president after the US Secret Service found his poem titled "The Sniper" on a white nationalist website called "NewSaxon.org." A portion of the poem reads, "The bullet that he has chambered is one of the purest pride. And the inspiration on the casing reads DIE negro DIE. He breathes out as he pulls the trigger releasing all his hate. And a smile appears upon his face as he seals that monkey's fate."[125]

The dehumanization of President Obama via the use of primate imagery raises the specter of personal threats to his safety from individuals who perceive him as being sufficiently subhuman to merit assassination. To the extent that such associations increase the number of threats to President Obama's life, 18 United States Code § 3056 is implicated. In 1994, Congress passed legislation stating that presidents elected to office after January 1, 1997, will receive Secret Service protection for ten years after they are out of office as opposed to lifetime protection. Originally known as the Treasury, Postal Service, and General Government Appropriations Act, it was later codified as section 3056.[126] To date, this legislation has received scant attention. Arguably, concerns about the safety of post-1997-elected presidents once they leave office have been, and maybe should be, negligible—that is, until the election of Barack Obama. In fact, there are numerous examples of threats on President Obama's life, so much so that by 2009 the Secret Service indicated that death threats against President Obama were four times those against President Bush.[127]

To date, scant attention has been paid to this law, but documented hostilities toward the first black president and the reality that he will someday be an ex-president beg for a revisiting of the law that would limit the amount of Secret Service protection he will receive. The paradox is that any future legislation would have to be passed, at least in part, by legislators who may have helped to foment the type of environment in which his assassination threat is elevated.

One Step Forward, Two Steps Back: Post-Racialism and Electoral Politics

The moment when the 2008 presidential election declared Senator Barack Obama the forty-fourth chief executive of the United States ushered in high public expectations of a post-racial America that would transcend the existing racial barriers. While some dominant media voices proclaimed that racism, as a societal problem, has been on the decline, a 2009 *Washington Post/ABC News* poll suggested that "44 percent of blacks and 22 percent of whites continue to see racism as a large societal problem" compared to an outstanding 70 percent of blacks and 52 percent of whites who held the same view in 1996.[128]

Yet, views on racism are not one dimensional. Professor Ron Walters argues that there are "two levels of identity with racism": the personal level and the national level that is "more symbolic."[129] Hence, personal experiences with racism can be at odds with views of racism as a larger, national problem affected by the body politic. For example, in 2009, 70 percent of African Americans indicated that they thought they would achieve or will achieve racial equality. Moreover, after the election of Obama, nearly two-thirds of Americans said the election was a sign of "black progress" and more than half of African Americans and 32 percent of whites reported being "more proud" of the 2008 election results.[130] This can be read as an improvement of racial perceptions under the Obama administration.

Since the 2008 election, public perceptions of race have positively altered daily interactions with individuals from other races. A 2010 Pew Research poll found that "black Americans are more satisfied with their situation than at any time in the past 25 years, and more than half say life will get better for them."[131] One of the reasons for this change in attitudes and trends is the "halo-effect."[132] Despite the fact that the recession had a disproportionate effect on African Americans in terms of high unemployment rates (from 9 percent in 2007 to 16 percent in 2009) and decrease in incomes, "39 percent of blacks say things are better for them than they were five years ago."[133] This number has nearly doubled since 2007. The National Urban League, a civil rights organization, also recognizes the poll results as reflecting an upbeat perception, wherein 54 percent of black Americans say race relations have improved since the 2008 elections. Furthermore, these polling results speak to the personable qualities of President Obama (95 percent approval ratings from African Americans versus 56 percent white ratings), which definitely help mold new perceptions of people of different races, particularly among black Americans.[134]

In a 2009 USA Today/Gallup poll, "six in ten Americans said that they expected that race relations would improve as a result of Obama's presidency, with four in ten believing that a difference has already been made."[135] As Dr. Martin Luther King Jr.'s historic "I Have a Dream" speech celebrates its forty-eighth anniversary on August 28, 2011, Americans see "progress in civil rights in their lifetime."[136] Despite the fact that 2011 USA Today/Gallup polls suggest that 52 percent of African Americans believe civil right laws are needed to reduce discrimination against blacks, the percentage of all Americans' opinion on the same view "dropped to 21% now from 38% in 1993, with similar changes among whites and blacks."[137] Nine out of ten reported that the Civil Rights Movement had positively improved race relations during their lifetime, regardless of opinions on government intervention in that area. Overall, today Americans are more positive about civil rights; the number of people saying that civil rights have "greatly" improved has risen eighteen percentage points since 1995.[138]

Whether one voted or did not vote for President Obama, one cannot deny the strides the nation has collectively made since the Civil Rights Movement. While many historians consider the Declaration of Independence the birth of America in 1776, others consider the inauguration of the first black president as the birth of a "post-racial" America. Yet, this belief may be quite harmful given that (1) there are still entrenched distinctions between whites' and racial minorities' perceptions of racial progress, (2) post-racialism may be a strong motivator toward harmful actions, and (3) such beliefs might obscure salient and objectively measurable racial inequities and progress.

For instance, research indicates that whites tend to perceive greater progress toward racial equality than do racial minorities.[139] This perception gap is associated with different reference points each group uses to assess progress. Whites focus on comparisons with the past; racial minorities focus on ideal standards.[140] Additional research shows that variability in whites' perceptions of racial progress could be explained by whites' self-reported racial prejudice. That is, whites who were less prejudiced focused more strongly on the ideal future than the past, whereas those higher in prejudice focused more strongly on the past than the ideal future.[141] It is no surprise, then, that whites' perceptions of racial progress predict their reactions to policies like affirmative action and social justice more broadly.[142] For example, people's perception that racism is less of a problem in the United States now than in times past has increased over time, and people now express less support for policies designed to address racial inequality.[143]

The perception, especially among the majority of Americans, that American race relations have largely been resolved could be particularly consequential in the rolling back of certain legal gains that African Americans have made—particularly as related to the Voting Rights Act (VRA). For example, in light of President Obama's election, some commentators suggest that the United States has reached a post-racial era in which race is relatively inconsequential.[144] Accordingly, there are those who have argued for the elimination of the VRA as well as the elimination of racial considerations in the districting process.[145]

The VRA, passed in 1965, outlawed discriminatory voting practices that had long been responsible for the widespread disenfranchisement of African American voters. Section 2 of the VRA provides voters with, inter alia, the ability to challenge racially discriminatory districting practices that dilute the minority group's ability to participate equally in the electoral process.[146] In *Thornburg v. Gingles*, the US Supreme Court established the framework for vote dilution claims. To challenge a method of election that allows for large voting districts, plaintiffs must demonstrate geographic compactness, political cohesion, and legally significant white bloc voting. After satisfying these preconditions, courts must consider the totality of the circumstances and determine—considering past and contemporary examples of discrimination—whether the political process is equally open to minority voters.[147]

Section 5 of the VRA provides a more preemptive remedy to racial discrimination in voting.[148] Pursuant to section 5 of the VRA, specific jurisdictions, commonly referred to as "covered jurisdictions," must submit all voting changes to either the US attorney general or the US District Court for the District of Columbia. Once the submission is received, it is reviewed to determine whether the change has the purpose or effect of being discriminatory against voters on the basis of race, color, or language.[149] In addition, the covered jurisdiction's submission is also reviewed for whether it places minority voters in a worse position than before the redistricting.[150] If the jurisdiction chooses to formally submit the change, it must demonstrate that the submitted change is not discriminatory.[151]

The use of race in redistricting has become increasingly suspicious when it is designed to improve the electoral prospects of racial minorities.[152] In *Shaw v. Reno*, plaintiffs (a group of white voters) charged that North Carolina created an unconstitutional racial gerrymander in violation of the Fourteenth Amendment. They argued that the two districts at issue were crafted "arbitrarily—without regard to considerations such as compactness, contiguousness, geographical boundaries, or political subdivisions, with the purpose to create congressional districts along racial lines and to assure the election of two black representatives to

Congress."[153] The Court stated that certain redistricting schemes that are "adopted with a discriminatory purpose and have the effect of diluting minority voting strength" will violate the Fourteenth Amendment.[154] However, the Court made clear that this was not a vote dilution case, because appellants never alleged that the plan "unconstitutionally diluted white voting strength."[155] The Court concluded that since the newly drawn districts were "so bizarre," they were "unexplainable on grounds other than race"; thus, strict scrutiny would be the appropriate standard of review.[156] The jurisdiction argued that its purpose in drawing the districts was to avoid putting minority groups in a worse position. The Court rejected this argument, finding that the plan was not narrowly tailored, and admonished jurisdictions to do only what is "reasonably necessary" to avoid retrogression.[157]

Four years after *Shaw*, the Supreme Court decided *Lawyer v. Department of Justice*.[158] In *Lawyer*, the Supreme Court examined whether Florida unconstitutionally considered race in drafting its redistricting plan. The Court found it did not. Appellants argued that race predominated because the district at issue encompassed more than one county, crossed a body of water, was oddly shaped, and had a much higher percentage of black voters than other counties. Nonetheless, the Court found that none of these factors was "different from what Florida's traditional districting principles could be expected to produce" and that race did not predominate.[159] Accordingly, in *Lawyer*, the Court appeared to reassure advocates that racial considerations were allowable in the redistricting process.

In *Georgia v. Ashcroft*, the Supreme Court allowed the fracturing of majority-minority districts.[160] In the 2001 redistricting cycle, Democrats in Georgia decided to "unpack" heavy majority-minority districts to create influence districts—i.e., districts requiring minority voters to rely upon whites to join them in voting for their preferred candidate in order to be successful. Yet, some argued that the fracturing of minority districts violated section 2 of the VRA. The Court refused "to equate a § 2 vote dilution inquiry with the § 5 retrogression standard."[161] The Court provided that states could create what it called "safe districts," which make it "highly likely that minority voters will be able to elect the candidate of their choice"; or create "influence districts," which allow for more districts but make it "not quite as likely as under the benchmark plan . . . that minority voters will be able to elect candidates of their choice."[162]

Then, in 2009, the Court seemed to move further away from majority-minority districts and the preservation of electoral gains in its *Bartlett v. Strickland* decision.[163] In *Bartlett*, a North Carolina county argued that section 2 of the VRA required it to split counties in order to maintain a majority-minority district that had fallen below 50 percent minority population. County officials attempted to maintain the district despite the fact that state law prohibited splitting counties because they believed that the VRA required it to draw a district that could sustain an opportunity for minorities to elect their candidate of choice. The Court reiterated that section 2 can require the creation of majority-minority districts, where the *Gingles* preconditions are met. But it also concluded that section 2 did not require states to maintain minority crossover and influence districts—i.e., to maintain minority districts where minorities constitute less than a majority. The problem with this approach, as articulated by law professor Gilda Daniels, is that "[t]he Supreme Court's idea of post-racial redistricting seems to lie in the hopes of crossover, influence, and coalition districts. These alternatives, however, do not offer minority voters a clear opportunity to elect. They merely offer an opportunity to influence an outcome that is reliant upon nonminority voters joining their preferred candidate."[164] However, nothing suggests that white voters are sufficiently post-racial to vote for black candidates to any large extent in the future. In fact, if there is anything that the 2008 presidential election taught us it is that (1) race played a role in voter attitudes and decision making leading up to and during the 2008 presidential election; (2) political leanings underscored the role of race and voting for Obama; and (3) the belief that we now live in, and even behavior that suggests an effort to move us toward, a post-racial society correlates with racial discrimination generally and quite possibly with voting specifically.

A December 2007 study found that racial resentment had much more of an adverse effect on candidate Obama's favorability ratings than on those of either candidate Clinton or candidate Edwards.[165] While racial resentment may, indeed, be quite explicit for some voters, for most it is probably automatic/implicit/unconscious. During the months preceding the 2008 election, B. Keith Payne and colleagues conducted three surveys of representative samples of American adults' explicit and implicit prejudice. They found that explicit and implicit prejudice significantly predicted later vote choice. Voters higher in explicit prejudice were less likely to vote for Obama and more likely to vote for McCain. After researchers controlled for explicit prejudice, citizens higher in implicit prejudice were less likely to vote for Obama, but were not more likely to vote for McCain. Instead, they were more likely either to abstain or to vote for a third-party candidate rather than Obama.[166] In a study conducted just prior to the 2008 presidential election, implicit racial attitudes were found to predict vote choice—with those with higher implicit pro-white biases choosing McCain over Obama for president.[167]

In their 2007 racial resentment study, researchers found that their distribution of racial resentment was skewed to the conservative side. One would suppose that a greater impact of racial resentment should typically diminish support for racially liberal candidates and policies. Obama managed to overcome the racial resentment by generating considerable support among the least racially resentful—i.e., those on the liberal side of the spectrum. Even after removing blacks (a group that was likely to be both racially liberal and supportive of Obama) from the analyses, researchers found that white racial conservatives still evaluated Obama less favorably than they did Clinton and Edwards.[168] Even more striking was their finding that although Democrats who were either racially resentful or simply ideologically conservative negatively evaluated Hillary Clinton in 1992, 1994, 2000, and 2004, in 2008, the racially resentful Democrats demonstrated more positive evaluations of Clinton while conservative Democrats maintained a negative evaluation of her.[169] Among Democrats, findings indicate that "racial conservatives were heavily voting their racial predispositions in opposing Barack Obama and therefore had to alter earlier evaluations of his main rival to make such votes congruent."[170] Hence, it is no surprise that Obama's race was a key factor in many Clinton supporters' defection to McCain. Racial resentment among Clinton primary voters predicted their support for McCain over Obama in March 2008, though they returned to Obama in October 2008.[171]

Other research, on moral credentialing, has found that racially egalitarian behavior can result in later racial discrimination. For example, in one study, given the chance to endorse Obama for president (as opposed to McCain), people were more likely to then choose a white candidate for a job in a racially charged police force.[172] The same effect was not found when participants were asked to endorse a white Democrat (in a Kerry/Bush version), or when the endorsement task was changed into an instruction to circle the picture of the younger candidate (still using the Obama/McCain option), suggesting that a combination of both the race and the act of endorsement led to the increased ability to then endorse a white person in the second task. In essence, endorsing President Obama resulted in individuals' discriminating against blacks.

In a related study, researchers first measured participants' prejudice using the Modern Racism Scale, then asked them to endorse either Obama or McCain (credential condition), or Kerry or Bush (political expression condition), and later asked participants to proportion tax funds to two antipoverty groups: one for a predominantly white neighborhood, the other for a predominantly black neighborhood. Endorsing Obama increased the proportion of funds allocated to whites at the expense of blacks, but only for those Obama supporters with higher levels of preexisting prejudice. Those who measured low levels of preexisting prejudice and endorsed Obama tended to favor more funds for the predominantly black neighborhood group.

The idea that endorsing Obama can provide voters with the "moral credentials" to discriminate against blacks in the future is further underscored by a recent study in the *Journal of Experimental Social Psychology*.[173] Examining participants' group dominance motivation, political orientation, perception of Obama's foreignness, belief that "racism is over," and reactions to the oath-of-office mistake, findings indicate a positive correlation with group-dominance motives and voting for Obama, but only among those who believed that an Obama victory meant that racism was virtually over. These findings suggest that the token act on the part of some white voters to vote for a black presidential candidate may undermine the political chances of future black political candidates.

There is little room for doubt that unconscious bias continues to correlate whiteness and authentic American identity and that bias is often activated by dehumanizing images of blacks and can often contain and enable differently politicized policy stances, may endanger the lives of

black elected officials, and can exercise a significant role on the (dis)
continuation of majority-minority districts as provided for in the Voting Rights Act. The significance of these phenomena will be unpacked
in the next, and last, chapter, in which we look into our social science
crystal ball to predict the next two years of our deeply racialized and
"post-racial" America.

Conclusion

On the evening of November 6, 2012, the presidential election results underscored what pollsters had projected, a victory for President Barack Obama. For those from the left to the middle-right of the political spectrum, these results were unsurprising. In the weeks leading up to the election, despite the small gain that Mitt Romney achieved following President Obama's poor debate performance on October 3, most nonpartisan polls had President Obama leading anywhere from three to six percentage points for the popular vote and having a lock in the Electoral College. In the end, the only swing states that went for Romney were Indiana and North Carolina; the swing states of Ohio and Florida were close but went Democrat. On the morning of November 7, the Electoral College recorded 332 votes for Obama and 206 for Romney. The first black president had decisively won both the popular and the electoral votes in his reelection bid.

Fear of a Black Planet

As President Obama's reelection was almost a certainty, Fox News became the site of a bizarre situation. By 11:15 p.m. (EST), Fox News statisticians had called Ohio for Obama, which meant he had the votes to win reelection. While the state had many votes still to count, those votes were in Democrat strongholds like Cuyahoga County and its county seat, Cleveland. Therefore, President Obama's reelection was a foregone conclusion. Obama won Ohio. As other news networks and Fox's own number crunchers reported the results, the Fox News backlash started. First, coanchors Megyn Kelly and Bret Baier appeared blindsided by, even disapproving of, the count. An agitated and confused Brit Hume reported that Romney's campaign had doubts about Fox News calling Ohio for Obama.

Karl Rove, the brain trust of the George W. Bush administration, chimed in, "Our network called it on the basis of about seventy-four percent of the vote being in. . . . a nine-hundred and eleven vote difference." Hume then pressed Rove on whether Ohio had been settled, to which Rove replied by describing the call as "premature." As the camera view switched to the scene of the celebration at Obama's campaign headquarters, we heard Rove's voice in the background, rebuking the Fox analysts for calling Ohio for Obama: "Thanks a lot. Thank you. It's great to have you guys here."

Before you knew it, Baier was pulling on the reigns and within seconds, Kelly was up from her desk, walking at a brisk pace through a backstage corridor with a cameraman in tow to seek out the statisticians at the "decision desk" to find out what was *really* going on in Ohio. Upon finally reaching the statistician after traversing the backstage labyrinth, Kelly asked him whether he stood by his call on Ohio. The soft-spoken political scientist replied,

> We're actually quite comfortable with our call in Ohio. Basically, right now, there's too much Obama vote that's outstanding there that we know is going to come in, that we know is going to be Obama. And while, yes, there are a number of counties out there that will be Romney, the largest thing that's outstanding is the Cleveland area, it's Cuyahoga. This is Democratic territory. And we're quite comfortable with the idea that Obama will carry Ohio.

Still, Rove was not persuaded.[1] Later that night, an exasperated Kelly looked at Rove and summed up the bizarre evening with a blunt question: "Is this just math that you do as a Republican to make yourself feel better, or is this real?"

Such an on-screen confrontation between Rove and the "Decision Desk" is indicative of the turmoil and angst among the Right that evening. At the University of Mississippi, bottles and rocks were thrown at cars while antiblack racial epithets were bandied about and an Obama/Biden sign was burned.[2] In New York City, Donald Trump tweeted a call for "revolution": "The election is a total sham and a travesty. We are not a democracy!" "More votes equals a loss . . . revolution!" "We can't let this happen. We should march on Washington and stop this travesty. Our nation is totally divided."[3] And just after the election results were announced, about forty white students gathered outside of the Minority Student Union at Hampden-Sydney College in Farmville, Virginia, to shout racial slurs, toss bottles, set off fireworks, and threaten physical violence.[4]

Whither Whiteness?

The aforementioned examples serve to punctuate a sobering reality. Fifty-nine percent of white voters supported Romney, and 88 percent of Romney's votes came from whites (compare with Obama's victory over John McCain in 2008, when 55 percent of white voters supported McCain). This is unsurprising given that the GOP and the radical groups that dance within or around its ranks worked diligently to become the party of whiteness: from the less-than-subtle Tea Party claim that *we* (and the "we" is anything but a vacant category, being decidedly white) must take *our* country back to the Birthers' bizarre and unhinged rationale that Obama was an alien constitutionally disqualified from holding office. Meanwhile, a large swath of the GOP worked diligently to characterize Obama as a black radical socialist food stamp president.

By the morning of November 7, 2012, this racial-othering strategy, replete with racial, dog-whistle politics and the covert playing of the race card, fell mightily short, at least in terms of presidential electoral politics. The party of whiteness had fallen. The decline in power was reflected in the discourse of various right-wing pontificators. For example, just hours before the election was called, Bill O'Reilly, the flagship commentator for Fox News, remarked that "[t]he white establishment is now the minority. . . . The demographics are changing. It's not a traditional America anymore."[5]

Days later, in attempting to clarify his comments, O'Reilly again bandied about the idea that white America was at the end of days and that groups like single women, Hispanic Americans, and African Americans no longer held a work ethic or a belief in "self-reliance":

If you look at the exit polling, you'll see that a coalition of voters put the President back into the oval office. That coalition was non-tradition, which means it veered away from things like traditional marriage, robust capitalism, and self-reliance. Instead, each constituency that voted for the President—whether it be single women, Hispanic Americans, African Americans, whatever—had very specific reasons for doing so. . . . Traditional American voters generally want a smaller government in Washington, more local control, some oversight on abortion, and believe in American exceptionalism.[6]

The day after the election, the normally on-the-offensive Ann Coulter called in to the conservative radio talk show host Laura Ingraham to state,

I'm pretty pessimistic about the country. . . . People are suffering. The country is in disarray. If Mitt Romney cannot win in this economy, then the tipping point has been reached. We have more takers than makers and it's over. There is no hope. . . . Mitt Romney was the president we needed right now, and I think it is so sad that we are going to be deprived of his brain power, of his skills in turning companies around, turning the Olympics around, his idea and his kindness for being able to push very conservative ideas on a country that no longer is interested in conservative ideas. It is interested in handouts.[7]

And in an unfiltered moment the day after the election, conservative pundit Pat Buchanan appeared on the G. Gordon Liddy radio show to state, "White America died last night. Obama's reelection killed it. Our 200 plus year history as a Western nation is over. We're a Socialist Latin American country now. Venezuela without the oil." Host George Liddy responded, "With what you just said right there. . . . You seem to imply that white people are better than other people. That's not really what you're saying is it?"

Of course that's what I'm saying. Isn't it obvious? Anything worth doing on this Earth was done first by white people. Who landed on the moon? White people. Who climbed Mount Everest? White people. Who invented the transistor? White people. Who invented paper?

White people. Who discovered algebra? White people. And don't give me all this nonsense about Martin Luther King and civil rights and all that. Who do you think freed the slaves? Abraham Lincoln. A white guy! But we're not led by Lincoln anymore, we're led by an affirmative-action mulatto who can't physically understand how great America once was. I cried last night G. I cried for hours. It's over for all of us. The great White nation will never survive another four years of Obama's leadership. . . . Of course I agree with half of what he does. He's half white! That's not the half I'm worried about.

The Right's hyperventilation over Obama's reelection continued over the next few weeks, and not only from those on the far right fringe of the GOP. On November 13, 2012, the former vice-presidential candidate, Paul Ryan, told WISC-TV of Wisconsin that they lost to Obama and Biden due to their lack of appeal in "urban areas"—a uniformly coded word for black voting blocs.[8] So also, the next day, on November 14, Mitt Romney stated that he was "troubled" by a defeat he attributed to "gifts" that Obama handed out to "the African-American community, the Hispanic community, and young people":

Free contraceptives were very big with young college-aged women. And then, finally, Obamacare also made a difference for them, because as you know, anybody now twenty-six years of age and younger was now going to be part of their parents' plan, and that was a big gift to young people. They turned out in large numbers, a larger share in this election even than in 2008. . . . You can imagine for somebody making $25,000 or $30,000 or $35,000 a year, being told you're now going to get free health care, particularly if you don't have it, getting free health care worth, what, $10,000 per family, in perpetuity, I mean, this is huge. Likewise with Hispanic voters, free health care was a big plus. But in addition with regards to Hispanic voters, the amnesty for children of illegals, the so-called Dream Act kids, was a huge plus for that voting group.[9]

The rhetoric was strong, but wrong. While exit poll data demonstrated that Obama did well in metropolitan areas, the interpretation by Ryan and Romney failed to take into account that the GOP lost overwhelmingly in many rural, mostly white states, like Iowa and New Hampshire.

Moreover, their version missed the fact that in big swing states, like Ohio for example, Obama received sixty-three thousand fewer votes in the three big urban counties in 2012 than he did in 2008. So also, Obama's 2012 victory was by much smaller margins (compared to 2008) in cities in swing states like Virginia, Colorado, Wisconsin, and Pennsylvania.[10]

But the facts about the election were beside their point. They grabbed onto the dominant white-victim narrative in which Obama effectively bought the election with handouts to special interest groups marked by age, race, and gender. This framing was used to eclipse the details that many whites did not vote for the GOP ticket. Hence, this alternate reality attempts to repackage the election result as one marred by the power of a racialized nanny state; people of color and their black president were in league against a meritocratic and bootstrapping white populace motivated by pure democratic idealism, rather than by unfair and earmarked government handouts for a lazy and undeserving underclass of women, the young, and people of color. The core weltanschauung of the Republican Party thus appears, even in defeat, as a package deal in which racist and reactionary views lay in consort with anti-immigrant, anti–working class, and anti-women policies.

Such issue constraint and discursive reframing is—as Sam Tenanhaus pointed out in his February 2013 *New Republic* article entitled "Why the GOP Is and Will Continue to Be the Party of White People"— a replay of the politics of nullification whereby a white populace is both encouraged to simply defy and delegitimize presidential authority and also interpolated as the quintessential voice and spirit of America. Tenanhaus thus writes that this bias is so profuse that

> [e]ven recent immigrants to this country sense . . . the extended lineage of rearguard politics, with its aggrieved call, heard so often today, "to take back America"—that is, to take America back to the "better" place it used to be. . . . In retreat, the nullifying spirit has been revived as a form of governance—or, more accurately, anti-governance. Its stronghold is the Tea Party–inflected House of Representatives, whose nullifiers would plunge us all over the "fiscal cliff." We see it too in continuing challenges to "Obamacare," even after it was validated by the Roberts Court. And we see it as well in Senator Rand Paul's promise to "nullify anything

the president does" to impose new gun controls. Each is presented not as a practical attempt to find a better answer, but as a "Constitutional" demand for restoration of the nation to its hallowed prior self. It is not a coincidence that the resurgence of nullification is happening while our first African American president is in office.

The Far Right's Faustian bargain with whiteness now ties it to a dwindling cohort of ideologically narrow and paranoid middle-aged white men who struggle against a nation that looks and acts much differently than their fathers' Grand Old Party. And for many, the party is over. This sociopolitical contractual conflation of whiteness with a true and authentic form of American citizenship and belonging is a point central to both Birtherism and many variants of Tea Party activism, and was continually but unsuccessfully driven home in the lead-up to Obama's first election, his first term in office, the path to his reelection, and the Far Right's post-reelection reaction. Yet, many may still feel that connecting the Right with whiteness is a bit oversimplified and dismissive of another discourse within the GOP, its allies, and its commentators: that of Republicans of color.

People of Color and the Janus Face of the GOP

The preceding chapters have spilled more than enough ink to demonstrate (1) the continued "othering" of African Americans generally and Barack Obama specifically, (2) the conflation of whiteness with morality and authentic citizenship, (3) the belief that whites are the proper administrators and paternalistic saviors of an increasingly diverse nation, and (4) the belief that whites are under unfair attack by an ungrateful mass of nonwhite people who refuse to live as contented servants in an increasingly stratified nation. What we have yet to address is how, illuminated on center stage in the wake of the 2012 election, the GOP is in a state of schizophrenic crisis over the decline of white hegemony and the place of people of color in the nation and the party.

One side of the Janus face turns toward the staunch old guard of the GOP that cannot stand the browning of America and the government refusal to turn away, at least not entirely, from helping the underserved and unprotected. These are the O'Reillys, the Coulters, and the

Buchanans. This cadre of folks trots out the old message that black people are lazy, that Latinos have too many children, and that white people are either biologically or culturally superior. This reactionary trope of black and brown pathologies is a tried and true device that scares white people into the ranks of the GOP, and they will most likely repeat it to their grave.

The anti-Latino specter haunts, if it is not fully alive within, the GOP. And this sentiment is not just an ideological approach to Latinos but exists in redistricting and gerrymandering, voter-identification requirements, and anti-immigration policies. These Republican-sponsored laws and tactics affect Latinos and other people of color disproportionately; and many Latinos see discrimination as deeply rooted among Republicans.[11] Writing in the *Atlantic*, Geraldo Cadava makes a salient point: "One of my students told me recently about her Latina grandmother, who—despite her conservative views on the economy, immigration, and marriage—always votes for Democratic candidates. Why? Because, she told her granddaughter, no matter how much she agreed with the Republicans, that party would never see her as an American."[12] Indeed, when then presidential candidate Mitt Romney famously suggested that undocumented immigrants would leave the United States voluntarily—that is, "self-deport"—if government eliminated incentives, many saw that interpretation as a precursor to a repeat of the 1930s removals of Mexican Americans, who were labeled as economic burdens and political subversives. Overall, the Republican Party aligns with policies that both result in and cause anti-Latino discrimination, and that orientation breeds distrust among many Latino voters.

But the other side of the GOP Janus face voices a different political rhetoric. In a world no longer marked by *absolute* white domination, some within the GOP seem to realize that if you can't beat 'em . . . then make 'em join you. This "solution" is predicated on catering to different racial demographics via rhetoric or symbolism thought to capture nonwhite attention. In this configuration, the propping up of black or brown faces—such as those of conservative Latino representatives Mario Diaz-Balart, Ruben Navarrette Jr., Senator Marco Rubio, or others such as Herman Cain or Bobby Jindal—will result in droves of nonwhites, on political autopilot, entering the tent of the Republican Party. Indeed, if the right side of the Janus face is the "Southern Strategy 2.0" due to its courting of white voters in the Deep South (Obama gained less than 20 percent of the white vote in Mississippi, Louisiana, Alabama, Georgia, and South Carolina.), then the left side is the "Illusion of Inclusion." In this second position, tokenism and the fetishism of diversity as a form of political correctness reigns supreme. Here, photo opportunities rather than equal opportunities emerge as the strategy for garnering votes. The newfound Janus-faced Republican strategy simultaneously courts nonwhite token candidates while chastising their attendant racial groups as dysfunctional entitlement classes. And while the former stratagem of playing to white anxieties is now well understood, we must further examine the strategy of tokenism

The Illusion of Inclusion: Tokenism

Racial-minority political candidates have been national-level contenders dating back to the post-Reconstruction era. With regard to the presidency, for example, in 1972, Shirley Chisholm was the first African American woman to run for president of the United States. Chisholm ran with limited resources but concentrated her efforts on "sympathetic" states and demographics, such as women, African Americans, and college students.[13] She won the New Jersey presidential primary with 66.9 percent of the vote and had strong showings in Florida, Massachusetts, and North Carolina. In the presidential primaries before the 1972 Democratic National Convention, Chisholm received 430,000 votes. At the convention, she received votes from 151 delegates on the first roll call ballot, and even though most of the 452 black delegates at the convention were already committed to other candidates, Chisholm picked off sixty-seven of those delegates.[14]

Chisholm's campaign faced an uphill battle. One of her biggest obstacles was African American sexism.[15] One black politician admitted, "In this first serious effort of blacks for high political office, it would be better if it were a man."[16] Other black leaders claimed, "A vote for Shirley Chisholm is a vote for George Wallace."[17] Despite facing criticism from the black community because of her commitment to women's rights, Chisholm also lacked support from feminists who refused to endorse her because they felt she never had a chance to win.[18] This seemed to be Chisholm's weakness—people took her seriously and as a result, most of those who would have supported her did not want to endorse a "doomed campaign."[19] However, Chisholm's goal was never to win; instead, she ran because "someone had to do it first."[20]

In 1984, Jesse Jackson became the second African American to make a run for the presidential nomination.[21] Jackson did well in the campaign, placed third in the Democratic primary voting, and received 3.5 million votes.[22] Jackson's campaign came under criticism when Jackson referred to Jews as "Hymies" in a *Washington Post* interview in January 1984. As a result, protests arose, and Jackson apologized for his statements a month later.[23] Jackson most likely contributed to the boost in black voter participation in 1984 but lost to Walter Mondale.[24]

In 1988, Jackson again made a bid for the Democratic presidential nomination.[25] He was one of eight presidential candidates and finished second in the primaries to Michael Dukakis. During the primaries, Jackson garnered more than seven million votes,[26] and because he enjoyed more national recognition, Jackson received greater support from both blacks and whites.[27]

In 2003, Carol Moseley Braun campaigned for a presidential bid. While her name had little recognition outside the African American community, Braun represented an important demographic within the Democratic Party—an African American woman against the Iraq War.[28] Because of this, Braun garnered support from the National Organization of Women and the National Women's Political Caucus.[29] In addition to support from women's groups, Braun also had more political experience than her male counterpart Al Sharpton. Braun is a lawyer, was formerly an assistant US attorney of Illinois, served in the Senate for six years, and was an ambassador to New Zealand.[30]

Despite these credentials, black voters were more willing to support a black man, whom 70 percent of black voters still found unfavorable.[31] Further, Braun participated in only one primary—the unofficial Washington, DC, contest—and Sharpton beat her, getting 34 percent of the vote to her 11 percent.[32] Braun's campaign also battled "controversial baggage."[33] In 1998, her bid for reelection to the Senate was undone by a scandal involving Moseley Braun and her siblings sharing an inheritance instead of reimbursing Medicaid. There were also accusations of misuse of campaign funds and a controversial visit to the military dictator of Nigeria that was not approved by the US State Department.[34]

Al Sharpton's 2003 presidential bid, from the beginning, suffered from disorganization. However, this was alleviated in April 2003 when Sharpton appointed Frank E. Watkins, who was a long-time aide to Jesse Jackson, as his campaign manager. While this helped his efforts, expanding his message to include education, health care, and women's rights, Sharpton's campaign also encountered "controversial baggage" such as his involvement in the Tawana Brawley case, in which he accused prosecutor Steven Pagones of participating in Brawley's rape,[35] which cost Sharpton sixty-five thousand dollars as a defamation claim award.[36]

Sharpton's campaign focused on the narrowing gap between Republicans and Democrats, stating that the parties had become "too similar on issues such as war, health care, business deregulation and taxes."[37] He was also concerned with affirmative action programs and anti–death penalty legislation; however, Sharpton's far-left perspective and his scandalous past ultimately cost him the election since most Democrats regarded him as too liberal.[38]

Not all national-level black political candidates have been Democrats. In fact, since President Obama's election, Republicans have been scurrying to find their own black and brown faces to run for office. Approximately a month after Obama claimed his second term, Republican governor Nikki Haley (herself a daughter of Sikh immigrants from Punjab, India, and the first female and first nonwhite governor of South Carolina) announced that Timothy Eugene Scott (a US representative for South Carolina's first congressional district) would serve as the United States senator-designate for South Carolina (replacing Jim DeMint, who resigned to run the Heritage Foundation). Scott was the first black Republican representative from South Carolina since 1901, and with Haley's appointment, became the first black senator from the South since Reconstruction (only the seventh African American ever to serve in the chamber). Across the nation, those on the right hailed the announcement as evidence of the GOP's laying claim to another black "first" and of the party still remaining, in the age of Obama, the party of Lincoln.

But as the political scientist Adolph Reed has written,

[T]his "first black" rhetoric tends to interpret African-American political successes—including that of President Obama—as part of a morality play that dramatizes "how far we have come." It obscures the fact that modern black Republicans have been more tokens than signs of progress. The cheerleading over racial symbolism plays to the Republicans' desperate need to woo (or at least appear to woo) minority voters, who favored Mr. Obama over Mitt Romney by huge margins.[39]

Indeed, there is good reason to doubt the racial sincerity of the Republicans given that many of the black politicians among their ranks support policies and laws that run in direct opposition to the preferences of most nonwhites, especially black Americans.[40] Given that disconnect, and that these select high-profile black politicians align more with white policy positions and political attitudes, it would seem that the appointment of black folks like now-senator Scott is directed more at whites who wish to distance their Grand Old Party from any claim of racism: "Look, one of our senators is black. We can't possibility be racist."

This logic obscures a fundamental fact of the supposed "post-racial" era: the crux of the situation no longer revolves around whether or not whites will vote for a black candidate (the two-time election of Obama settled that); rather, the question remains whether black candidates can construct strong multiracial coalitions around policies that support black interests. That seems very much in doubt, regardless of the black tokens put forward by the GOP and the continued fetishization, by those on the right *and* the left, of black politicians as potent token-symbols of "progress" that strategically ignores their policies.

Simply put, tokenism is "the policy or practice of making only a symbolic effort (as to desegregate)."[41] Legal scholar Linda Greene describes tokenism as a "phenomenon of disproportionate numbers associated with isolation, increased visibility, and disproportionate burdens."[42] Greene further explains tokenism as "a model of limited integration in which institutions include a minimal number of people of color without altering the presumptively White character of an institution."[43] Not only does tokenism labor to preserve the status quo, but it often has a deleterious effect on those who occupy tokenized positions. According to Rosabeth Moss Kanter, tokens are often treated as representative of their respective category instead of as individuals.[44] Kanter argues that individuals who occupy token positions in their work settings experience three sources of stress: performance pressures, boundary heightening, and role entrapment.[45] Performance pressure is the high visibility and scrutiny tokens face because of their differences and the added pressure to perform well due to the belief that their performance may determine employment opportunities for other members of their group in the future.[46] Boundary heightening is the exaggeration of the differences between the dominant group and the token group. Oftentimes it results in isolation or in downplaying of characteristics associated with the token group as a way of gaining acceptance.[47] Role entrapment is a form of typecasting in which tokens are placed into a tightly constrained role. The resistance to the role may lead to those in the dominant group viewing the token as "militant" or abrasive.[48] Sociologist Pamela Braboy Jackson demonstrates that such stresses can have quite a negative social-psychological effect on members of token groups. In various settings, Jackson believes tokens are more likely to be asked to serve on additional panels or committees or in high-profile positions as representatives for their "type," consequently adding more pressure and time commitments to their workload.[49]

Not all token groups experience the same type of negative effects. For example, individuals who are racial tokens are more likely to experience depression, and individuals who experience high opposite-gender representation in their workplace are significantly more likely to experience anxiety.[50] Racial tokens also experience more token stress, which in turn increases depression.[51] As might be expected, the proportion of the token group to the dominant group does have a relation to the negative effects experienced. Black individuals working in settings with higher percentages of black coworkers and clients experienced fewer problems with loss of black identity, sense of isolation, and feelings of having to demonstrate more competence than their peers.[52]

Indeed, the black electoral success narrative often voiced by the GOP ignores problems of tokenism and promotes an idea of equality of opportunity.[53] Yet, legal scholar Lani Guinier sees three major problems with this line of thought. First, blacks cannot escape disadvantaged-minority status by mobilizing the vote to elect more black candidates, as simply being a member of the group does not necessarily make an individual an effective advocate for legislative action in the interests of the disadvantaged. Second, the creation of majority-black single-member districts from which black legislators can be elected will not rid society of hostility and prejudice. Finally, real change cannot be had until a move is made toward proportional interest representation and away from winner-take-all majority rule.[54] Simply electing a few representatives from majority-black districts does not mean any effect will occur among the legislative body as a whole. Without allies in the legislature, without cooperation and an open exchange of ideas, these elected officials can become no more than tokens.[55] While the chance to elect a representative to an all-white body may mobilize a minority voter base, the role of minorities as token representatives who are incapable of influencing policy outcomes reduces the ability of minority representatives to energize a voter base.[56]

Social science research tends to show that a minimum of 35 to 40 percent minority group members as compared to nonminority group member is an important ratio in attempts to overcome negative effects associated with tokenism, such as social isolation, stereotyping, and performance pressure.[57] It may be important to note that this critical mass does not need to consist of one minority group. In fact, it would be extremely difficult in many situations to create such a mass. Rather, the grouping of different nondominant groups to create a critical mass and lessen the effects of tokenism should be a workable remedy.[58]

Tokenism and the Curious Case of Herman Cain

In September of 2010, Herman Cain, a 64-year-old African American and former CEO of Godfather's Pizza, announced his consideration of a 2012 Republican run to unseat Obama.[59] In the months that followed, Cain became somewhat of a darling with the extreme right-wing Tea Party movement and was a "YouTube sensation."[60] By May of 2011, Cain officially announced his candidacy—a proclamation given to a raucous conservative crowd in Atlanta, Georgia, at which he stated, "I'm running for President of the United States and I'm not running for second."[61]

However, after rising and falling in the polls in relation to other Republican candidates, with mounting skepticism of his "9-9-9" tax plan, with serious media gaffes related to foreign policy, and most notably following several allegations of sexual harassment and adultery,

Cain's poll numbers plummeted. By December of 2011, Cain announced the suspension of his presidential campaign.[62]

The meteoric rise and fall of Herman Cain represents a curious case study for the modern intersection of race, tokenism, and politics. The match-up of an incumbent nonwhite candidate (represented by Barack Obama) against a formerly obscure black conservative (represented by Herman Cain) with the support of an already racially charged and white-dominated Tea Party was an episode barely imaginable just a few years prior. While some claimed that Cain attempted to run a "color-blind" and "post-racial" campaign,[63] we contend that Cain performed a meticulously managed version of black masculinity and crafted a narrative about US race relations and racial (in)equality that absolved—and proved palatable to—a white and conservative reactionary electorate. Cain did not transcend the dominant meanings of race; he attempted to bend them to his will. Yet in the end, Cain's attempts to court a racially antagonistic Tea Party base backfired upon him.

From the outset, Cain ran what can best be described as a racially schizophrenic campaign. On the one hand, he often sidestepped discussions about his own race or policies geared toward specific racial groups. On the other hand, Cain would spontaneously insert racialized commentary into his analysis of the policies of his chief competitor—Barack Obama. Before we can understand the latter, we need to explore the former.

Cain quickly established himself as a color-blind candidate unlike any other. He seemed comfortable amid hyper-conservatives and Tea Partiers who had already garnered both academic and lay suspicion for their implicit racism. "I talk very plainly and very clearly about what I'd do about the economy, about energy—getting us to energy independence—about illegal immigration. I'm very specific about my plans, and that's what people are responding to."[64] Accordingly Cain often referenced himself in respect to his inspirational "rags-to-riches" storyline and often avoided the topic of race. When Cain did bring up the specter of race during his childhood in the Jim Crow South, he would bring it up as a straw man easily burnt to the ground. Writing in his presumptuously titled *This Is Herman Cain! My Journey to the White House*, he penned the following:

One of the most important lessons Dad taught us was not to feel like victims. He never felt like a victim; he never talked like a victim; he never expressed one "victim" attitude the whole while I knew him. It was his inner self-determination. He just never had that attitude, so *we* didn't have that attitude. And both of our parents [his mother worked as a maid and his father was a chauffeur] taught us not to think that the government owed us something. They didn't teach us to be mad at this country. They would say to us: "If you want something just work hard enough, focus on it, and guess what? You can make it *happen!*"[65]

When discussing his attendance at the prestigious African American Morehouse College during the Civil Rights Movement (he was a freshman in 1963), Cain said that he largely ignored the opportunity to join the movement. "I wasn't determined to make social change." He instead "wanted to earn some change" and "make some money."[66] He even claimed not to have remembered when Dr. Martin Luther King Jr. came to Morehouse.[67] Cain repeatedly dismissed the significance of race throughout his campaign. In October of 2011, he stated on CNN,

I don't believe racism in this country today holds anybody back in a big way. Is there some—are there some elements of racism? Yes. It gets back to if we don't grow this economy, that is a ripple effect for every economic level, and because blacks are more disproportionately unemployed, they get hit the worst when economic policies don't work. That's where it starts. Grow this economy, and it's going to help everybody to get jobs and to get back in the workforce.[68]

Time and time again, Cain asserted that blacks now walk upon a level playing field—often citing his own life story to ground his commentary. When discussing racial inequality, Cain dismissed charges of racism to insert a lack of work ethic on the part of African Americans. "They weren't held back because of racism," Cain said. "People sometimes hold themselves back because they want to use racism as an excuse for them not being able to achieve what they want to achieve."[69] By and large, his campaign centered on color-blind economic issues. As the *Washington Post* remarked in October 2011,

That Cain's campaign is so studiously scrubbed free of race is a commentary on the very racialization he eschews. His Web site features his stances on immigration, national security, taxation, energy and health care. There is no reference to civil rights concerns, disproportionate incarceration or what is, at this point, a racialized unemployment crisis. This is curious only because, unlike the other Republican candidates, Cain believes that he can win a solid third of the black vote.[70]

Moreover, when it came to light that Rick Perry's family leased a property known as "Niggerhead" (complete with a large rock painted with the name) and that Ron Paul had authored a series of racist pamphlets in years prior, Cain barely raised an eyebrow, calling the Perry issue "insensitive" and ignoring Paul's racial diatribes.[71] Early on, Cain portrayed a personality and campaign in which race was barely a noteworthy issue. At most, he seemed to think race the specter of a bygone age that only reared its head from time to time in "insensitive" ways.

And this was a line that Cain, as a GOP token, had to toe carefully. Even after Cain's less-than-powerful reply to Perry's racist property name, conservative voices (e.g., *RedState's* Erick Erickson, *InstaPundit's* Glenn Reynolds, and *Daily Caller's* Matt Lewis) chided Cain for "playing the race card."[72] As Clarence Page wrote in the *Chicago Tribune,*

> Yet we did not hear conservatives complain about a race card when Cain previously suggested President Barack Obama was not a "real black man" or "a strong black man." Or when he labeled Planned Parenthood clinics in black communities as "Planned Genocide." The implicit message from conservatives to Cain: It is OK for you to talk about race, as long as you only criticize black people.

So while Tea Party supporters of Cain are not necessarily racist, a recent study indicates that Tea Partiers are 25 percent more likely to be racially resentful than those who do not support the Tea Party.[73] Accordingly, courting the Tea Party as a black candidate means walking a narrowly constructed color-blind line. Cain responded to this political myopia by "lacing his policy pitches with jokes and colloquialisms."[74] For example, he referred to the current policies on taxes as the "21st-century version of slavery."[75] Throughout his campaign, Cain intertwined racial comments with political policies that he, and the Tea Party, promoted.

Playing the "Race Card"

While Cain seemed to master the color-blind tack in charting out his campaign strategy, he would selectively evoke the concept of race when advantageous (and in line with Tea Party political goals). He sometimes jokingly referred to himself as the GOP flavor of the week, "black walnut," a self-depreciating statement that paints him as a nonthreatening black man in contradistinction to the monstrous caricature of Obama constructed by the Right.[76] Cain's campaign seemed to imply that he could beat Obama simply because he was black, too. And in courting a largely hyper-conservative and white electorate, Cain mentioned race and politics in ways that his Tea Party supporters seemingly adored. In September 2011 on CNN, Cain stated that black voters have been "brainwashed" into not "thinking for themselves" or "even considering a conservative point of view."[77] A month later, Cain appeared on Fox News and stated, "I left the Democratic plantation a long time ago."[78] In such a framing, Cain emerges as the nouveau runaway slave, with the Democrats being the modern racists and the Republicans being fresh abolitionists.

Cain's race baiting and social conservatism worked well with many white Tea Partiers and the new social movements opposing them. When the Occupy Wall Street protests took hold of the nation's attention in October of 2011, Cain responded, "If you don't have a job and you're not rich, blame yourself!"[79] Such deployment of race and harsh, hyper-individualistic rhetoric seemed to weaken Cain's support among other African Americans. Edward DuBose, a leader within the NAACP, concluded that Cain's statements stem from his desire to associate with people other than African Americans.[80] Toward that end, Cain has eschewed the term "African American," instead preferring "American black conservative."[81]

Perhaps the most audacious race-conscious rhetoric of Cain's has been his racialized comparisons between himself and Barack Obama. Such a discourse has revolved around the notion of black racial *authenticity.* Cain consistently brought up his African American roots in order to criticize Obama as less "authentic" than himself. Cain frequently brought up Obama's white mother and his travels between Hawaii and Indonesia as a reason to discount his authenticity as an African American.[82] So also, Cain has repeated claimed to be a "real black man" in comparison to Obama and has maligned Obama's mixed-race identity, saying that Obama "has never been part of the black experience in America"[83] and that Democrats are "doubly scared that a real black man might run against Barack Obama."[84]

From Courting to Canning Cain

Cain is a "Black candidate manufactured to run against the sitting black man in the White House. . . . Harvard to Morehouse; elite to average, Democratic to Republican. Cain is up for the occasion. The 2008 mantra, 'Yes we can,' now moves to 'Yes we Cain.'"[85] Cain quickly became the contrived black darling of the Tea Party because of his overall color-blind policy positions, his racialized critiques of Obama's blackness and Americanness, and his twofold symbolic power. First, Cain could say the things about race that Tea Partiers wanted to but couldn't without risking charges of "racism." And second, the Tea Party's support of Cain (a black man) shows a decisive response to the charges of antiblack racism already leveled against the TPM.

The use of Cain as a tokenized figurehead of the hyper-conservative Right was more than apparent after several November and December 2011 allegations of at least three instances of sexual harassment and adultery (with white and light-skinned women). In recent years, Republicans have argued that there is little to no bigotry in the world— a position that Cain often took. But that position was quickly reversed when the sexual allegations were made public. On the heels of the allegation, Jordan Gehrke of AmericansforHermanCain.com wrote, "Just like they did to Clarence Thomas, they are engaging in a 'high-tech lynching' by smearing Herman Cain's reputation and character."[86] Moreover, on Fox News conservative talking head Ann Coulter accused the Democrats of exacerbating the situation due to their hatred of black conservatives. Comparing the accusations against Cain to Anita Hill's allegations against Clarence Thomas years earlier, she stated, "If you are a conservative black they will believe the most horrible sexualized fantasies of these uptight white feminists." She continued, "Our blacks are so much better than their blacks. . . . To become a black Republican, you don't just roll into it. You're not going with the flow . . . and that's why we have very impressive blacks in the Republican Party."[87] Coulter's generalization materializes a potent symbolic boundary between conservative and liberal African Americans in which the latter are deemed weak, unthinking, and predatory upon the astute, respectable, and independent blacks of the GOP. When asked to clarify her remarks, Coulter later said that black conservatives have had to fight an uphill battle against the predominantly black liberals and Democrats. In her words, black conservatives have fought against "your family members, probably your neighbors, you have thought everything out and that's why we have very impressive blacks in our party."[88]

Yet, when Cain offered his own response to the allegations—that they were motivated by racism from either the Left or his Republican presidential competitors—the Right turned on Cain. In denying the sex harassment allegations, Cain used his race as a shield. On Fox News he responded to a question of whether his race influenced the public allegations. "I believe the answer is yes, but we do not have any evidence to support it." So also, the black conservative commentator Armstrong Williams, who worked for Clarence Thomas when he headed the Equal Employment Opportunity Commission, said some Republicans were put off by Cain's claims of racism because they so dislike claims of racism when they are directed at the Right. "Why is the first response from some conservatives that this must have to do with Cain's race? That makes them guilty of the same race-baiting we accuse Democrats of," Williams said.[89] Moreover, "I think we need to get past the language of race on both sides," said Condoleezza Rice.[90]

It should be no surprise that Tea Partiers liked Cain (prior to his claims of racism) given that it is easier for conservative whites to favor blacks who prefer policies that favor whites, and simply given that he was a black man who opposed Obama.[91] But this political commitment may have become a problem for Cain given that white conservative political attitudes predict less support for interracial romantic desires, while black political conservatives hold preferences for interracial romantic relationships.[92] While Cain's demise could have resulted from his lack of command of the facts and weak grasp on policy, it could have resulted from the still-taboo romance across the color line; the growing number of white women whom he allegedly sexually harassed or with whom he had affairs derailed the narrative and persona of the proper black token.

The Republicans' Racial Irony

The predicament in which the GOP finds itself is far from lost on the American mainstream. And the courting of white voters via policies and laws that work against the interests of many darker-skinned Americans is a mark that the GOP may find hard to erase. The critique of the GOP in this regard has been biting. Colin Powell, a high-profile black Republican and George W. Bush cabinet member, stated the following in 2013:

> There's also a dark—a dark vein of intolerance in some parts of the Party. What I do mean by that? I mean by that is they still sort of look down on minorities. How can I evidence that? When I see a former governor say that the president is shuckin' and jivin', that's a racial era slave term.[93]

Others have injected an air of humor in the analysis. During the 2011 White House Correspondents' Dinner, Seth Meyers observed that "[Trump has] said he's got a great relationship with 'the blacks.' Unless 'the Blacks' are a family of white people, I bet he's mistaken."[94] He went on to quip that "[w]hen [Obama was] sworn in [he] looked like the guy from the Old Spice commercials. Now [he] look[s] like Louis Gosset Sr. If the President's hair gets any whiter, the tea party is going to endorse it."[95]

Even Obama has poked fun at himself in light of the racialized attacks from the political Right. During the 2011 White House Correspondents' Dinner, Obama's presentation began after professional wrestler Hulk Hogan's anthem—"Real American"—was played. Video images of Uncle Sam and Mount Rushmore were displayed alongside his birth certificate. Obama then offered to show his birth video, which was a clip from Disney's *Lion King*,[96] alluding to the myth that he was born in Kenya.[97]

It is against this backdrop that the future for the Republican Party looks bleak. In order to be a viable party in the twenty-first century, the

GOP needs what President Obama brought to the Democratic Party—a diverse constituency. In an ever-browning America, that means that the GOP is caught in a catch-22. It must either work to place token black and brown people in key positions within the party or reinvent itself. In consideration of the former tactic, the GOP has run a few token black and brown faces, but they have generally been seen for what they are. For example, it may seem like a coup for the GOP to have African American Tim Scott appointed a United States senator. Yet, NAACP president Ben Jealous threw cold water on that feat when he noted that Scott is less than a supporter of civil rights, given Scott's attitudes on policies that disproportionally impact the racial underclass, such as his lack of support for federal government contracting only with employers who pay prevailing wages, oppose collective bargaining, oppose funding to Planned Parenthood, and oppose the Affordable Care Act.

In consideration of the former option, the CPAC (Conservative Political Action Conference) motto for 2013 was "America's Future: The Next Generation of Conservatives," yet its headliners were decisively old faces: Sarah Palin, Paul Ryan, Rand Paul, and a (slight) newcomer in the form of Marco Rubio, a Latino senator from Florida—whose election recalls the aforementioned tokenism. In this sense, the GOP is not taking active strides to present a fundamentally different racial ideology as it looks forward to 2016. Put simply, for the GOP to remain relevant in a post-Obama era, it will have to fundamentally change its policies around issues central to people of color, in particular, African Americans and Latinos. It will also have to forsake racial, dog-whistle politics. Such an approach would be taking the high road, but in turn the GOP could lose a sizeable portion of its base. Without that 20 or 30 percent, the GOP as we know it may no longer be a viable party. Time will tell which route it will take.

NOTES

NOTE TO THE INTRODUCTION

1. Cited in George Winslow, *Capital Crimes* (New York: Monthly Review Press, 1999).

NOTES TO CHAPTER 1

1. Tasha S. Philpot, *Race, Republicans, and the Return of the Party of Lincoln (The Politics of Race and Ethnicity)* (Ann Arbor: University of Michigan Press, 2007), 38. Philpot demonstrates how formative scholars like Elmer Schattschneider omitted race from his landmark 1956 political history of the early Democratic and Republican parties. Moreover, while James Sundquist and Sidney Milkis briefly discussed race in their noteworthy texts, race was more of an afterthought than a central feature of the analysis.

2. Eric Foner, *Free Soil, Free Labor, Free Men: The Ideology of the Republican Party before the Civil War* (New York: Oxford University Press, 1995).

3. Roger Daniels, *Coming to America: A History of Immigration and Ethnicity in American Life* (New York: HarperCollins, 2002).

4. Jules Witcover, *Party of the People* (New York: Random House, 2003), 7.

5. Daniels, *Coming to America.*

6. Ibid.

7. Kenneth Morgan, *Slavery in America: A Reader and Guide* (Athens: University of Georgia Press, 2005).

8. Ibid., 133–66.

9. Foner, *Free Soil, Free Labor, Free Men,* 89.

10. Witcover, *Party of the People,* 11.

11. Alexander Deconde, "Washington's Farewell, the French Alliance, and the Election of 1796," *Mississippi Valley Historical Review* 43.4 (1957): 641–58.

12. Deconde, "Washington's Farewell, the French Alliance, and the Election of 1796."

13. Wiliam Nisbet Chambers, *Political Parties in a New Nation: The American Experience, 1776–1809* (New York: Oxford University Press, 1963).

14. Stanley M. Elkins and Eric McKitrick, *The Age of Federalism: The Early American Republic, 1788–1800* (New York: Oxford University Press, 1995).

15. John Craig Hammond, *Slavery, Freedom, and Expansion in the Early American West* (Charlottesville: University of Virginia Press, 2007).

16. John R. Vile, *The Constitutional Convention of 1787: A Comprehensive Encyclopedia of America's Founding*, vol. 2 (Santa Barbara, CA: ABC-CLIO, 2005), 269.

17. Ibid., 265–75.

18. John E. Ferling, *Adams versus Jefferson: The Tumultuous Election of 1800* (New York: Oxford University Press, 2004).

19. Witcover, *Party of the People*, 24–25.

20. Ibid.

21. Joseph J. Ellis, *American Sphinx: The Character of Thomas Jefferson* (New York: Vintage, 1994), 50. It is said that during the three-day congressional debate over Jefferson's draft of the Declaration, Jefferson spoke not one word for or against any of the proposed revisions to his document.

22. Witcover, *Party of the People*, 11.

23. Thomas Jefferson, *Notes on the State of Virginia* (New York: Library of America, 1984 [1787]), 264–65. One of the most famous passages on race in *Notes* is as follows:

> It will probably be asked, Why not retain and incorporate the blacks into the state, and thus save the expense of supplying, by importation of white settlers, the vacancies they will leave? Deep rooted prejudices entertained by the whites; ten thousand recollections, by the blacks, of the injuries they have sustained; new provocations; the real distinctions which nature has made; and many other circumstances, will divide us into parties, and produce convulsions which will probably never end but in the extermination of the one or the other race. —To these objections, which are political, may be added others, which are physical and moral. The first difference which strikes us is that of colour. Whether the black of the negro resides in the reticular membrane between the skin and scarf-skin, or in the scarf-skin itself; whether it proceeds from the colour of the blood, the colour of the bile, or from that of some other secretion, the difference is fixed in nature, and is as real as if its seat and cause were better known to us. And is this difference of no importance? Is it not the foundation of a greater or less share of beauty in the two races? Are not the fine mixtures of red and white, the expressions of every passion by greater or less suffusions of colour in the one, preferable to that eternal monotony, which reigns in the countenances, that immoveable veil of black which covers all the emotions of the other race? Add to these, flowing hair, a more elegant symmetry of form, their own judgment in favour of the whites, declared by their preference of them, as uniformly as is the preference of the Oranootan for the black women over those of his own species. (264–65)

24. James Madison and James Monroe were staunch supporters of the American Colonization Society, which raised funds to send blacks, both slave and free, to Africa and to the Caribbean.

25. Foner, *Free Soil, Free Labor, Free Men*, 94–95.

26. The early part of the War of 1812 did not go well for the United States. The war was especially unpopular in New England; due to its dependence on trade and the British blockade of New England ports, the Federalist Party sent delegates to the Hartford Convention of 1814 to discuss secession from the United States. Moreover, Federalists constructed a list of demands from Washington, including that they provide New England states with financial assistance to compensate for lost trade and proposed constitutional amendments requiring a two-thirds vote in Congress before an embargo could be imposed, new states admitted, or war declared. Meanwhile, the Federalists secretly sent word to England to broker a separate peace accord. However, by the time the Federalist delegates delivered these demands to Washington, the war was over. The Federalists returned to New England as parochial disloyalists. They were destroyed as a political force. See James M. Banner, *To the Hartford Convention: The Federalists and the Origins of Party Politics in Massachusetts, 1789–1815* (New York: Knopf, 1970).

27. Foner, *Free Soil, Free Labor, Free Men*, 149–85.

28. Chase Curran Mooney, *William H. Crawford, 1772–1834* (Lexington: University Press of Kentucky, 1974).

29. Arthur Meier Schlesinger and Fred L. Israel, *History of American Presidential Elections, 1789–1968*. Volume 1, *1789–1844* (New York: Chelsea House, 1971), 379–81.

30. J. William Harris, *The Making of the American South: A Short History, 1500–1877* (New York: Wiley-Blackwell, 2006), 145–46.

31. Ibid.

32. Witcover, *Party of the People*, 137.

33. Ronald H. Brown, *Of the People: The 200-Year History of the Democratic Party* (Darby, PA: Diane Publishing, 1992).

34. Ibid.

35. David W. Galenson, *Traders, Planters, and Slaves: Market Behavior in Early English America* (Cambridge: Cambridge University Press, 2002).

36. Foner, *Free Soil, Free Labor, Free Men*, 103–48.

37. Ibid., 124–25, 153–60.

38. Laird W. Bergad, *The Comparative Histories of Slavery in Brazil, Cuba, and the United States* (Cambridge: Cambridge University Press, 2007), 261.

39. Foner, *Free Soil, Free Labor, Free Men*.

40. Ibid., 225.

41. Foner, *Free Soil, Free Labor, Free Men*.

42. Statistical View of the United States (Washington, DC: Beverly Tucker, Senate Printer, 1854), http://www2.census.gov/prod2/decennial/documents/1850c-01.pdf.

43. Campbell J. Gibson and Emily Lennon, "Historical Census Statistics on the Foreign-born Population of the United States: 1850–1990" (Washington, DC:

US Bureau of the Census, 1999), http://www.census.gov/population/www/documentation/twps0029/twps0029.html.

44. L. Edward Purcell, *Immigration* (New York: Greenwood, 1995), 72–84.

45. Lewis L. Gould, *Grand Old Party* (New York: Random House, 2007), 11.

46. Tyler Anbinder, *Nativism and Slavery: The Northern Know Nothings and the Politics of the 1850s* (New York: Oxford University Press, 1994), 70–74.

47. Foner, *Free Soil, Free Labor, Free Men*, 307.

48. Shane Mountjoy, *Manifest Destiny: Westward Expansion* (New York: Infobase Publishing, 2009), 111–12.

49. Gould, *Grand Old Party*, 14.

50. Ibid.

51. Ibid.

52. Ibid., 16.

53. Ambrose Lane Sr., *For Whites Only? How and Why America Became a Racist Nation* (Bloomington, IN: AuthorHouse, 2008).

54. James Oakes, *The Radical and the Republican: Frederick Douglass, Abraham Lincoln, and the Triumph of Antislavery Politics* (New York: Norton, 2007).

55. J. William Harris, *The Making of the American South: A Short History, 1500–1877* (New York: Wiley-Blackwell, 2006), 138–44.

56. Gould, *Grand Old Party*, 21.

57. Oakes, *The Radical and the Republican*.

58. Ibid.

59. Gould, *Grand Old Party*, 21.

60. Ibid., 20.

61. David Brown, *Southern Outcast: Hinton Rowan Helper and the Impending Crisis of the South* (Baton Rouge: Louisiana State University, 2006), 159–61.

62. Oakes, *The Radical and the Republican*.

63. Albert P. Blaustein and Robert L. Zangrando, *Civil Rights and African Americans: A Documentary History* (Chicago: Northwestern University Press, 1991), 244.

64. Ibid., 244–67.

65. Bruce Bartlett, *Wrong on Race: The Democratic Party's Buried Past* (New York: Palgrave Macmillan, 2008).

66. Gould, *Grand Old Party*, 44.

67. Ibid., 47.

68. Zoltan Hajnal and Taeku Lee, *Why Americans Don't Join the Party: Race, Immigration, and the Failure (of Political Parties) to Engage the Electorate* (Princeton, NJ: Princeton University Press, 2011), 105.

69. Brian R. Farmer, *American Conservatism: History, Theory, and Practice* (Cambridge: Cambridge Scholars Press, 2005), 177.

70. Ibid.

71. Gould, *Grand Old Party*, 52.

72. Philpot, *Race, Republicans, and the Return of the Party of Lincoln*, 41.

73. Ibid.

74. Adam Fairclough, *Better Day Coming: Blacks and Equality, 1890–2000* (New York: Penguin, 2002).
75. Witcover, *Party of the People*, 312.
76. Ibid.
77. Ibid.
78. Fairclough, *Better Day Coming*.
79. Ibid.
80. Ibid.
81. Philpot, *Race, Republicans, and the Return of the Party of Lincoln*, 42.
82. Dan T. Carter, *The Politics of Rage* (Baton Rouge: Louisiana State University Press, 2000).
83. Karl Frederickson, *The Dixiecrat Revolt and the End of the Solid South* (Chapel Hill: University of North Carolina Press, 2001), 13.
84. Earl Black and Merle Black, *The Rise of the Southern Republicans* (Cambridge, MA: Belknap Press of Harvard University Press, 2003), 42.
85. Richard K. Scher, *Politics in the New South: Republicanism, Race, and Leadership in the Twentieth Century* (Armonk, NY: Sharpe, 1997).
86. Ibid.
87. Ibid.
88. Witcover, *Party of the People*, 373.
89. Joyce B. Ross, "Mary McLeod Bethune and the National Youth Administration: A Case Study of Power Relationships in the Black Cabinet of Franklin D. Roosevelt," *Journal of Negro History* 60 (1975): 1–28.
90. Witcover, *Party of the People*, 375.
91. Frederickson, *The Dixiecrat Revolt and the End of the Solid South*, 24.
92. Nancy Joan Weiss, *Farewell to the Party of Lincoln: Black Politics in the Age of F.D.R.* (Princeton, NJ: Princeton University Press, 1983), 222.
93. Carter, *The Politics of Rage*, 71.
94. Witcover, *Party of the People*, 426–27, 429–31.
95. Ibid.
96. Mary C. Brennan, *Turning Right in the Sixties: The Conservative Capture* (Chapel Hill: University of North Carolina Press, 1995), 42.
97. Black and Black, *The Rise of the Southern Republicans*, 54.
98. Ibid.
99. Ibid.
100. Bruce H. Kalk, *The Origins of the Southern Strategy: Two-Party Competition in South Carolina, 1950–1972* (Lanham, MD: Lexington Books, 2001).
101. Frederickson, *The Dixiecrat Revolt and the End of the Solid South*, 5.
102. Ibid., 6.
103. Ibid., 31–32.
104. Ibid., 21–22.
105. Ibid., 9.
106. Ibid., 39.

107. Ibid., 32.
108. Black and Black, *The Rise of the Southern Republicans*.
109. Ibid.
110. Ibid.
111. Brennan, *Turning Right in the Sixties*, 6.
112. Ibid., 25.
113. Brennan, *Turning Right in the Sixties*, 21–22.
114. Sara Diamond, *Roads to Dominion: Right-Wing Movements and Political Power in the United States* (New York: Guilford Press, 1995), 324.
115. Brennan, *Turning Right in the Sixties*, 13.
116. Ibid.
117. Ibid., 61.
118. Ibid., 40.
119. Ibid., 55.
120. Witcover, *Party of the People*, 492.
121. Black and Black, *The Rise of the Southern Republicans*, 28.
122. Ibid., 83.
123. Ibid., 117.
124. Brennan, *Turning Right in the Sixties*, 1–2.
125. Ibid., 83.
126. Tali Mendelberg, *The Race Card: Campaign Strategy, Implicit Messages, and the Norm of Equality* (Princeton, NJ: Princeton University Press, 2001), 14.
127. Ibid., 17, 75–76.
128. Ibid., 14–15.
129. R. W. Apple Jr., "G.O.P. Tries Hard to Win Black Votes, but Recent History Works against It," *New York Times*, September 19, 1996, http://www.nytimes.com/1996/09/19/us/gop-tries-hard-to-win-black-votes-but-recent-history-works-against-it.html.
130. Ibid.
131. Godfrey Mwakikagile, *Black Conservatives in the United States* (Dar es Salaam, Tanzania: New Africa Press, 2006).
132. Jack White, "Lott, Reagan, and the Republican Party," *Time*, December 14, 2002, http://www.time.com/time/nation/article/0,8599,399921,00.html.
133. Black and Black, *The Rise of the Southern Republicans*, 13.
134. Mendelberg, *The Race Card*, 7.
135. Ibid., 7.
136. Philpot, *Race, Republicans, and the Return of the Party of Lincoln*, 37.
137. Mendelberg, *The Race Card*, 15.
138. Witcover, *Party of the People*, 665; Gregory S. Parks and Matthew W. Hughey, *The Obamas and a (Post)Racial America?* (New York: Oxford University Press, 2011).
139. Ibid., 134.
140. Ibid.

141. Ibid., 379.

142. Mendelberg, *The Race Card*, 105.

143. Ibid.

144. Ibid., 19.

145. Philpot, *Race, Republicans, and the Return of the Party of Lincoln.*

146. Ibid.

147. Ibid., 29.

148. Ibid.

149. James M. Glaser, *Race, Campaign Politics, and the Realignment in the South* (New Haven, CT: Yale University Press, 1996), 20–24.

NOTES TO CHAPTER 2

1. Glynnis MacNicol, "Glenn Beck: If Tea Party Votes for Gingrich It's Because Obama's Black," *Business Insider*, December 12, 2011, http://www.businessinsider.com/glenn-beck-tea-party-doesnt-like-obama-because-hes-black-2011-12.

2. Cited in Ari Melber, "The Nation: Confronting Trump's Coded Racism," *National Public Radio*, April 27, 2011, http://www.npr.org/2011/04/27/135777342/the-nation-confronting-trumps-coded-racism.

3. Evelyn Nakano Glenn, "Constructing Citizenship: Exclusion, Subordination, and Resistance," *American Sociological Review* 76.1 (2011): 1–24, 3.

4. Kathryn M. Bartol, Charles L. Evans, and Melvin T. Stith, "Black versus White Leaders: A Comparative Review of the Literature, "*Academy of Management Review* 3.2 (1978): 293–304.

5. Stephen Labaton, "Agency's '04 Rule Let Banks Pile Up New Debt," *New York Times*, October 3, 2008, retrieved on April 17, 2010, from www.nytimes.com/2008/10/03/business/03sec.html?_r=2&em&oref=slogin.

6. Matthew W. Hughey, "The (Dis)Similarities of White Racial Identities: The Conceptual Framework of 'Hegemonic Whiteness,'" *Ethnic and Racial Studies* 33.8 (2010): 1289–1309.

7. Charles W. Mills, *The Racial Contract* (Ithaca, NY: Cornell University Press, 1997).

8. Patrick J. Buchanan, "Has the Bell Begun to Toll for the GOP?" *Buchanan.org*, May 18, 2012, http://buchanan.org/blog/has-the-bell-begun-to-toll-for-the-gop-5077.

9. John Blake, "Are Whites Racially Oppressed?" *CNN*, March 4, 2011, retrieved on March 5, 2011, from www.cnn.com/2010/US/12/21/white.persecution/index.html?hpt=T2.

10. Devin Burghart and Leonard Zeskind, "Tea Party Nationalism: A Critical Examination of the Tea Party Movement and the Size, Scope, and Focus of Its National Factions" (Kansas City, MO: Institute for Research & Education on Human Rights, 2010), 7.

11. Adele M. Stan, 2010. "Dismiss the Tea Parties at Your Peril: They're a Force to Be Reckoned With," *AlterNet*, May 4, 2010, http://www.alternet.org/

news/146707/dismiss_the_tea_parties_at_your_peril__they%27re_a_force_to_be_reckoned_with.

12. Burghart and Zeskind, "Tea Party Nationalism."

13. Sundiata K. Cha-Jua, "Introduction to the Special Issue Defending Ethnic Studies in Arizona: Obama, the Rise of the Hard Right, Arizona and Texas, and the Attack on Racialized Communities Studies," *Black Scholar* 40.4 (2010), http://works.bepress.com/sundiata_chajua/20.

14. Vanessa Williamson, Theda Skocpol, and John Coggin, "The Tea Party and the Remaking of Republican Conservatism," *Perspectives on Politics* 9.1 (2011): 26.

15. Jill Lepore, *The Whites of Their Eyes: The Tea Party's Revolution and the Battle over American History* (Princeton, NJ: Princeton University Press, 2010), 3.

16. Daniel Libit, "For the Tea Party Movement, Sturdy Roots in the Chicago Area," *New York Times*, February 18, 2010, http://www.nytimes.com/2010/02/19/us/19cncodom.html?ref=us.

17. Steve Eichler, "We Agree on Most Points! Fight On!" *TeaParty.org*, May 16, 2010, http://teapartyorg.ning.com/profiles/blogs/we-agree-on-most-points-fight?xg_source=activity.

18. "'Tea Party' and 'Anti-Pork' Protest Rally in Lafayette, Louisiana," *ResistNet*, February 24, 2009, www.resistnet.com/events/tea-party-and-antipork-protest.

19. Rob Jordan, "FreedomWorks Launches Nationwide 'Tea Party' Tour," *FreedomWorks*, March 9, 2009, http://www.freedomworks.org/publications/freedomworks-launches-nationwide-%E2%80%9Cteaparty%E2%80%9D-tour.

20. Burghart and Zeskind, "Tea Party Nationalism," 41.

21. Ibid., 33.

22. Zachary Courser, "The Tea Party at the Election," *Forum* 8.4 (2010): 1–18, 12; Scott Rasmussen and Douglas Schoen, *Mad as Hell: How the Tea Party Movement Is Fundamentally Remaking Our Two-Party System* (New York: HarperCollins, 2010), 36.

23. Frank Davies, "Primary Preview: Ron Paul's Anti-War Bid Powered by Net Activists," *Mercury News*, January 20, 2008, http://www.mercurynews.com/elections/ci_8025814?nclick_check=1.

24. Judson Berger, "Modern-Day Tea Parties Give Taxpayers Chance to Scream for Better Representation," *Fox News*, April 9, 2009, http://www.foxnews.com/politics/2009/04/09/modern-day-tea-parties-taxpayers-chance-scream-better-representation.

25. Dick Armey, "'Tea Parties': The Next Grass-Roots Movement?" *Atlanta Journal Constitution*, April 15, 2009, http://www.freedomworks.org/news/'tea-parties'-the-next-grass-roots-movement.

26. Courser, "The Tea Party at the Election," 5.

27. Darrel Enck-Wanzer, "Barack Obama, the Tea Party, and the Threat of Race: On Neoliberalism and Born-Again Racism," *Communication, Culture, and Critique* 4.1 (2011): 23–30, 25.

28. Rasmussen and Schoen, *Mad as Hell,* 38.

29. Enck-Wanzer, "Barack Obama, the Tea Party, and the Threat of Race," 24.
30. Ibid., 24.
31. Burghart and Zeskind, "Tea Party Nationalism," 21; Alex Pappas, "Tea Party Leaders Release List of Targeted Races at FreedomWorks Summit," *Daily Caller*, January 25, 2010, http://www.freedomworks.org/news/tea-party-leaders-release-list-of-targeted-races-a.
32. Williamson, Skocpol, and Coggin, "The Tea Party and the Remaking of Republican Conservatism," 38.
33. Rasmussen and Schoen, *Mad as Hell*, 53.
34. Burghart and Zeskind, "Tea Party Nationalism," 11.
35. Cf. Enck-Wanzer, "Barack Obama, the Tea Party, and the Threat of Race." The paper contains an excellent discussion of racist imagery directed at Obama that has been used in Tea Party rallies and organizations.
36. Justin Elliott, "Man Charged with Death Threats Apparently Attended Tea Party Protest Targeting Murray," *Talking Points Memo*, April 7, 2010; Philip Rucker, "Former Militiaman Unapologetic for Calls to Vandalize Offices over Health Care," *Washington Post*, March 25, 2010; William Douglas, "Tea Party Protesters Scream 'n**ger' at Black Congressman," *McClatchy Washington Bureau*, March 20, 2010; cf. Burghart and Zeskind, "Tea Party Nationalism," 63–64.
37. Kate Zernike, "N.A.A.C.P. Report Raises Concerns about Racism within Tea Party Groups," *New York Times*, October 20, 2010, http://www.nytimes.com/2010/10/21/us/politics/21naacp.html.
38. David Weigel, "'N-Word' Sign Dogs Would-Be Tea Party Leader," *Washington Independent*, January 4, 2010, http://washingtonindependent.com/73036/n-word-sign-dogs-would-be-tea-party-leader.
39. Mark Potok, "TeaParty.org Founder Labels Obama with Racial Terms," *Southern Poverty Law Center*, May 28, 2010, http://www.splcenter.org/blog/2010/05/28/teaparty-org-founder-labels-obama-with-racial-terms.
40. Burghart and Zeskind, "Tea Party Nationalism," 23.
41. "Constitution Suspended in 1933," *TakeAmericaBack.org*, accessed August 17, 2011 from http://www.takeamericaback-org/id102.html.
42. Karen Pack, "An Ardent Plea," *Winnsboro, Texas Tea Party*, http://winnsborotexasteaparty.org; cf. Burghart and Zeskind, "Tea Party Nationalism," 44–45.
43. Robert Steinback, "Race Continued to Dog Tea Party Representatives and Events," *Southern Poverty Law Center*, May 16, 2011, http://www.splcenter.org/blog/2011/05/16/race-continues-to-dog-tea-party-representatives-and-events.
44. Burghart and Zeskind, "Tea Party Nationalism," 60.
45. Ibid.
46. Edythe Jensen, "Gabrielle Giffords' Arizona Shooting Prompts Resignations," *Arizona Republic*, January 11, 2011, http://www.azcentral.com/community/ahwatukee/articles/2011/01/11/20110111gabrielle-giffords-arizona-shooting-resignations.html.
47. Burghart and Zeskind, "Tea Party Nationalism," 62.

48. Ibid., 8; Robert P. Jones and Daniel Cox. "Religion and the Tea Party in the 2010 Election: An Analysis of the Third Biennial American Values Survey" (Washington, DC: Public Religion Research Institute, 2010), 1.

49. Burghart and Zeskind, "Tea Party Nationalism," 8.

50. Ibid.

51. "National Survey of Tea Party Supporters," *New York Times/CBS News* Poll, April 5–12, 2010, question 72; *Newsweek* Poll conducted by Princeton Survey Research Associates May 21–22, 2008, cited at http://www.pollingreport.com/race.htm.

52. Jones and Cox, "Religion and the Tea Party in the 2010 Election," 1.

53. David Campbell and Robert Putnam, "Crashing the Tea Party," *New York Times*, August 16, 2011, http://www.nytimes.com/2011/08/17/opinion/crashing-the-tea-party.html.

54. Ibid.

55. Jones and Cox, "Religion and the Tea Party in the 2010 Election," 1.

56. Trey Ellis, "There's No Taming the Tea Party Dragon," *Root*, October 20, 2010, http://www.theroot.com/views/grave-danger-conservative-blindness.

57. Christopher Parker and Christopher C. Towler, "Tea Party Content Analysis: 2010 Multi-state Survey on Race & Politics Content Analysis," *WISER: University of Washington Institute for the Study of Ethnicity, Race, and Sexuality*, 2010, http://depts.washington.edu/uwiser/tp_content_analysis.htm. Data for the analysis on Tea Party websites was collected from five states identified as top Tea Party venues by a Rasmussen report conducted in June 2010 as well as from six more battleground states. One thousand and seventy-nine articles and postings from thirty-one official Tea Party websites (websites that represent the state in its entirety such as the Colorado Tea Party, or websites from a major city or region of the state) were examined, dating back no further than 2009. The content from these websites, if not analyzed in its entirety, was randomly sampled in order to accurately represent all of the content within the website over time.

58. Jonathan Kay, *Among the Truthers: A Journey through America's Growing Conspiracist Underground* (New York: Harper, 2011).

59. Andrew Perrin, Steven Tepper, Neal Caren, and Sally Morris, "Cultures of the Tea Party." Conference Presentation, American Sociological Association, Las Vegas, NV, August 2011.

60. Jennifer Rubin, "What's behind Tea Party Approval Numbers," *Washington Post*, March 31, 2011, http://www.washingtonpost.com/blogs/right-turn/post/whats-behind-tea-party-approval-numbers/2011/03/29/AF878Q9B_blog.html.

61. Campbell and Putnam, "Crashing the Tea Party."

62. Matthew W. Hughey, "Show Me Your Papers! Obama's Birth and the Whiteness of Belonging," *Qualitative Sociology* 35.2 (2012): 163–81.

63. George Lipsitz, *The Possessive Investment in Whiteness: How White People Profit from Identity Politics* (Philadelphia: Temple University Press, 1998).

64. W. E. B. Du Bois, *Black Reconstruction in America, 1860–1880* (Millwood, NY: Kraus-Thomson, 1976 [1935]).

65. Glenn Feldman, *The Disfranchisement Myth: Poor Whites and Suffrage Restriction in Alabama* (Athens: University of Georgia Press, 2004).

66. Eric Foner, *Reconstruction: America's Unfinished Revolution, 1863–1877* (New York: Harper & Row, 1988).

67. Karen S. Glover, *Racial Profiling: Research, Racism, and Resistance* (Lanham, MD: Rowman & Littlefield, 2009); Gregory S. Parks and Matthew W. Hughey, *12 Angry Men: True Stories of Being a Black Man in America Today* (New York: New Press, 2010).

68. Ari Berman, "The GOP War on Voting," *RollingStone*, August 30, 2011, http://action.democraticgovernors.org/page/s/stop-vote-suppression-outbrain.

69. Michael Kramer, "Lott & Strom: Time for Both to Pack It In," *Daily News*, December 11, 2002, http://articles.nydailynews.com/2002-12-11/news/18214470_1_states-rights-party-al-gore-incoming-senate-majority-leader.

70. Ibid.

71. phenry, "Ron Paul, In His Own Words," *Daily Kos*, May 15, 2007, http://www.dailykos.com/story/2007/05/15/335036/-Ron-Paul-In-His-Own-Words.

72. Amy Hollyfield, "For True Disbelievers, the Facts Are Just Not Enough," *St. Petersburg Times*, June 29, 2008, http://www.pulitzer.org/archives/8406; Ben Smith, "Birtherism: Where It All Began," *Politico*, April 22, 2011, http://www.politico.com/news/stories/0411/53563.html.

73. Jim Geraghty, "Obama Could Debunk Some Rumors by Releasing His Birth Certificate," *National Review Online*, June 9, 2008, http://www.nationalreview.com/campaign-spot/9490/obama-could-debunk-some-rumors-releasing-his-birth-certificate.

74. Kay, *Among the Truthers*.

75. Ibid.

76. Ibid.

77. Ibid.

78. Ibid.

79. Ibid.

80. Patrick McCreless, "Update: Shelby Comments Draw Fire Nationally," *Cullman Times*, February 23, 2009, http://www.cullmantimes.com/breakingnews/x1116141508/UPDATE-Shelby-comments-draw-fire-nationally; Jim Galloway, "Nathan Deal Says He'll Ask for Barack Obama's Birth Certificate," *Atlanta Journal-Constitution*, November 5, 2009, http://blogs.ajc.com/political-insider-jim-galloway/2009/11/05/nathan-deal-says-hell-ask-for-barack-obamas-birth-certificate; David Weigel, "And Now, Roy Blunt," *Washington Independent*, July 29, 2009, http://washingtonindependent.com/53127/and-now-roy-blunt.

81. Patrik Jonsson, "A Last Electoral Hurdle for Obama," *Christian Science Monitor*, November 26, 2008, http://www.csmonitor.com/USA/Politics/2008/1126/a-last-electoral-hurdle-for-obama; David Weigel, "How Many Southern Whites Believe Obama Was Born in America?" *Washington Independent*, September 31, 2009, http://washingtonindependent.com/53396/

how-many-southern-whites-believe-obama-was-born-in-america; David Weigel, "Change They Can Litigate: The Fringe Movement to Keep Barack Obama from Becoming President," *Slate,* December 4, 2008, http://www.slate.com/id/2206033/pagenum/all.

82. Dan Fletcher, "Orly Taitz," *Time,* August 10, 2009, http://www.time.com/time/nation/article/0,8599,1915285,00.html.

83. Kay, *Among the Truthers: A Journey through America's Growing Conspiracist Underground,* 3.

84. Ibid.

85. Ibid.

86. Cf. Adam Liptak, "A Citizen, but 'Natural Born'?" *New York Times,* July 11, 2008, http://www.nytimes.com/2008/07/11/us/politics/11mccain.html?_r=2&oref=slogin&oref=slogin; Congressional Research Service, Memorandum 41131059, "What to Tell Your Constituents in Answer to Obama Eligibility," April 3, 2009, http://www.scribd.com/doc/41197555/41131059-MoC-Memo-What-to-Tell-Your-Constituents-in-Answer-to-Obama-Eligibility.

87. "The Truth about Barack's Birth Certificate," *Obama for America,* June 12, 2008, http://fightthesmears.com/articles/5/birthcertificate; Michael Isikoff, "Ex-Hawaii Official Denounces 'Ludicrous' Birther Claims," *MSNBC.com,* April 19, 2011, http://www.msnbc.msn.com/id/42519951/ns/politics-more_politics/#.Tmo7u-yRoS4; June Watanabe, "Born Identity," *Honolulu Star-Bulletin,* June 6, 2009, http://archives.starbulletin.com/content/20090606_kokua_line.

88. "Barack Obama's Long Form Birth Certificate" accessed on 8 September 2011, http://www.whitehouse.gov/sites/default/files/rss_viewer/birth-certificate-long-form.pdf.

89. "Birther Movement (Obama Birth Certificate)," *New York Times,* April 27, 2011, http://topics.nytimes.com/top/reference/timestopics/subjects/b/birther_movement/index.html.

90. Ibid., 5.

91. Donald Trump, interview by Meredith Vieira, *Today Exclusive,* National Broadcasting Company, April 7, 2011.

92. Donald Trump, "Donald Trump to Release Financial, Tax Information at the 'Appropriate Time.'" *ABC News,* April 27, 2011, http://abcnews.go.com/Politics/donald-trump-glee-obama-birth-certificate-release/story?id=13465438.

93. Robert Steinback, "Race Continued to Dog Tea Party Representatives and Events," *Southern Poverty Law Center,* May 16, 2011, http://www.splcenter.org/blog/2011/05/16/race-continues-to-dog-tea-party-representatives-and-events; Marcus Lloyd has made a small career out of framing himself as an exception to the black masses that suckle from government welfare, and in so doing, deteriorate their own spirit and waste their lives. Lloyd wrote in *The Guardian,*

> Several of my cousins stayed enslaved to the system and the bigotry of low expectations. Because true self-esteem comes from personal achievement, they possessed very little. They lived angry and bitter lives, consumed with

serial impregnating, out-of-wedlock births and substance abuse. An outrageously high number died prematurely. . . . So, when I hear politicians, such as Barack Obama, pandering to the so-called poor of America, it turns my stomach. I've witnessed the deterioration of the human spirit, wasted lives and suffering that happens when government becomes "daddy."

See Marcus Lloyd, "Why I Am a Black Tea Party Patriot Opposed to Barack Obama," *Guardian*, October 8, 2010, http://www.guardian.co.uk/commentisfree/lloyd-marcus-tea-party-blog/2010/oct/08/lloyd-marcus-tea-party.

94. Tali Mendelberg, *The Race Card: Campaign Strategy, Implicit Messages, and the Norm of Equality* (Princeton, NJ: Princeton University Press, 2001).

95. Cited in "Chris Matthews, Pat Buchanan Fight over Obama's Academic Qualifications" (video), *Huffington Post*, accessed on September 11, 2011, http://www.huffingtonpost.com/2011/04/27/chris-matthews-pat-buchanan-obama_n_854219.html.

96. "An Open Letter to Barack Obama: Are You a Natural Born Citizen of the U.S.? Are You Legally Eligible to Hold the Office of President?" *We the People Foundation*, November 2008, http://www.wethepeoplefoundation.org/UPDATE/misc2008/ChicagoTribune-ObamaLtr-Nov-2008.pdf.

97. Mark Williams, "Taking Back America One Tea Party at a Time," *MarkTalk.com*, 2010, 40.

98. Ibid., 152.

99. Amy Kremer, "Welcome Y'all," *SouthernBellePolitics.com*, October 9, 2008, http://www.southernbellepolitics.com/2008/10/welcome-yall.html.

100. "GOP Official Defends Obama Chimpanzee Email: Party Leader Calls It 'Racist,'" *Los Angeles Times*, April 17, 2011, http://latimesblogs.latimes.com/lanow/2011/04/gop-official-defends-obama-chimpanzee-email-party-leader-calls-it-racist.html.

101. R. Scott Moxley, "KTLA Gets Davenport Scoop: Racist Orange County Republican Email; President Obama and His Parents Are Apes," *OC Weekly*, April 20, 2011, http://blogs.ocweekly.com/navelgazing/2011/04/racist_orange_county_republica.php.

102. Mary Mitchell, "Monkeys, Watermelons, and Black People," *Chicago Sun-Times*, February 26, 2009, http://blogs.suntimes.com/mitchell/2009/02/monkeys_watermelons_and_black.html.

103. David A. Love, "Bachmann Can't Run from Her Birther Bona Fides," *Grio*, June 15, 2011, http://www.thegrio.com/politics/bachmann-cant-run-from-her-birther-bona-fides.php.

104. Mark Potok, "Let's Call the 'Birthers' What They Are," *Huffington Post*, April 28, 2011, http://www.huffingtonpost.com/mark-potok/lets-call-the-birthers-wh_b_855095.html.

105. E. Hehman, S. L. Gaertner, and J. F. Dovidio, "Evaluations of Presidential Performance: Race, Prejudice, and Perceptions of Americanism," *Journal of Experimental Social Psychology* 47 (2011): 430–35.

106. Hughey, "Show Me Your Papers! Obama's Birth and the Whiteness of Belonging."

107. Glenn Thrush, "58 Percent of GOP Not Sure/Doubt Obama Born in US," *Politico.com*, July 30, 2009, http://www.politico.com/blogs/glennthrush/0709/58_of_GOP_not_suredont_beleive_Obama_born_in_US.html.

108. David Weigel, "How Many Southern Whites Believe Obama Was Born in America?" *Washington Independent*, September 31, 2009, http://washingtonindependent.com/53396/how-many-southern-whites-believe-obama-was-born-in-america.

109. Ibid.

110. Of respondents interviewed on September 21, 2009, by Public Policy Polling, 59 percent said Obama was born in the United States, with 23 percent saying he was not and 18 percent unsure. For full poll results and crosstabs see http://www.publicpolicypolling.com/pdf/surveys/2009_Archives/PPP_Release_National_9231210.pdf.

111. Harris Interactive, "'Wingnuts' and President Obama," *Harris Poll* #42, March 23, 2010, http://www.harrisinteractive.com/NewsRoom/HarrisPolls/tabid/447/ctl/ReadCustom%20Default/mid/1508/ArticleId/223/Default.aspx.

112. Susan Page, "Poll: What Kind of President Would Donald Trump Make?" *USA Today*, April 26, 2011, http://www.usatoday.com/news/politics/2011-04-25-trump-president-poll.htm.

113. Brendan Nyhan, "Why Did Birther Support Drop So Much?" *Huffington Post*, May 13, 2011, http://www.huffingtonpost.com/brendan-nyhan/why-did-birther-support-d_b_861639.html.

114. Michael Eric Dyson, "Real Time with Bill Maher," *HBO*, May 6, 2011, http://www.hbo.com/real-time-with-bill-maher/episodes/0/212-episode/synopsis/quotes.html.

115. Lymari Morales, "Obama's Birth Certificate Convinces Some, but Not All, Skeptics," *Gallup Poll*, May 13, 2011, http://www.gallup.com/poll/147530/Obama-Birth-Certificate-Convinces-Not-Skeptics.aspx.

116. Cf. Theodore Allen, *The Invention of the White Race*. Vol. 1, *Racial Oppression and Social Control* (London: Verso, 1994); Theodore Allen, *The Invention of the White Race*. Vol. 2, *The Origins of Racial Oppression in Anglo-America* (London: Verso, 1997); Nell Irvin Painter, *The History of White People* (New York: Norton, 2010); Karen Brodkin, *How Jews Became White Folks and What That Says about Race in America* (New Brunswick, NJ: Rutgers University Press, 1998); Noel Ignatiev, *How the Irish Became White* (New York: Routledge, 1995); Matthew Frye Jacobson, *Roots Too: White Ethnic Revival in Post–Civil Rights America* (Cambridge, MA: Harvard University Press, 2006); David R. Roediger, *The Wages of Whiteness: Race and the Making of the American Working Class* (New York: Verso, 1996).

117. Mark A. Graber, *Dred Scott and the Problem of Constitutional Evil* (Cambridge: Cambridge University Press, 2006), 46–58.

118. Burghart and Zeskind, "Tea Party Nationalism."

NOTES TO CHAPTER 3

1. Robert Entman and Andrew Rojecki, *The Black Image in the White Mind: Media and Race in America* (Chicago: University of Chicago Press, 2000), xi.

2. Stefano DellaVigna and Ethan Kaplan, "The Fox News Effect: Media Bias and Voting," *NBER Working Paper,* no. 12169, National Bureau of Economic Research.

3. Matthew A. Baum, *Soft News Goes to War: Public Opinion and American Foreign Policy in the New Media Age* (Princeton, NJ: Princeton University Press, 2003); Matthew A. Baum, "Talking the Vote: Why Presidential Candidates Hit the Talk Show Circuit," *American Journal of Political Science* 49 (2005): 213–34; Scott Collins, *Crazy Like a FOX: The Inside Story of How Fox News Beat CNN* (New York: Penguin, 2004).

4. Kyle Leighton, "Pew: Cable Still Dominates as Internet News Consumers Are Unenthusiastic about 2012," *TPM,* February 8, 2012, http://2012.talkingpoints-memo.com/2012/02/cable-news-dominates-as-net-users-unenthusiastic-about-2012.php.

5. Bill Carter, "Fox News Marks a Decade at No. 1 in Cable News," *New York Times,* January 31, 2012, http://mediadecoder.blogs.nytimes.com/2012/01/31/fox-news-marks-a-decade-at-no-1-in-cable-news.

6. Jonathon Morris, "The Fox News Factor," *Harvard International Journal of Press/Politics* 10.3 (2005): 56–79, 57.

7. "News Audiences Increasingly Politicized," *Pew Research Center for the People and the Press,* June 8, 2004, http://people-press.org/reports/display.php3?ReportID=215.

8. Ibid.

9. Collins, *Crazy Like a FOX.*

10. Ken Auletta, "Vox Fox: How Roger Ailes and Fox News Are Changing Cable News," *New Yorker,* May 26, 2003, 58–73.

11. Tim Dickinson, "How Roger Ailes Built the Fox News Fear Factory," *Rolling Stone,* May 25, 2011, http://www.rollingstone.com/politics/news/how-roger-ailes-built-the-fox-news-fear-factory-20110525.

12. Ibid.

13. Ibid.

14. Alexander Zaitchik, *Common Nonsense: Glenn Beck and the Triumph of Ignorance* (Hoboken, NJ: Wiley, 2011), 164–65.

15. Rick Perlstein, *Nixonland: The Rise of a President and the Fracturing of America* (New York: Simon & Schuster, 2008), 331.

16. Jim Rutenberg, "War or No, News on Cable Already Provides the Drama," *New York Times,* January 15, 2003, http://www.nytimes.com/2003/01/15/business/media/15TUBE.html.

17. Morris, "The Fox News Factor," 61.

18. Dickinson, "How Roger Ailes Built the Fox News Fear Factory."

19. Lucy Madison, "Palin Attacks 'Lamestream Media' for Forcing Gingrich Apology; Calls for Tea Party Candidate in 2012 Election," *CBS News*, May 19, 2011, http://www.cbsnews.com/8301-503544_162-20064322-503544.html.

20. Scott Conroy, "'Gotcha Journalism' or a Double Standard," *CBS News*, September 29, 2008, http://www.cbsnews.com/8301-502443_162-4487987-502443.html.

21. Jim Burkee, "Even Rush Limbaugh Needs the Mainstream Press," *Wisconsin State Journal*, May 17, 2009, page B3, through LexisNexis Academic.

22. Ibid.

23. Stefano DellaVigna and Ethan Kaplan, "The Fox News Effect: Media Bias and Voting," *Quarterly Journal of Economics* 122.3 (2007): 1187–1234; Tim Groeling, "Who's the Fairest of Them All? An Empirical Test for Partisan Bias on ABC, CBS, NBC, and Fox News," *Presidential Studies Quarterly* 38.4 (2008): 628–54; Morris, "The Fox News Factor."

24. Morris, "The Fox News Factor," 68–69.

25. Groeling, "Who's the Fairest of Them All," 649.

26. MSNBC's Keith Olbermann and the liberal organization Media Matters, for instance, regularly call attention to racially insensitive comments appearing on conservative talk radio and the Fox News Channel.

27. See Michael Tesler and David Sears, "Is the Obama Presidency Post Racial? Evidence from His First Year in Office," *Annual Meeting of the Midwest Political Science Association*, April 22–25, 2010. (Much of this paper appears as chapter 8 in Michael Tesler and David Sears, *Obama's Race: The 2008 Election and the Dream of a Post-Racial America* [Chicago: University of Chicago Press, 2010].) This study replicated questions from their CCAP reinterviews and a July 2009 Pew Poll. The Pew question was only asked of respondents who get most of their news from TV. Of this group, 27 percent said they get most of their information about national and international affairs from Fox News. Survey by Pew Research Center for the People and the Press. Methodology: Conducted by Princeton Survey Research Associates International, July 22–July 26, 2009, and based on telephone interviews with a national adult sample of 1,506. Of these, 1,129 respondents were interviewed on a landline telephone and 377 were interviewed on a cell phone, including 114 who had no landline telephone. Percentages accessed from iPOLL. When asked what televised source respondents get most of their news from, 26 percent of these respondents said they get most of their information about national and international affairs from Fox News.

28. Tesler and Sears, "Is the Obama Presidency Post Racial?" 15.

29. Ibid., 16.

30. Chelsea Rudman, "Coulter Absurdly Claims 'No One on Fox Ever Mentioned' Birtherism," *Grate Wire*, June 11, 2011, http://gratewire.com/topic/foxs-ann-coulter-claims-no-one-on-network-that-obsessively-hyped-birtherism.

31. "Report: Fox Promotes Birther Myth in at Least 52 Segments," *Newscorpwatch*, April 27, 2011, http://newscorpwatch.org/research/201104270009.

32. Ibid.

33. Theda Skocpol and Vanessa Williamson, *The Tea Party and the Remaking of Republican Conservatism* (New York: Oxford University Press, 2012), 130.

34. Ibid.

35. DellaVigna and Kaplan, "The Fox News Effect: Media Bias and Voting."

36. Cited in James Loewen, *Lies My Teacher Told Me* (New York: Touchstone, 1995).

37. Peter Hart, *The Oh Really? Factor: Unspinning Fox News Channel's Bill O'Reilly* (New York: Seven Stories Press, 2003), 28–29.

38. Bill O'Reilly, "Smearing Fox News," *Fox News*, July 23, 2008, http://www.foxnews.com/story/0,2933,390078,00.html.

39. "Beck Said 'To Be Consistent,' Clinton Should Give Obama '5 Percentage Points' Because of Affirmative Action," *Media Matters*, January 28, 2008, http://mediamatters.org/mobile/research/200801280005.

40. "Beck: 'You Know What This President Is Doing Right Now? He is Addicting This Country to Heroin—the Heroin That Is Government Slavery,'" *News Corp Watch*, February 11, 2009, http://newscorpwatch.org/clips/200902110028.

41. "Glenn Beck: What's Driving President Obama's Agenda," *Glennbeck.com*, July 24, 2009, http://www.glennbeck.com/content/articles/article/198/28330.

42. "Limbaugh's 'Colorblind' History of Racially Charged Comments," *Media Matters*, October 13, 2009, http://mediamatters.org/research/200910130049.

43. Nassira Nicola, "Black Face, White Voice: Rush Limbaugh and the 'Message' of Race," *Journal of Language and Politics* 9.2 (2010): 281–309.

44. Casey Gane-McCalla, "Top 10 Racist Limbaugh Quotes," *NewsOne*, July 16, 2010, http://newsone.com/nation/casey-gane-mccalla/top-10-racist-limbaugh-quotes.

45. Ibid.

46. Ibid.

47. "Dick Morris Uses Phony New Black Panthers Scandal to Declare Obama Is 'Stereotyping Himself as a Racial President,'" *Media Matters*, July 16, 2010, http://mediamatters.org/video/2010/07/16/dick-morris-uses-phony-new-black-panthers-scand/167786.

48. Todd Gregory, "Fox Baselessly Links Obama and Holder to New Black Panthers Case, but Their Key Witness Says Otherwise," *Media Matters*, July 16, 2010, http://mediamatters.org/research/2010/07/16/fox-baselessly-links-obama-and-holder-to-new-bl/167820.

49. Erick Schroeck, "Bipartisan Agreement: Fox-Hyped New Black Panthers Case Is a Phony Scandal," *Media Matters*, July 17, 2010, http://mediamatters.org/research/2010/07/17/bipartisan-agreement-fox-hyped-new-black-panthe/167847.

50. Fae Jencks, Terry Krepel, and Matt McLaughlin, "Fox News' Long History of Race-Baiting," *Media Matters*, July 27, 2010, http://mediamatters.org/research/2010/07/27/fox-news-long-history-of-race-baiting/168312.

51. Editorial, "Politics of Attack," *New York Times*, October 8, 2008, http://www.nytimes.com/2008/10/08/opinion/08wed1.html?_r=1&ref=opinion&pagewanted=print&oref=slogin.

52. Sean Hannity, "Evaluating the State of the Presidential Race," *Fox News*, October 9, 2008.

53. Paul Kane, "'Tea Party' Protesters Accused of Spitting on Lawmaker, Using Slurs," *Washington Post*, March 20, 2010, http://www.washingtonpost.com/wp-dyn/content/article/2010/03/20/AR2010032002556.html.

54. Ann Coulter, "Obama's Poll Numbers Down, Imaginary Racism Up," *Anncoulter.com*, July 21, 2010, http://www.anncoulter.com/columns/2010-07-21.html.

55. Ibid.

56. Andrew Breitbart, "Andrew Breitbart on 'Hannity': 'This Is Not about Shirley Sherrod,'" *Fox News*, July 20, 2010, http://www.foxnews.com/on-air/hannity/transcript/andrew-breitbart-hannity-not-about-shirley-sherrod.

57. Ed O'Keefe and Krissah Thompson, "NAACP, White House Respond to Ouster of USDA Worker Shirley Sherrod," *Washington Post*, July 20, 2010, http://voices.washingtonpost.com/federal-eye/2010/07/usda_worker_quits_over_racism.html.

58. Glenn Beck, "Video Shows ACORN Stopping Health Care Protestors: U.S. Changes Immigration Policy; Service Employees Union Fights for Health Care; Beck and Guns," *Fox News*, July 27, 2010.

59. Mark Levin, "Mark Levin: Racism Abounds over There at MSNBC and NBC," *Real Clear Politics*, May 17, 2011, http://www.realclearpolitics.com/video/2011/05/17/mark_levin_racism_abounds_over_there_at_msnbc_and_nbc.html.

60. "'Please Let Me Speak': Reporter Heckles Obama in the Rose Garden for 'Favoring Immigrant Workers over Americans' as President Unveils Work Permit Break for 800,000 Young Migrants," *Daily Mail*, June 15, 2012, http://www.dailymail.co.uk/news/article-2160019/Neil-Munro-Obama-bickers-heckler-speech-favouring-immigrant-workers.html.

61. Simon Maloy, "I Call Him a Monkey," *Media Matters*, June 21, 2012, http://mediamatters.org/blog/2012/06/21/i-call-him-a-monkey/185475.

62. "Tucker Carlson on Sam Donaldson's 'Right-Wing' Media and Race Remarks: 'Anyone Who Charges Racism with No Evidence Shouldn't Be Taken Seriously,'" *Fox News Insider*, June 19, 2012, http://foxnewsinsider.com/2012/06/19/tucker-carlson-on-sam-donaldsons-right-wing-media-and-race-remarks-anyone-who-charges-racism-with-no-evidence-shouldnt-be-taken-seriously.

63. "Remarks by the President on Immigration," *Whitehouse.gov*, June 15, 2012, http://www.whitehouse.gov/the-press-office/2012/06/15/remarks-president-immigration.

64. "Please Let Me Speak.'"

65. "Fox Host O'Reilly Says Restaurant Comments Not Racist," *CNN*, September 26, 2007, http://articles.cnn.com/2007-09-26/entertainment/oreilly.race_1_primarily-black-patronship-bill-o-reilly-glorifying-violence?_s=PM:SHOWBIZ.

66. Ali Moossavi, "What Are We Going to Do about Racism," *Arab American News*, August 18, 2007, http://www.arabamericannews.com/news/index.php?mod=article&cat=OtherOpinions&article=73.

67. "O'Reilly: 'Many, Many, Many' Hurricane Victims Who Failed to Evacuate New Orleans Are 'Drug-Addicted . . . Thugs.'" *Media Matters*, September 15, 2005, http://mediamatters.org/mmtv/200509150001.

68. Lesie Rosenberg and Eric Schroeck. "Right-Wing Media Predictably Attack Obama for Going to Europe after Tornadoes," *Media Matters*, May 24, 2011, http://mediamatters.org/research/2011/05/24/right-wing-media-predictably-attack-obama-for-g/179960.

69. Aliyah Shahid, "Laura Ingraham Slams Obama for Drinking Guinness in Ireland while Tornado-Ravaged Missourians Suffer," *New York Daily News*, May 24, 2011, http://articles.nydailynews.com/2011-05-24/news/29597832_1_president-obama-liberal-press-guinness.

70. Marc H. Morial, "Imus Redux: Talk Radio Needs to Clean Up Act," *New York Beacon*, March 6, 2008, 8–9.

71. Glynnis MacNicol, "Hoods in the House: Fox Business Host Slammed for Overtly Racist Obama Remark," *Business Insider*, June 13, 2011, http://articles.businessinsider.com/2011-06-13/entertainment/29999579_1_obama-shares-chyron-fox-business-network.

72. Fox Nation, "Bill O'Reilly and Sarah Palin Weigh In on Rapper Controversy," *Fox News*, May 12, 2011, http://nation.foxnews.com/oreilly-factor/2011/05/11/factor-preview-nj-state-police-slam-insensitive-and-stupid-wh-cop-killer-ra.

73. "Sean Hannity: Obama 'Back to His Radical Roots' with Common Invite," *Huffington Post*, May 11, 2011, http://www.huffingtonpost.com/2011/05/11/sean-hannity-obama-common-radical_n_860446.html.

74. Fox Nation, "Obama's Hip-Hop BBQ Didn't Create Jobs," *Fox News*, August 5, 2011, http://nation.foxnews.com/president-obama/2011/08/05/obama-parties-chris-rock-jay-z-and-whoopi-while-rome-burns.

75. Clarence Page, "Obama's Brew-ha-ha: Removing Conflict between the Police and Citizens," *Chicago Tribune*, August 2, 2009, http://articles.chicagotribune.com/2009-08-02/news/0908010203_1_obama-spokesman-working-class-whites-brew-ha-ha.

76. Joe Windish, "Murdoch Doesn't Get It," *Moderate Voice*, November 9, 2009, http://themoderatevoice.com/52472/murdoch-doesnt-get-it.

77. Sean Hannity, "Story of Resigning Congressman Changing: Dan Rather Comment Raises Questions," *Fox News*, March 9, 2010.

78. Mark R. Levin, "The Obama Temptation," *National Review Online*, October 28, 2009, http://www.nationalreview.com/corner/172652/obama-temptation/mark-r-levin.

79. Greg Lewis, "Savage: 'I Fear That Obama Will Stir Up a Race War . . . in Order to Seize Absolute Power,'" *Media Matters*, October 9, 2008, http://mediamatters.org/mmtv/200810090008.

80. Michael Saul, "Glenn Beck Draws Fire from Civil Rights Leaders over African-American Flap," *New York Daily News*, January 9, 2010, http://articles

.nydailynews.com/2010-01-09/news/17945472_1_rev-al-sharpton-glenn-beck-african-american.

81. Bill O'Reilly, "The Politics of Prejudice," *Fox News*, February 5, 2007.

82. Leonard Pitts Jr., "This Is Who 'We' Really Is, Glenn," *Alameda* (CA) *Times-Star*, August 30, 2010.

83. Andrew Ironside, "On MLK Day, Savage Called Civil Rights a 'Racket' Designed to Steal 'White Males' Birthright,'" January 16, 2007, http://mediamatters.org/research/2007/01/16/on-mlk-day-savage-called-civil-rights-a-racket/137746.

84. "Beck: 'The Health Care Bill Is Reparations. It's the Beginning of Reparations,'" *Media Matters*, July 22, 2009, http://mediamatters.org/mmtv/200907220015.

85. Glenn Beck, "What's Driving President Obama's Agenda?" *Fox News*, July 23, 2009, http://www.foxnews.com/story/0,2933,534643,00.html.

86. "President Obama Delivers Remarks on Ft. Hood Shooting at End of Tribal Leaders Conference," *Washington Post*, November 5, 2009, www.washingtonpost.com/wp-dyn/content/article/2009/11/05/AR2009110504202.html.

87. Glenn Beck, "Beck for November 11, 2009—Part 1," *Fox News*, November 11, 2009.

88. "Trouble Brews on Sharpton Show," *Rush Limbaugh Show*, July 22, 2009, http://www.rushlimbaugh.com/daily/2009/07/22/trouble_brews_on_sharpton_show.

89. Paula Zahn, "Rutgers Basketball Team Speaks Out: Father of Anna Nicole Smith's Baby Revealed—Part 2," *CNN*, April 10, 2007.

90. Joseph A. Palermo, "Ann Coulter Starts Early with Racist Slurs against Obama," *Huffington Post*, February 15, 2008, http://www.huffingtonpost.com/joseph-a-palermo/ann-coulter-starts-early-_1_b_86849.html.

91. Todd Gregory, "Fox Baselessly Links Obama and Holder to New Black Panthers Case, but Their Key Witness Says Otherwise," *Media Matters*, July 16, 2010, http://mediamatters.org/research/2010/07/16/fox-baselessly-links-obama-and-holder-to-new-bl/167820.

92. Bill O'Reilly, "Talking Points Memo and Top Story," *Fox News*, July 22, 2010.

93. Betty Winston Bayé, "The Trashing of a Good Woman, Shirley Sherrod," (Lexington, KY) *Courier-Journal,* July 22, 2010, http://www.courier-journal.com/article/20100722/COLUMNISTS09/307220009/Betty-Winston-Bay-trashing-good-woman-Shirley-Sherrod.

94. Bill O'Reilly, "Talking Points Memo and Top Story," *Fox News*, July 20, 2010, http://www.billoreilly.com/show?action=viewTVShow&showID=2649.

95. Larry King, "Interview with T. Boone Pickens: Is Tea Party Racist?" *CNN*, July 19, 2010, http://transcripts.cnn.com/TRANSCRIPTS/1007/19/lkl.01.html.

96. Ibid.

97. Ibid.

98. "Sherrod: White House Worried about Glenn Beck," *CNN*, July 20, 2010, http://politicalticker.blogs.cnn.com/2010/07/20/sherrod-white-house-worried-about-glenn-beck/?fbid=GmSiFGmDEyY.

99. Mary Clare Jalonick, "Contrite, Obama Asks Sherrod to Come Back," *Charleston* (WV) *Gazette*, July 23, 2010.

100. Jonathan Capehart, "Shirley Sherrod: Sacrificial Lamb on the Altar of Race," *Washington Post*, July 20, 2010, http://voices.washingtonpost.com/postpartisan/2010/07/shirley_sherrod_sacrificial_la.html.

101. Ibid.

102. Cited in Jessie Washington, "Black Racism Suddenly Topic of Debate," *Post and Courier*, July 22, 2010, http://www.postandcourier.com/news/2010/jul/22/black-racism-suddenly-topic-of-debate/?print.

103. Ann Coulter, "Obama's Dimestore 'Mein Kampf,'" *Anncoulter.com*, April 2, 2008, http://www.anncoulter.com/columns/2008-04-02.html.

104. "Conservative Radio Hosts Repeat Discredited Claim That Obama Has Not Produced Valid U.S. Birth Certificate," *Media Matters*, October 14, 2008, http://mediamatters.org/video/2008/10/14/conservative-radio-hosts-repeat-discredited-cla/145650.

105. Eli Clifton, "Glenn Beck Addresses the Israeli Knesset, Admits He 'Doesn't Know Many Palestinians or Jewish People,'" *Think Progress*, July 11, 2011, http://thinkprogress.org/security/2011/07/11/265195/glenn-beck-addresses-the-israeli-knesset-admits-he-doesnt-know-many-palestinians-or-jewish-people.

106. Sean Hannity, *Conservative Victory: Defeating Obama's Radical Agenda* (New York: Harper Paperbacks, 2010), 195.

107. Sean Hannity and Alan Colmes, "Barack Obama Highlights Issues of Religion and Politics: Should Fairness Doctrine Be Revived," *Fox News*, June 25, 2007.

108. Bob Herbert, "America Is Better Than This," *New York Times*, August 28, 2010, A19.

109. Joseph A. Palermo, "Ann Coulter Starts Early with Racist Slurs against Obama," *Huffington Post*, February 15, 2008, http://www.huffingtonpost.com/joseph-a-palermo/ann-coulter-starts-early-_1_b_86849.html.

110. Nathan Thornburgh, "Why Is Obama's Middle Name Taboo?" *Time*, February 28, 2008, http://www.time.com/time/politics/article/0,8599,1718255,00.html.

111. Bill O'Reilly, "Obama Pastor Controversy Continues," *Fox News*, March 17, 2008, http://www.foxnews.com/on-air/oreilly/2008/03/17/obama-pastor-controversy-continues#ixzz1Z5ybEsnW.

112. Sean Hannity, "Interview with Mark Levin," *Fox News*, July 1, 2009.

113. Canadian Press, "Obama's Laugh Riles the Right," *Waterloo Region Record* (Canada), May 12, 2009.

114. Joseph Wyatt, "The Party of Rush Is Troubled," *Charleston* (WV) *Gazette*, April 16, 2009.

115. Janet Shan, "Rush Limbaugh Says Barack Obama a Veritable Rookie Whose Only Chance of Winning Is Because He's Black," *Hinterland Gazette*, http://hinterlandgazette.com/2008/06/rush-limbaugh-says-barack-obama.html?utm_source=rss&utm_medium=rss&utm_campaign=rush-limbaugh-says-barack-obama.

116. Casey Gane-McCalla, "Limbaugh: Obama and Oprah Are Only Successful Because They're Black," *News One*, July 7, 2010, http://newsone.com/582245/limbaugh-says-obama-and-oprah-are-only-successful-because-theyre-black.

117. Contra Nilanjana Dasgupta and Anthony G. Greenwald, "On the Malleability of Automatic Attitudes: Combating Automatic Prejudice with Images of Admired and Disliked Individuals," *Journal of Personality and Social Psychology* 81.5 (2001): 800–814.

118. Laurie A. Rudman and Matthew R. Lee, "Implicit and Explicit Consequences of Exposure to Violent and Misogynous Rap Music," *Group Processes & Intergroup Relations* 5.2 (2002): 133–50.

119. Franklin D. Gilliam Jr. and Shanto Iyengar, "Prime Suspects: The Influence of Local Television News on the Viewing Public," *American Journal of Political Science* 44.3 (2000): 560–73.

NOTES TO CHAPTER 4

1. For more on the constant dichotomization and "good vs. evil" of racialized politics, see Matthew W. Hughey, *White Bound: Nationalists, Antiracists, and the Shared Meanings of Race* (Stanford, CA: Stanford University Press, 2012).

2. Lucy Morgan, "Jim Greer Denounces Florida Republican Party Officials as Liars, 'Right-Wing Crazies' in Deposition," *Tampa Bay Times*, July 26, 2012, http://www.tampabay.com/news/politics/national/jim-greer-denounces-florida-republican-party-officials-as-liars-and/1242157.

3. Brendan Farrington, "Ex-Fla. GOP Head Jim Greer Claims Embarrassing Party Secrets," *Ledger*, July 26, 2012, http://www.theledger.com/article/20120726/POLI TICS/120729446/1374?p=2&tc=pg.

4. "Voter ID: 2012 Legislation," *National Conference of State Legislatures*, July 13, 2012, http://www.ncsl.org/legislatures-elections/elections/voter-id-2012-legisla-tion.aspx.

5. Justin Levitt, "The Truth about Voter Fraud," Paper, Brenner Center for Justice at New York University Law School, 2007.

6. Lynette Holloway, "Racist Imagery Used to Push for Minn. Voter-ID Law," *Root*, February 21, 2012, http://www.theroot.com/buzz/gop-use-racist-imagery-push-minn-voter-id-law.

7. David C. Wilson and Paul Brewer, "Poll: Racial Resentment Tied to Voter ID Support," *University of Delaware*, July 18, 2012, http://www.eurekalert.org/pub_ releases/2012-07/uod-prr071812.php.

8. Tali Mendelberg, *The Race Card: Campaign Strategy, Implicit Messages, and the Norm of Equality* (Princeton, NJ: Princeton University Press, 2001), 28.

9. Ibid., 29.

10. James McPherson, *The Struggle for Equality* (Princeton, NJ: Princeton University Press, 1964), 30–31.

11. Leon F. Litwak, *North of Slavery* (Chicago: University of Chicago Press, 1961); August Meier and Elliott Rudwick, *From Plantation to Ghetto* (New York: Hill and Wang, 1996), 92–93; Christopher Malone, *Between Freedom and Bondage: Racial Voting Restrictions in the Antebellum North* (New York: Routledge, 2008).

12. Louis Ruchames, *Racial Thought in America: From the Puritans to Abraham Lincoln* (Amherst: University of Massachusetts Press, 1969), 421.

13. Mendelberg, *The Race Card*, 34–36.

14. Donald G. Nieman, *Promises to Keep: African-Americans and the Constitutional Order, 1776 to the Present* (Oxford: Oxford University Press, 1991), 42–43.

15. Mendelberg, *The Race Card*, 39–42.

16. Eric Foner, *A Short History of Reconstruction, 1863–1877* (New York: Harper and Row, 1990), 43–48.

17. Mendelberg, *The Race Card*, 49–51.

18. J. Steven Rosenstone, Roy L. Behr, and Edward H. Lazarus, *Third Parties in America: Citizen Response to Major Party Failure* (Princeton, NJ: Princeton University Press, 1984), 64–65; C. Van Woodward, *The Strange Career of Jim Crow* (New York: Oxford University Press, 1966), 36.

19. Mendelberg, *The Race Card*, 56–59.

20. William D. Barnard, *Dixiecrats and Democrats: Alabama Politics, 1942–1950* (Tuscaloosa: University of Alabama Press, 1974), 9–10 (explaining James E. Folsom's use of populism in his campaign for Alabama governor in 1946).

21. W. Fitzhugh Brundage, *Lynching in the New South: Georgia and Virginia* (Urbana: University of Illinois Press, 1993), 231, 252.

22. Karl Frederickson, *The Dixiecrat Revolt and the End of the Solid South, 1932–1968* (Chapel Hill: University of North Carolina Press, 2001), 3–7.

23. Celeste M. Condit and John L. Lucaites, *Crafting Equality: America's Anglo-African Word* (Chicago: University of Chicago Press, 1993), 161, 179–80.

24. Celeste M. Condit and John L. Lucaites, *The Retreat of Scientific Racism: Changing Concepts of Race in Britain and the United States between World Wars* (Cambridge: Cambridge University Press, 1992).

25. Howard Schuman, Charlotte Steeh, and Lawrence Bobo, *Racial Attitudes in America: Trends and Interpretation* (Cambridge, MA: Harvard University Press, 1985), 106, table 3.3.

26. Mendelberg, *The Race Card*, 75–81.

27. Mendelberg, *The Race Card*, 76.

28. Mendelberg, *The Race Card*, 78.

29. Mendelberg, *The Race Card*, 80.

30. "Voter ID Legislation in the States," *Brennan Center for Justice*, last updated June 9, 2011, http://brennan.3cdn.net/74138fe01a34d22af0_ n7m6bny5d.pdf.

31. "The Law Regarding Voting Photo Identification Laws," *Lawyers Committee for Civil Rights under Law*, June 2011, http:// www.lawyerscommittee.org/admin/ voting-rights/documents/files/state-of-voter-ID-laws-for-web.pdf.

32. "Citizens without Proof: A Survey of Americans' Possession of Documentary Proof of Citizenship and Photo Identification," *Brennan Center for Justice*, November 2006, http://www.brennancenter.org/page/-/d/download_ file_39242. pdf.

33. Ibid.

34. Michael J. Pitts, "Photo ID, Provisional Balloting, and Indiana's 2012 Primary Election," *University of Richmond Law Review* 47 (2013): 943 (citing Richard L. Hasen, *The Voting Wars* [2012], 6).

35. Tony Norman, "Black Voters a Surprise, Especially to GOP," *Pittsburgh Post-Gazette*, May 10, 2013, A2.

36. Daniel N. Lipson, "The Resilience of Affirmative Action in the 1980s: Innovation, Isomorphism, and Institutionalization in University Admissions," *Political Research Quarterly* (March 1, 2012): 132 (citing Terry H. Anderson, *The Pursuit of Fairness: The History of Affirmative Action* [2004]).

37. Aaron Blake, "Romney Wanders into the Slippery Slope of Birtherism," *WashingtonPost.com,* August 24, 2012.

38. Ibid.

39. Ibid.

40. Mendelberg, *The Race Card*, 91.

41. Ibid.

42. Mendelberg, *The Race Card*, 88–93.

43. Mary C. Brennan, *Turning Right in the Sixties: The Conservative Capture of the GOP* (Chapel Hill: University of North Carolina Press, 1995), 121–37.

44. Mendelberg, *The Race Card*, 93–95.

45. George Poague, "Clinton Was Right in Her LBJ-MLK Remark," *Leaf-Chronicle,* January 27, 2007.

46. Mendelberg, *The Race Card*, 99–101.

47. Mendelberg, *The Race Card*, 105.

48. Bob Herbert, "Impossible, Ridiculous, Repugnant," *New York Times*, October 6, 2005, http://query.nytimes.com/gst/fullpage.html?res=9C04E6DF1E30F935A357 53C1A9639C8B63.

49. Susan Douglas and Meredith W. Michaels, *The Mommy Myth: The Idealization of Motherhood and How It Has Undermined All Women* (New York: Free Press, 2005), 178.

50. Jon Hurwitz and Mark Peffley, "Public Perception of Race and Crime: The Role of Racial Stereotypes," *American Journal of Political Science* 41.2 (1997): 383–91; Fred Slocum, "White Racial Attitudes and Implicit Racial Appeals: An Experimental Study of 'Race Coding' in Political Discourse," *Politics & Policy* 29.4 (2001): 650.

51. See Tali Mendelberg, *The Race Card: Campaign Strategy, Implicit Messages, and the Norm of Equality* (Princeton, NJ: Princeton University Press, 2001).

52. Fred Slocum and Yeuh-Ting Lee, "Racism, Racial Stereotypes, and American Politics," in *The Psychology of Prejudice and Discrimination*, ed. Jean Lau Chin (Santa Barbara, CA: Greenwood, 2004), 72–73.

53. Mendelberg, *The Race Card*, 143–44.

54. James M. Glaser, *Race, Campaign Politics, and the Realignment in the South* (New Haven, CT: Yale University Press, 1996), 185.

55. Ibid.
56. Slocum, "Racism, Racial Stereotypes, and American Politics," 73.
57. Glaser, *Race, Campaign Politics, and the Realignment in the South,* 185.
58. John Nichols, "Jesse Helms, John McCain, and the Mark of the White Hands," *Nation,* July 4, 2008, http://www.thenation.com/blog/jesse-helms-john-mccain-and-mark-white-hands.
59. Slocum, "Racism, Racial Stereotypes, and American Politics," 72.
60. Ibid.
61. Glaser, *Race, Campaign Politics, and the Realignment in the South,* 203.
62. Bill Curry, "Rove Leaves Long Trail of Dirty Tricks," *Hartford Courant,* August 19, 2007, C3.
63. Jennifer Steinhauer, "Confronting Ghosts of 2000 in South Carolina," *New York Times,* October 19, 2007.
64. Ibid.
65. Ibid.
66. Jesse Jackson, "Does GOP Mean Gutter-Oriented Politics," *Chicago Sun-Times,* October 31, 2006, 27; Peter Wallsten, "Democrats Say GOP Ad Appeals to Racist Fears," *Los Angeles Times,* October 24, 2006, A5.
67. Richard T. Middleton IV and Sekou Franklin, "Southern Racial Etiquette and the 2006 Tennessee Senate Race: The Racialization of Harold Ford's Deracialized Campaign," *National Political Science Review* 12 (2008): 63–81.
68. Stephanie McCrummen, "At Rick Perry's Texas Hunting Spot, Camp's Old Racially Charged Name Lingered," *Washington Post,* October 1, 2011.
69. Trey Ellis, "Santorum's Sticky Views on Entitlements," *Root,* January 5, 2012, available online.
70. Lucy Madison, "Santorum Targets Blacks in Entitlement Reform," *CBS News,* January 2, 2012, http://www.cbsnews.com/8301-503544_162-57350990-503544/santorum-targets-blacks-in-entitlement-reform.
71. Ashley Killough, "Santorum on Controversial Remark: I Was 'Tongue-Tied,'" *CNN,* January 4, 2012, http://politicalticker.blogs.cnn.com/2012/01/04/santorum-on-controversial-remark-i-was-tongue-tied.
72. Jonathan Chait, "News Bulletin: Ron Paul Is a Huge Racist," *New York Magazine,* December 15, 2011, http://nymag.com/daily/intel/2011/12/news-bulletin-ron-paul-is-a-huge-racist.html.
73. James Kirchick, "Angry White Man," *New Republic,* January 8, 2008, http://www.tnr.com/article/politics/angry-white-man.
74. Ibid.
75. Ibid.
76. Jackie Kucinich, "Paul's Story Changes on Racial Comments," *USA Today,* December 21, 2011, http://www.usatoday.com/news/politics/story/2011-12-21/ron-paul-racist-newsletters/52147878/1.
77. Ibid.

78. Ibid.

79. Jenee Desmond-Harris, "Paul Walks Out over Racist-Newsletter Probe," *Root*, December 22, 2011, http://www.theroot.com/buzz/paul-walks-out-over-racist-newsletter-probe.

80. Ibid.

81. Amanda Terkel, "Ron Paul: I'm the Only Candidate 'That Understands True Racism,'" *Huffington Post*, January 7, 2012, http://www.huffingtonpost.com/2012/01/07/ron-paul-new-hampshire-debate_n_1191953.html.

82. "Bush-era efforts to increase participation and broaden the program 'produced consistent increases in the number of average monthly beneficiaries. The number rose in seven out of the eight years of Bush's presidency—most of which were years not considered recessionary. All told, the number of recipients rose by a cumulative 63 percent during Bush's eight-year presidency" (Charles Blow, "The G.O.P.'s 'Black People' Platform," *New York Times*, January 6, 2012, http://www.nytimes.com/2012/01/07/opinion/blow-the-gops-black-people-platform.html).

83. Associated Press, "GOP Campaign Rhetoric Raising Racial Concerns," *Fox News*, January 18, 2012, http://www.foxnews.com/us/2012/01/18/gop-campaign-rhetoric-raising-racial-concerns.

84. Ibid.

85. Susan Reimer, "Gingrich's Really Poor Idea for 'Really Poor Children,'" *Baltimore Sun*, December 12, 2011, http://articles.baltimoresun.com/2011-12-12/news/bs-ed-reimer-gingrich-20111212_1_poor-children-poor-idea-herman-cain.

86. Frances Martel, "Newt Gingrich and Juan Williams Rumble over Proposed 'Child Janitors' Claim," *Mediaite*, January 16, 2012, http://www.mediaite.com/tv/newt-gingrich-and-juan-williams-rumble-over-proposed-child-janitors-claim.

87. Charles M. Blow, "Newt's Southern Strategy," *New York Times*, January 20, 2012, http://www.nytimes.com/2012/01/21/opinion/blow-newts-southern-strategy.html.

88. "Matthews Fawns over Obama: Romney Entitled; Obama Had to Work," *Real Clear Politics*, December 29, 2011, http://www.realclearpolitics.com/video/2011/12/29/matthews_fawns_over_obama_romney_had_entitled_life_obama_had_to_work.html.

89. Emily Friedman, "Mitt Romney Launches Fresh Attack on President Obama, Dubbing Him 'the Great Complainer,'" *ABC News*, January 2, 2012, http://abcnews.go.com/blogs/politics/2012/01/mitt-romney-launches-fresh-attack-on-president-obama-dubbing-him-the-great-complainer.

90. Matthew Jaffe, "Mitt Romney Ripped for DREAM Act Veto Threat, Alienates Some Latinos," *ABC News*, January 5, 2012, http://abcnews.go.com/blogs/politics/2012/01/mitt-romney-ripped-for-dream-act-veto-alienates-some-latinos.

91. James Oliphant, "Herman Cain Drops out of Presidential Race," *L.A. Times*, December 3, 2011.

92. Jackie Kucinich and Susan Page, "Texas Gov. Rick Perry Stumbles Badly in Republican Debate," November 11, 2011, http://www.usatoday.com/news/politics/story/2011-11-09/Republican-debate-michigan-herman-cain-economy/51145714/1.

93. Jeff Zeleny and Michael D. Shear, "Perry Ends Bid for Presidency," *New York Times*, January 19, 2012.

94. Blow, "Newt's Southern Strategy."

95. Paul West, "Newt Gingrich Ends 'Truly Wild Ride' of a Presidential Campaign," *L.A. Times*, May 2, 2012.

96. "Rick Santorum Finishes Ahead of Mitt Romney: Iowa Caucus Results," *Huffington Post*, January 19, 2012, http://www.huffingtonpost.com/2012/01/19/rick-santorum-iowa-caucus-results-certified-_n_1215690.html.

97. Rosalind S. Helderman and Nia-Malika Henderson, "Rick Santorum's Strategy of Focusing on Low-Key Races Paid Off," *Washington Post*, February 8, 2012.

98. Ibid.

99. John Ward, "Rick Santorum Drops Out: Why He Couldn't Get over the Hump," *Huffington Post*, April 10, 2012, http://www.huffingtonpost.com/2012/04/10/rick-santorum-drops-out_n_1416488.html.

100. Kim Geiger, "Rick Santorum Suspends Presidential Campaign, Is 'Not Done Fighting,'" *L.A. Times*, April 10, 2012.

101. Seema Mehta, "Ron Paul's Army May Have Loud Voice at GOP Convention," *L.A. Times*, June 18, 2012.

102. Rachel Weiner, "Ron Paul's Stealth State Convention Takeover," *Washington Post*, May 2, 2012.

103. Liz Halloran, "Romney and GOP Strike Deal with Ron Paul Loyalists before Convention," *NPR*, August 22, 2012, http://www.npr.org/blogs/itsallpolitics/2012/08/21/159594780/romney-and-gop-strike-deal-with-ron-paul-loyalists-before-convention.

104. Nate Silver, "The Myth of 'Anybody but Romney,'" *New York Times*, January 17, 2012.

105. Ari Berman, "Super PAC, Big Donors Propel Romney to Florida Victory," *Nation*, February 1, 2012, http://www.thenation.com/blog/165985/super-pac-big-donors-propel-romney-florida-victory.

106. Michael D. Shear, "Super Tuesday Victories for Romney, but Questions, Too," *New York Times*, March 7, 2012.

107. Tony Schinella, "Romney's Son's Birth Certificate Comment Causes National Firestorm," *Concord Patch*, December 30, 2011, http://concord-nh.patch.com/articles/romney-s-son-s-birth-certificate-comment-causes-national-firestorm.

108. Peter Grier, "Was Mitt Romney Hoping to Be Booed during NAACP Speech?" *Christian Science Monitor*, July 12, 2012, http://www.csmonitor.com/USA/DC-Decoder/Decoder-Wire/2012/0712/Was-Mitt-Romney-hoping-to-be-booed-during-NAACP-speech-video.

109. Charles Babington, "Romney Seeks to Undercut Obama's Likability Lead," *Boston.com*, August 15, 2012, http://www.boston.com/news/politics/ articles/2012/08/15/romney_tells_obama_to_change_tone_of_campaign_now.

110. Ashley Parker, "Romney Comments on Palestinians Draw Criticism," *New York Times*, July 30, 2012, http://thecaucus.blogs.nytimes.com/2012/07/30/ romney-comments-on-palestinians-draw-criticism.

111. See Karen Brodkin, *How Jews Became White Folks: And What That Says about Race in America* (New Brunswick, NJ: Rutgers University Press, 2008); Christopher Allen, *Islamophobia* (Surrey, England: Ashgate, 2010).

112. Ashley Parker, "Romney Comments on Palestinians Draw Criticism," *New York Times*, July 30, 2012, http://thecaucus.blogs.nytimes.com/2012/07/30/ romney-comments-on-palestinians-draw-criticism.

113. Associated Press, "Romney's Attacks on Obama and Welfare Deemed False by Fact Checkers," *Christian Science Monitor*, August 20, 2012, http://www.csmonitor.com/USA/Latest-News-Wires/2012/0820/ Romney-s-attacks-on-Obama-and-welfare-deemed-false-by-fact-checkers.

114. Michael Tesler, "Testing the Racializing Influence of Romney's Welfare Ad," *YouGov*, August 20, 2012, http://today.yougov.com/news/2012/08/20/ testing-racializing-influence-romneys-welfare-ad.

115. Ibid.

116. Ashley Parker and Trip Gabriel, "Romney Makes a Birth Certificate Joke While Campaigning in Michigan," *New York Times*, August 24, 2012, http://thecaucus. blogs.nytimes.com/2012/08/24/romney-makes-a-birther-joke-while- campaigning/?smid=fb-share.

117. Joe Feagin, *White Party, White Government: Race, Class, and U.S. Politics* (New York: Routledge, 2012), viii.

118. Tali Mendelberg, "Racial Priming Revived," *Perspectives on Politics* 6.1 (2008): 109–23.

119. Vincent L. Hutchings and Ashley E. Jardina, "Experiments on Racial Priming in Political Campaigns," *Annual Review of Political Science* 12 (2009): 397–402.

120. Ibid.

121. Ibid.

122. Ibid.

123. Ibid.

124. Ibid.

125. Ibid.

126. Stephen Caliendo and Charlton D. McIlwan, "Black Messages, White Messages: The Differential Use of Racial Appeals by Black and White Candidates," *Journal of Black Studies* 39.5 (2009): 732–43.

NOTES TO CHAPTER 5

1. Fred Slocum and Yeuh-Ting Lee, "Racism, Racial Stereotypes, and American Politics," in *The Psychology of Prejudice and Discrimination*, ed. Jean Lau Chin (Santa Barbara, CA: Greenwood, 2009), 15–30, quoting Stanley Greenberg, 1985.

2. Theodor W. Adorno et al., "Authoritarianism: 'Right' and 'Left,'" in *The Authoritarian Personality*, ed. Edward A. Shils (New York: Harper & Brothers, 1950), 28–42.

3. Bob Altemeyer, "The Other Authoritarian Personality," in *Advances in Experimental Social Psychology*, ed. Mark P. Zanna (San Diego, CA: Academic Press, 1998), 47–92; Bernard E. Whitley Jr., "Right-Wing Authoritarianism, Social Dominance Orientation, and Prejudice," *Journal of Personality and Social Psychology* 77.1 (1999): 126.

4. Bo Ekehammar and Nazar Akrami, "The Relation between Personality and Prejudice: A Variable- and a Person-Centered Approach," *European Journal of Personality* 17.6 (2003): 459.

5. Francis J. Flynn, "Having an Open Mind: The Impact of Openness to Experience on Interracial Attitudes and Impression Formation," *Journal of Personality and Social Psychology* 88.5 (2005): 816.

6. Alain van Hiel, Malgorzata Kossowska, and Ivan Mervielde, "The Relationship between Openness to Experience and Political Ideology," *Personality and Individual Differences* 28.4 (2000): 742.

7. Paul D. Trapnell, "Openness versus Intellect: A Lexical Left Turn," *European Journal of Personality* 8.4 (1994): 282.

8. Michael Tesler and David O. Sears, *Obama's Race: The 2008 Election and the Dream of a Post-Racial America* (Chicago: University of Chicago Press, 2010), 17–18.

9. See Paul M. Sniderman and Philip E. Tetlock, "Symbolic Racism: Problems of Motive Attribution in Political Analysis," *Journal of Social Issues* 42.2 (1986).

10. Maryon F. King and Gordon C. Bruner, "Social Desirability Bias: A Neglected Aspect of Validity Testing," *Psychology and Marketing* 17.2 (2000): 80; Douglas P. Crowne and David Marlowe, "A New Scale of Social Desirability Independent of Psychopathology," *Journal of Consulting Psychology* 24.4 (1960): 349.

11. Erving Goffman, "Embarrassment and Social Interaction," *American Journal of Sociology* 62.3 (1956): 265.

12. Brent Weiss and Robert S. Feldman, "Looking Good and Lying to Do It: Deception as an Impression Management Strategy in Job Interviews," *Journal of Applied Social Psychology* 36.4 (2006): 1074.

13. Hilary B. Bergsieker et al., "To Be Liked versus Respected: Divergent Goals in Interracial Interactions," *Journal of Personality and Social Psychology* 99.2 (2010): 249.

14. Jacquie D. Vorauer et al., "How Do Individuals Expect to Be Viewed by Members of Lower-Status Groups? Content and Implications of Meta-Stereotypes," *Journal of Personality and Social Psychology* 75.4 (1998): 917.

15. Anthony G. Greenwald and Mahzarin R. Banaji, "Implicit Social Cognition: Attitudes, Self-Esteem, and Stereotypes," *Psychological Review* 102.1 (1995): 10–11. Anthony G. Greenwald et al., "A Unified Theory of Implicit Attitudes, Stereotypes, Self-Esteem, and Self-Concept," *Psychological Review* 109.1 (2002): 18.

16. Daniel Kahneman and Shane Frederick, "Representativeness Revisited: Attribute Substitution in Intuitive Judgment," in *Heuristics and Biases: The Psychology of Intuitive Judgment*, ed. Thomas Gilovich et al. (New York: Cambridge University Press, 2002), 49–81; see also Steven A. Sloman, "Two Systems of Reasoning," in *Heuristics and Biases: The Psychology of Intuitive Judgment*, ed. Thomas Gilovich et al. (New York: Cambridge University Press, 2002), 379–96.

17. Ibid., 383.

18. *See* Richard E. Nisbett and Timothy D. Wilson, "Telling More Than We Can Know: Verbal Reports on Mental Processes," *Psychological Review* 84.3 (1977): 231 (noting that people's "reports are based on a priori, implicit causal theories, or judgments about the extent to which a particular stimulus is a plausible cause of a given response"); cf. Steven A. Sloman, "Two Systems of Reasoning," *Psychological Bulletin* 119.1 (1996): 15 (finding that "[t]he associative system however always has its opinion heard and, because of its speed and efficiency, often precedes and thus neutralizes the rule-based response").

19. Nisbett and Wilson, "Telling More Than We Can Know: Verbal Reports on Mental Processes," 231.

20. Timothy DeCamp Wilson and Richard E. Nisbett, "The Accuracy of Verbal Reports about the Effects of Stimuli on Evaluations and Behavior," *Social Psychology* 41.2 (1978): 123–24.

21. Ibid., 124.

22. Matthew Ratcliffe, *Rethinking Commonsense Psychology: A Critique of Folk Psychology, Theory of Mind, and Simulation* (New York: Palgrave MacMillan, 2007), 42; Daniel D. Hutto and Matthew Ratcliffe, *Folk Psychology Re-Assessed* (Dordrecht, The Netherlands: Springer, 2007), 2; Terrence Horgan and James Woodward, "Folk Psychology Is Here to Stay," in *Mind and Cognition: An Anthology*, ed. William G. Lycan and Jesse J. Prinz (Malden, MA: Wiley-Blackwell, 2008), 419–36.

23. Anna Wierzbicka, "Folk Conceptions of Mind, Agency, and Morality," *Journal of Cognition and Culture* 6.1–2 (2006): 169.

24. Martin T. Orne, "On the Social Psychology of the Psychological Experiment: With Particular Reference to Demand Characteristics and Their Implications," *American Psychologist* 17 (1962): 779; Milton J. Rosenberg, "The Conditions and Consequences of Evaluation Apprehension," in *Artifact in Behavioral Research*, ed. Robert Rosenthal and Ralph L. Rosnow (New York: Oxford University Press, 2009), 276–83; Stephen J. Weber and Thomas D. Cook, "Subject Effects

in Laboratory Research: An Examination of Subject Roles, Demand Characteristics, and Valid Inference," *Psychological Bulletin* 77.4 (1972): 278; see also Leon Festinger, *A Theory of Cognitive Dissonance* (Stanford, CA: Stanford University Press, 1957), 230–31 (aiding our understanding of individuals' inability to accurately identify the causes of their thought and behavior).

25. Daniel Kahneman, *Thinking Fast and Slow* (New York: Farrar, Straus, and Giroux, 2013).

26. Mahzarin R. Banaji and Anthony G. Greenwald, *Blindspot: Hidden Biases of Good People* (New York: Delacorte, 2013).

27. See Alice H. Eagly and Shelly Chaiken, "Attitude Structure and Function," in *The Handbook of Social Psychology*, ed. Daniel T. Gilbert, Susan T. Fiske, and Gardner Lindzey (New York: McGraw-Hill, 1998), 269–322.

28. Anthony G. Greenwald and Mahzarin R. Banaji, "Implicit Social Cognition," *Psychological Review* 102.1 (1995): 6.

29. Michael A. Olson and Russell H. Fazio, "Implicit and Explicit Measures of Attitudes: The Perspective of the MODE Model," in *Attitudes: Insights from the New Implicit Measures*, ed. Richard E. Petty et al. (New York: Psychology Press, 2009), 19–64.

30. Richard E. Petty, Russell H. Fazio, and Pablo Brinol, *Attitudes: Insights from the New Implicit Measures* (Abingdon, UK: Psychology Press, 2008).

31. Luigi Castelli, "Implicit In-group Metafavoritism: Subtle Preference for Ingroup Members Displaying In-group Bias," *Personality and Social Psychology Bulletin* 34.6 (2008): 807–18.

32. *See* supra note 30.

33. Roger Tourangeau, Lance J. Rips, and Kenneth Rasinski, *The Psychology of Survey Response* (Cambridge: Cambridge University Press, 2000), 302; Seymour Sudman, Norman M. Bradburn, and Norbert Schwarz, *Thinking about Answers: The Application of Cognitive Processes to Survey Methodology* (New York: Wiley, 1995), 75.

34. Bernd Wittenbrink and Norbert Schwartz, "Introduction," in *Implicit Measures of Attitudes*, ed. Bernd Wittenbrink and Norbert Schwartz (New York: Guilford, 2007), 1–16.

35. Russell H. Fazio, "On the Automatic Activation of Attitudes," *Journal of Personality and Social Psychology* 50.2 (1986): 229.

36. Ibid.

37. Russell H. Fazio et al., "Variability in Automatic Activation as an Unobtrusive Measure of Racial Attitudes: A Bona Fide Pipeline?" *Journal of Personality and Social Psychology* 69.6 (1995): 1015.

38. Dominika Maison, Anthony G. Greenwald, and Ralph H. Bruin, "Predictive Validity of the Implicit Association Test in Studies of Brands, Consumer Attitudes, and Behavior," *Journal of Consumer Psychology* 14.4 (2005): 405.

39. Malte Friese, Michaela Wanke, and Henning Plessner, "Implicit Consumer Preferences and Their Influences on Product Choice," *Psychology and Marketing* 23.9

(2006): 727. Finding that participants who possessed incongruent explicit and implicit preferences in regard to generic food products and well-known food brands were more likely to choose the implicitly preferred brand when choices were made under time pressure.

40. Anthony G. Greenwald and Linda Hamilton Krieger, "Implicit Bias: Scientific Foundations," *California Law Review* 94.4 (2006): 945–67, 958.

41. "Teaching Tolerance," *Southern Poverty Law Center*, http://tolerance.org.

42. John T. Jost, Mahzarin R. Banaji, and Brian A. Nosek, "A Decade of System Justification Theory: Accumulated Evidence of Conscious and Unconscious Bolstering of the Status Quo," *Political Psychology* 25.6 (2004): 881–919, 897.

43. Jack Citrin and Donald Green, "The Self-Interest Motive in American Public Opinion," *Research in Micropolitics* 3 (1990); Donald R. Kinder and Lynn M. Sanders, *Divided by Color: Racial Politics and Democratic Ideals* (Chicago: University of Chicago Press, 1996), 203; John B. McConahay, "Modern Racism and Modern Discrimination: The Effects of Race, Racial Attitudes, and Context on Simulated Hiring Decisions," *Personality and Social Psychology Bulletin* 9.4 (1983): 551; David O. Sears, "Symbolic Racism," in *Eliminating Racism: Profiles in Controversy*, ed. Phyllis A. Katz and Dalmas A. Taylor (New York: Springer-Verlag, 1988), 53–84.

44. Howard Schuman et al., *Racial Attitudes in America: Trends and Interpretations*, rev. ed. (Cambridge, MA: Harvard University Press, 1997); Sears, "Symbolic Racism."

45. Kristina A. Lane and John T. Jost, "Black Man in the White House: Ideology and Implicit Racial Bias in the Age of Obama," in *The Obamas and a (Post) Racial America?* ed. Gregory S. Parks and Matthew W. Hughey (New York: Oxford University Press, 2011), 48–69.

46. Paul M. Sniderman, Gretchen C. Crosby, and William G. Howell, "The Politics of Race," in *Racialized Politics: The Debate about Racism in America*, ed. David O. Sears, Jim Sidanius, and Lawrence Bobo (Chicago: University of Chicago Press, 2000), 236–79; Paul M. Sniderman and Edward G. Carmines, *Reaching beyond Race* (Cambridge, MA: Harvard University Press, 1997), 78.

47. Ibid.

48. Paul M. Sniderman, Richard A. Brody, and James H. Kuklinski, "Policy Reasoning and Political Values: The Problem of Racial Equality," *American Journal of Political Science* 28.1 (1984): 84; Paul M. Sniderman et al., "The New Racism," *American Journal of Political Science* 35.2 (1991): 426.

49. Sniderman and Carmines, *Reaching Beyond Race*, 91; Paul M. Sniderman and Thomas Piazza, *The Scar of Race* (Cambridge, MA: Harvard University Press, 1993), 112; Sniderman et al., "The New Racism," 426.

50. Ibid.

51. Christopher M. Frederico and James Sidanius, "Racism, Ideology, and Affirmative Action Revisited: The Antecedents and Consequences of 'Principled

Objections' to Affirmative Action," *Journal of Personality and Social Psychology* 82.4 (2002): 488–502, 489.

52. Paul M. Sniderman et al., "Reasoning Chains: Causal Models of Policy Reasoning in Mass Publics," *British Journal of Political Science* 16.4 (1986): 417; Sniderman et al., "The New Racism," 437.

53. Jerry Z. Muller, "Conservatism: Historical Aspects," in *International Encyclopedia of the Social and Behavioral Sciences*, ed. Neil J. Smelser and Paul B. Baltes (Oxford, England: Elsevier, 2001), 2624–28; Fred N. Kerlinger, *Liberalism and Conservatism: The Nature and Structure of Social Attitudes* (Hillsdale, NJ: Erlbaum, 1984); Samuel P. Huntington, "Conservatism as an Ideology," *American Political Science Review* 51.2 (1957): 455.

54. Brian A. Nosek, Mahzarin R. Banaji, and John T. Jost, "The Politics of Intergroup Attitudes," in *The Social and Psychological Bases of Ideology and System Justification*, ed. John T. Jost, Aaron C. Kay, and Hulda Thorisdottir (New York: Oxford University Press, 2009), 486–87.

55. Ibid.

56. William A. Cunningham, John B. Nezlek, and Mahzarin R. Banaji, "Implicit and Explicit Ethnocentrism: Revisiting the Ideologies of Prejudice," *Personality and Social Psychology Bulletin* 30.10 (2004): 1333; John T. Jost, Mahzarin R. Banaji, and Brian A. Nosek, "A Decade of System Justification Theory: Accumulated Evidence of Conscious and Unconscious Bolstering of the Status Quo," *Political Psychology* 25.6 (2004): 881.

57. Ibid., 902. So also, some research does indicate that while liberals and conservatives differ substantially in their explicit preferences, they are much more similar at the implicit level. Still, at both the explicit and implicit levels, conservatives showed little discrepancy in their strong preference for higher-status groups. In contrast, liberals demonstrated a larger discrepancy between their implicit preference for higher-status persons and their relatively weaker explicit preference for higher-status persons.

58. Andrew Scott Baron and Mahzarin R. Banaji, "The Development of Implicit Attitudes: Evidence of Race Evaluations from Age 6 and 10 and Adulthood," *Psychological Science* 17.1 (2006): 53–58, 55–56.

59. Stacey Sinclair, Elizabeth Dunn, and Brian S. Lowery, "The Relationship between Parental Racial Attitudes and Children's Implicit Prejudice," *Journal of Experimental Social Psychology* 41.3 (2005): 283.

60. Luigi Castelli, Cristina Zogmaister, and Silvia Tomelleri, "The Transmission of Racial Attitudes within the Family," *Developmental Psychology* 45.2 (2009): 586.

NOTES TO CHAPTER 6

1. Kirk Johnson, "Despite the Evidence, 'Birther' Bills Advance," *New York Times*, April 22, 2011, A11.

2. Stewart M. Powell and Hillary Sorin, "Texas Lawmakers Fan Flames over Candidate Citizenship Bill," *Houston Chronicle*, August 2, 2009, http://www.

chron.com/news/houston-texas/article/Texas-lawmakers-fan-flames-over-candidate-1720081.php.

3. "Arizona Gov. Vetoes Presidential Birther Bill," *Carroll County Times*, April 19, 2011.

4. "Congressman to Introduce Birther Bill," *UPI NewsTrack*, April 29, 2011, http://www.upi.com/Top_News/US/2011/04/29/Congressman-to-introduce-birther-bill/UPI-84581304118259.

5. James Oliphant and Christi Parsons, "Obama Seeks to Defuse 'Birthers': Release of His Long-Form Birth Certificate Is Called an Attempt to Get On with More Serious Issues," *Philadelphia Inquirer*, April 28, 2011, http://articles.philly.com/2011-04-28/news/29483101_1_birther-theories-president-obama-independent-voters.

6. Johnson, "Despite the Evidence, 'Birther' Bills Advance."

7. Powell and Sorin, "Texas Lawmakers Fan Flames over Candidate Citizenship Bill."

8. Ibid.

9. Ibid.

10. John Distaso, "'Birther' Bill Effective Date Moved to after 2012 Election," *New Hampshire Union Leader*, March 9, 2011.

11. Brad Bumsted, "Pa. Birther Bill's Odds Improve, Analyst Says," *Pittsburgh Tribune-Review*, April 19, 2011.

12. "Arizona Gov. Vetoes Presidential Birther Bill," *CBS News,* April 18, 2011, http://www.cbsnews.com/2100-250_162-20055129.html.

13. Ibid.

14. Kirk Johnson, "State Legislatures Take Up 'Birther' Bills: Lawmakers from Conservative Regions Push Measures," *San Jose Mercury News*, April 22, 2011.

15. Johnson, "Despite the Evidence, 'Birther' Bills Advance."

16. Nathanael Yowell, "Birther Going Forward Despite That Obama Released His Birth Certificate," *Shreveport Examiner*, April 30, 2011, http://www.examiner.com/article/birther-bill-going-forward-despite-that-obama-released-his-birth-certificate.

17. Nathanael Yowell, "Governor Jindal Will Sign Birther Bill, If Passed by State Legislature," *Shreveport Examiner*, April 20, 2011, http://www.examiner.com/article/governor-jindal-will-sign-birther-bill-if-passed-by-state-legislature.

18. Ibid.

19. John Pirro, "Democrats Attack Filing of State 'Birther' Bill," *Chronicle*, February 28, 2011.

20. Ibid.

21. Eloisa Ruano Gonzalez, "Make Presidential Candidates Have Parents Born in U.S.?" *Orlando Sentinel*, February 28, 2011.

22. Duge Butler Jr., "Birtherism Comes to Indiana," *Indianapolis Examiner*, May 1, 2011.

23. Matthew W. Hughey, "The (Dis)Similarities of White Racial Identities: The Conceptual Framework of 'Hegemonic Whiteness,'" *Ethnic and Racial Studies*

33.8 (2010): 1300; Matthew W. Hughey, "Show Me Your Papers! Obama's Birth and the Whiteness of Belonging," *Qualitative Sociology* 35.2 (2012): 165.

24. Michael Mello, "Buena Park Pastor Files Lawsuit to Keep Obama from Taking Office," *Orange County Register*, November 20, 2008.

25. Keyes v. Bowen, 189 Cal.App.4th 647, 654 (Cal. App. 2010).

26. Ibid., 662.

27. James Jenega, "Lawsuit Contesting Barack Obama's Citizenship Heads to Supreme Court," *Pittsburgh Post-Gazette*, December 5, 2008.

28. David G. Savage, "Dual Lawsuits Attack Obama's U.S. Citizenship," *Los Angeles Times*, December 8, 2008.

29. Ibid.

30. Ewa Kochanska, "Georgia 'Birther Soldier' Lawsuit Thrown Out," *Atlanta Examiner*, September 19, 2009, http://www.examiner.com/article/georgia-birther-soldier-lawsuit-thrown-out.

31. Ibid.

32. Ibid.

33. Ibid.

34. Ibid.

35. Reggie Oh and Frank Wu, "The Evolution of Race in the Law: The Supreme Court Moves from Approving Internment of Japanese Americans to Disapproving Affirmative Action for African Americans," *Michigan Journal of Race and the Law* 1 (1996): 173.

36. Hussein Ibish and Anne Stewart, *Against Arab Americans: The Post–September 11 Backlash (September 11, 2001–October 11, 2002)* (Washington, DC: American-Arab Anti-Discrimination Committee, 2003), http://www.adc.org/PDF/hcr02.pdf; Jack Levin and Jack McDevitt, *Hate Crimes Revisited: America's War on Those Who Are Different* (New York: Basic Books, 2002), 48.

37. Studs Terkel, *Race: How Blacks and Whites Think and Feel about the American Obsession* (New York: New Press, 1992), v (quoting a 1990 University of Chicago National Opinion Research Center survey).

38. Thierry Devos and Mahzarin R. Banaji, "American = White," *Journal of Personality and Social Psychology* 88 (2005): 452–53.

39. Thierry Devos et al., *Is Barack Obama American Enough to Be the Next President? The Role of Racial and National Identity in American Politics* (San Diego State University, 2008), http://www.rohan.sdsu.edu/~tdevos/thd/Devos_spsp2008.pdf.

40. Ran R. Hassin et al., "Précis of Implicit Nationalism," *Annals of the New York Academy of Sciences* 1167 (2009): 143.

41. Kristel Gerow et al., "Is Obama the Anti-Christ? Racial Priming, Extreme Criticisms of Barack Obama, and Attitudes toward the 2008 US Presidential Candidates," *Journal of Experimental Social Psychology* 46 (2010): 864.

42. Lee Harris, "The Tea Party vs. the Intellectuals," *Policy Review* no. 161 (2010): 3.

43. Ibid., 9.

44. Vanessa Williamson, Theda Skocpol, and John Coggin, "The Tea Party and the Remaking of Republican Conservatism," *Perspectives on Politics* 9.1 (2011): 25.

45. Zachary Courser, "The Tea Party at the Election," *Forum* 8.4 (2010): 1.

46. Williamson, Skocpol, and Coggin, "The Tea Party and the Remaking of Republican Conservatism," 26.

47. Harris, "The Tea Party vs. the Intellectuals," 4–5.

48. Ibid., 3.

49. Charles M. Blow, "Genuflecting to the Tea Party," *New York Times*, August 13, 2011, A19.

50. DeWayne Wickham, "GOP's Disrespect of Obama Goes beyond the Debt Fight," *USA Today*, August 2, 2011.

51. John Larson on *Hardball with Chris Matthews*, MSNBC, July 28, 2011, http://www.msnbc.msn.com/id/43989577/ns/msnbc-hardball_with_chris_matthews/t/hardball-chris-matthews-thursday-july/#.UIOBHIb-2KI.

52. Frank Newport, "Tea Party Supporters Overlap Republican Base," *Gallup*, July 2, 2010, http://www.gallup.com/poll/141098/tea-party-supporters-overlap-republican-base.aspx.

53. Alexander Bolton, "Tea Party's Heyday Could Be Nearing End, Say Political Experts," *Hill*, August 14, 2011, http://thehill.com/homenews/news/176799-tea-partys-heyday-may-be-coming-to-an-end-say-political-experts.

54. Paul Kane, "'Tea Party' Protesters Accused of Spitting on Lawmaker, Using Slurs," *Washington Post*, March 20, 2010, http://www.washingtonpost.com/wp-dyn/content/article/2010/03/20/AR2010032002556.html.

55. Patrik Jonsson, "Why Tea Party Defenders Won't Let N-word Claims Rest," *Christian Science Monitor*, April 28, 2010, http://www.csmonitor.com/USA/2010/0428/Why-tea-party-defenders-won-t-let-N-word-claims-rest.

56. Paul Kane, "'Tea Party' Protesters Accused of Spitting on Lawmaker, Using Slurs."

57. Ibid.

58. Kate Zernike, "Republicans Strain to Ride Tea Party Tiger," *New York Times*, January 23, 2010, A1.

59. Patrik Jonsson, "Amid Harsh Criticisms, 'Tea Party' Slips into the Mainstream," *Christian Science Monitor*, April 3, 2010, http://www.csmonitor.com/USA/Politics/2010/0403/Amid-harsh-criticisms-tea-party-slips-into-the-mainstream.

60. Ibid.

61. Steven Rattner, "Republican Extremism, Bad Economics," *New York Times*, August 15, 2011, http://www.nytimes.com/2011/08/16/opinion/republican-extremism-bad-economics.html.

62. Alex Altman, "In Ohio, the Tea Party Rallies around Opposition to Health Care Mandate," *Time*, July 6, 2011, http://swampland.time.com/2011/07/06/in-ohio-the-tea-party-rallies-around-opposition-to-health-care-mandate.

63. Carl Hulse and David M. Herszenhorn, "A Quick Move from Tea Party to Flex Muscle," *New York Times*, November 5, 2010, A1.

64. Laurie A. Rudman and Richard D. Ashmore, "Discrimination and the Implicit Association Test," *Group Processes & Intergroup Relations* 10.3 (2007): 363–68.

65. Efrén O. Pérez, "Explicit Evidence on the Import of Implicit Attitudes: The IAT and Immigration Policy Judgments," *Political Behavior* 32.4 (2010): 517.

66. Jon Hurwitz and Mark Peffley, "Playing the Race Card in a Post–Willie Horton Era: The Impact of Racialized Code Words on Support for Punitive Crime Policy," *Policy Opinion Quarterly* 69.1(2005): 109.

67. Eric D. Knowles et al., "Racial Prejudice Predicts Opposition to Obama and His Health Care Reform Plan," *Journal of Experimental Social Psychology* 46 (2009): 423.

68. Theda Skocpol and Vanessa Williamson, *The Tea Party and the Remaking of Republican Conservatism* (New York: Oxford University Press, 2012), 155.

69. Geoffrey Kabaservice, *Rule and Ruin: The Downfall of Moderation and the Destruction of the Republican Party, from Eisenhower to the Tea Party* (New York: Oxford University Press, 2012), 389.

70. Ibid.

71. Robert Seltzer, "Bigotry Unveiled on the Campaign Trail," *San Antonio Express-News*, October 19, 2008.

72. Ibid.

73. Ibid.

74. Bo Emerson, "Politically Correct? Not This Bar Owner," *Atlanta Journal-Constitution*, May 15, 2008, B1.

75. "Doll 'Pure Racism,'" *Grand Rapids Press*, June 15, 2008, A4.

76. Sean Delonas, "Sean Delonas Cartoon," *New York Post*, February 18, 2009, http://www.nypost.com/opinion/cartoons/delonas.htm.

77. Dora Apel, "Just Joking? Chimps, Obama, and Racial Stereotype," *Journal of Visual Culture* 8.2 (2009): 134.

78. Ibid.

79. See Sarah Kershaw, "Police Shooting Reunites Circle of Common Law," *New York Times*, December 2, 2006, A1. (This article also mentions black shooting victims Patrick M. Dorismond, Gidone Busch, Malcolm Ferguson, Timothy Stansbury Jr., and thirteen-year-old Nicholas Heyward Jr., as well as Abner Louima, a Haitian immigrant who was brutalized and sodomized with a toilet plunger by New York City police officers outside a Brooklyn nightclub in 2007.)

80. Apel, "Just Joking? Chimps, Obama, and Racial Stereotype," 134.

81. Ibid.

82. Elaine De Valle, "'Monkeys' amid Display of Obama Books Outrages," *Miami Herald*, March 8, 2009.

83. Ibid.

84. Monica Drake, "Clarkston Residents: Racism Is a Problem within Community," *Oakland Press*, April 6, 2011, http://theoaklandpress.com/articles/2011/04/06/news/local_news/doc4d9bc3ed68f0a545672946.txt?viewmode=fullstory.

85. Brian Martinez, "OC Republican Allegedly Sent Offensive Email," *Orange County Register*, April 17, 2011, http://www.ocregister.com/articles/davenport-296732-county-party.html.
86. Ibid.
87. "California GOP Member Censured over Joke," *UPI NewsTrack*, May 5, 2011, http://www.upi.com/Top_News/US/2011/05/05/California-GOP-member-censured-over-joke/UPI-25501304612069.
88. "Republican Denounced for Racist Email," *UPI News Service*, April 17, 2011, http://www.upi.com/Top_News/US/2011/04/17/Republican-denounced-for-racist-e-mail/UPI-73041303071387.
89. "California GOP Member Censured over Joke."
90. "Republican Denounced for Racist Email," *Black Radio Network,* April 18, 2011, http://www.blackradionetwork.com/republican_denounced_for_racist_email.
91. Ibid.
92. Martin Wisckol, "Obama Chimp Photo: GOP Boss Wants Action Now," *Orange County Register*, April 18, 2011.
93. "Sergeant Suspended for Obama Note in Scripture," *Sarasota Herald-Tribune*, January 4, 2012, http://www.heraldtribune.com/article/20110104/ARTICLE/101041044/2055/NEWS?Title=Sergeant-suspended-for-Obama-note-in-scripture&tc=ar.
94. Nick Wings, "Florida Corrections Officer Suspended for 'Obama Prayer' Calling for President's Death," *Huffington Post,* January 4, 2011, http://www.huffingtonpost.com/2011/01/04/florida-obama-prayer-psalm-109_n_804221.html.
95. Ralina L. Joseph, "Imagining Obama: Reading Overtly and Inferentially Racist Images of our 44th President, 2007–2008," *Communication Studies* 62.4 (2011): 389.
96. Ibid.
97. Ibid.
98. Ibid.
99. Gregory S. Parks and Danielle C. Heard, "'Assassinate the Nigger Ape': Obama, Implicit Imagery, and the Dire Consequences of Racist Jokes," *Rutgers Race and Law Review* 11.2 (2010): 270.
100. Ibid., 270.
101. Ibid., 272.
102. Ibid., 274.
103. Ibid.
104. Ibid., 275.
105. Ibid, 276.
106. Ibid., 277.
107. Phillip Atiba Goff et al., "Not Yet Human: Implicit Knowledge, Historical Dehumanization, and Contemporary Consequences," *Journal of Personality & Social Psychology* 94.2 (2008): 295.
108. Ibid.

109. Ibid.
110. Arlen C. Moller and Edward L. Deci, "Interpersonal Control, Dehumaniza-tion, and Violence: A Self-Determination Theory Perspective," *Group Process & Intergroup Relations* 13.1 (2009): 43.
111. Tobias Greitemeyer and Neil McLatchie, "Denying Humanness to Others: A Newly Discovered Mechanism by Which Violent Video Games Increase Aggres-sive Behavior," *Psychological Science* 22.5 (2011): 659.
112. Emmanuele Castano and Roger Giner-Sorolla, "Not Quite Human: Infrahu-manization in Response to Intergroup Killing," *Journal of Personality and Social Psychology* 90.5 (2006): 804.
113. Moller and Deci, "Interpersonal Control, Dehumanization, and Violence: A Self-Determination Theory Perspective," 44.
114. Greitemeyer and McLatchie, "Denying Humanness to Others: A Newly Discov-ered Mechanism by Which Violent Video Games Increase Aggressive Behavior," 659.
115. Ibid., 805.
116. Albert Bandura, Bill Underwood, and Michael E. Fromson, "Disinhibition of Aggression through Diffusion of Responsibility and Dehumanization of Vic-tims," *Journal of Research in Personality* 9.4 (1975): 253.
117. Ibid., 255.
118. Ibid.
119. Ibid., 254.
120. Ibid., 43–44.
121. Ibid.
122. Ibid., 664.
123. Castano and Giner-Sorolla, "Not Quite Human: Infrahumanization in Response to Intergroup Killing," 805.
124. Ibid., 806.
125. "40 Violent Incidents and the Right-Wing Rhetoric That Presaged Them," *Alter-net,* January 10, 2011, http://www.alternet.org/story/149468/40_violent_inci-dents_and_the_right-wing_rhetoric_that_presaged_them.
126. See *Treasury, Postal Service and General Government Appropriations Act.* Public Law 103–329, *U.S. Statutes at Large* 108 (1994): 2382.
127. See Ronald Kessler, *In the President's Secret Service: Behind the Scenes with Agents in the Line of Fire and the Presidents They Protect* (New York: Crown, 2009), 225.
128. Jon Cohen and Michael Fletcher, "Far Fewer Consider Racism Big Problem: Little Change, However, at Local Level," *Washington Post,* January 19, 2009, A6.
129. Ibid.
130. Ibid.
131. Marisol Bello, "Blacks in Poll More Optimistic about the Future, Respondents Say Their Lives Have Gotten Better since 5 Years Ago," *New York Times,* January 13, 2000, 2A.
132. Ibid.

133. Ibid.
134. Thompson Krissah, "Blacks' View of Race Relations Surging, Pew Study Finds," *Washington Post*, January 12, 2010, Business section.
135. Lola Adesioye, "Change, for Good and Ill," *Guardian*, November 1, 2009, http://www.guardian.co.uk/commentisfree/cifamerica/2009/oct/30/barack-obama-race.
136. Frank Newport, "Blacks, Whites Differ on Government's Role in Civil Rights," *Gallup*, August 19, 2011, http://www.gallup.com/poll/149087/blacks-whites-differ-government-role-civil-rights.aspx.
137. Ibid.
138. Ibid.
139. Richard P. Eibach and Joyce Ehrlinger, "Keep Your Eyes on the Prize: Reference Points and Racial Differences in Assessing Progress toward Equality," *Personality and Social Psychology Bulletin* 32.1 (2006): 70.
140. Ibid.
141. Amanda B. Brodish et al., "More Eyes on the Prize: Variability in White Americans' Perceptions of Progress toward Racial Equality," *Personality and Social Psychology Bulletin* 34.4 (2008): 514.
142. Cheryl R. Kaiser et al., "The Ironic Consequences of Obama's Election: Decreased Support for Social Justice," *Journal of Experimental Social Psychology* 45 (2009): 556.
143. Ibid.
144. See, e.g., Shelby Steele, "Obama's Post-Racial Promise: Barack Obama Seduced Whites with a Vision of Their Racial Innocence Precisely to Coerce Them into Acting out of a Racial Motivation," *Los Angeles Times*, November 5, 2008, A31.
145. Roger Clegg, "Voting Rights and Equal Protection: The Future of the Voting Rights Act after Bartlett and NAMUDNO," *Cato Supreme Court Review* 35 (2009): 50 (arguing that both section 2 and section 5 have been so successful that it makes sense at this point "to scrap the law altogether and start anew").
146. *Voting Rights Act*, U.S. Code 42 (2006), § 1973(b).
147. Thornburg v. Gingles, 478 U.S. 30 (1986).
148. Gilda R. Daniels, "A Vote Delayed Is a Vote Denied: A Proactive Approach to Eliminating Election Administration Legislation That Disenfranchises Unwanted Voters," *University of Louisville Law Review* 47 (2008): 66.
149. *Voting Rights Act*, U.S. Code 42 (2000) § 1973c(a).
150. Beer v. United States, 425 U.S. 130, 141 (1976).
151. *Voting Rights Act*, U.S. Code 42 (1973) § 1973c(a).
152. Gilda R. Daniels, "Racial Redistricting in a Post-Racial World," *Cardozo Law Review* 32.3 (2011): 947.
153. Shaw v. Reno, 509 U.S. 630, 637 (1993).
154. Ibid., 641.
155. Ibid.
156. Ibid., 644.

157. *See* ibid., 642, 655.

158. Lawyer v. Department of Justice, 521 U.S. 567 (1997).

159. Ibid., 582.

160. Georgia v. Ashcroft, 539 U.S. 461, 461 (2003).

161. Ibid., 478.

162. Ibid., 480.

163. Bartlett v. Strickland, 129 S. Ct. 1231, 1240 (2009).

164. Daniels, "Racial Redistricting in a Post-Racial World," 960.

165. Michael Tesler and David O. Sears, *Obama's Race: The 2008 Election and the Dream of a Post-Racial America* (Chicago: University of Chicago Press, 2010), 36.

166. B. Keith Payne et al., "Implicit and Explicit Prejudice in the 2008 American Presidential Election," *Journal of Experimental Social Psychology* 46.2 (2010): 367.

167. Anthony G. Greenwald et al., "Implicit Race Attitudes Predicted Vote in the 2008 U.S. Presidential Election," *Analyses of Social Issues and Public Policy* 9.1 (2009): 241–42.

168. Tesler and Sears, *Obama's Race: The 2008 Election and the Dream of a Post-Racial America,* 36–37.

169. Ibid., 48–49.

170. Ibid., 50.

171. Ibid., 72.

172. Daniel A. Effron, Jessica S. Cameron, and Benoît Monin, "Endorsing Obama Licenses Favoring Whites," *Journal of Experimental Social Psychology* 45 (2009): 590.

173. Eric D. Knowles, Brian S. Lowery, and Rebecca L. Schaumberg, "Anti-Egalitarians for Obama? Group-Dominance Motivation and the Obama Vote," *Journal of Experimental Social Psychology* 45 (2009): 965.

NOTES TO THE CONCLUSION

1. Eli Epstein, "Karl Rove and Fox News Argue over Who Won the Election," *International Business Times,* November 7, 2012.

2. Robbie Brown, "Anti-Obama Protest at Ole Miss Turns Unruly," *New York Times,* November 8, 2012, P9.

3. Nick Wing, "Donald Trump: Election Is 'Total Sham and a Travesty,' Suggests 'Revolution' Is Necessary," *Huffington Post,* November 7, 2012.

4. Yamiche Alcindor, "Slurs, Protests at Colleges Unveil Racial Animosities: Post-Election Incidents Show Setbacks in Relations Despite Progress," *USA Today,* November 12, 2012.

5. Eugene Robinson, "A New America Spoke in Tuesday's Election," *Lawton Constitution,* November 12, 2012.

6. Jenée Desmond-Harris, "Crazy Talk: O'Reilly on Blacks and Self-Reliance," *Michigan Chronicle,* November 20, 2012.

7. "'Demoralized' Ann Coulter to Laura Ingraham: 'It's Over, There Is No Hope,'" *Huffington Post,* November 8, 2012.

8. Michael Shear and Jennifer Steinhauer, "Ryan Sees Urban Vote as Reason G.O.P. Lost," *New York Times*, 13 November, 2012, http://www.nytimes.com/2012/11/14/us/politics/ryan-sees-urban-vote-as-reason-gop-lost.html?_r=0.

9. Ashley Parker, "Romney Blames Loss on Obama's 'Gifts' to Minorities and Young Voters," *Caucus*, November 14, 2012, http://thecaucus.blogs.nytimes.com/2012/11/14/romney-blames-loss-on-obamas-gifts-to-minorities-and-young-voters.

10. Shear and Steinhauer, "Ryan Sees Urban Vote as Reason G.O.P. Lost."

11. Mark Hugo Lopez, Rich Morin, and Paul Taylor, "Illegal Immigration Backlash Worries, Divides Latinos," *Pew Hispanic*, October 28, 2010, http://www.pewhispanic.org/2010/10/28/illegal-immigration-backlash-worries-divides-latinos.

12. Geraldo Cadava, "The GOP Doesn't Need Hispanic Outreach—It Needs a Hispanic Takeover," *Atlantic*, May 1, 2013, http://www.theatlantic.com/politics/archive/2013/05/the-gop-doesnt-need-hispanic-outreach-it-needs-a-hispanic-takeover/275401.

13. Paula D. McClain, Niambi M. Carter, and Michael C. Brad, "Gender and Black Presidential Politics: From Chisholm to Moseley Braun," *Journal of Women, Politics, and Policy* (2005): 56.

14. Ibid., 57.

15. Id.

16. James Haskins, *Fighting Shirley Chisholm* (New York: Dial, 1985), 158.

17. Brad Koplinski, *Hats in the Ring: Conversations with Presidential Candidates* (Sacramento, CA: Presidential, 2000), 100.

18. McClain, Carter, and Brad, "Gender and Black Presidential Politics: From Chisholm to Mosely Braun," 57.

19. Ibid., 57–58.

20. Ibid., 56 (citing Shirley Chisholm, *Fighting the Good Fight* [New York: Harper & Row, 1973], 3).

21. "Jesse Jackson: Biography," *Biography.com*, n.d., http://www.biography.com/people/jesse-jackson-9351181?page=2 (last visited May 23, 2013).

22. Ibid.

23. Ibid.

24. Katherine Tate, "Black Political Participation in the 1984 and 1988 Presidential Elections," *American Political Science Review* (1991): 1159, 1160, 1168.

25. Ibid., 1168; "Jesse Jackson."

26. "Jesse Jackson."

27. Tate, "Black Political Participation in the 1984 and 1988 Presidential Elections," 1169.

28. McClain, Carter, and Brad, "Gender and Black Presidential Politics: From Chisholm to Mosely Braun," 58.

29. Ibid., 60.

30. Ibid., 59.

31. Ibid., 60.

32. Ibid., 59.
33. Ibid.
34. Ibid.
35. Seth Gitell, "Al Sharpton for President?" *Phoenix*, September 28, 2013, http://bostonphoenix.com/boston/news_features/top/features/documents/02179035.htm (last visited May 23, 2013).
36. "Candidates: Al Sharpton," *CNN.com*, n.d., http://www.cnn.com/ELECTION/2004/special/president/candidates/sharpton.html (last visited May 23, 2013).
37. Ibid.
38. Ibid.
39. Adolph Reed Jr., "The Puzzle of Black Republicans," *New York Times*, December 18, 2012.
40. B. D. Orey, "Explaining Black Conservatives: Racial Uplift or Racial Resentment?" *Black Scholar* 34.1 (2004): 18–22.
41. Linda Greene, "From Tokenism to Emancipatory Politics: The Conferences and Meetings of Law Professors of Color," *Michigan Journal of Race and Law* 5 (1999): 178.
42. Ibid., 179.
43. Ibid., 179.
44. Pamela Braboy Jackson et al., "Composition of the Workplace and Psychological Well-Being: The Effects of Tokenism on America's Black Elite," *Social Forces* 74 (1995): 544–45.
45. Ibid., 543.
46. Ibid., 545.
47. Ibid.
48. Ibid.
49. Ibid., 549.
50. Ibid., 550.
51. Ibid., 551.
52. Ibid., 552–53.
53. Lani Guinier, "The Triumph of Tokenism: The Voting Rights Act and the Theory of Black Electoral Success," *Michigan Law Review* 89 (1991): 1079–80.
54. Ibid.
55. Ibid., 1117.
56. Ibid., 1111.
57. Roger W. Reinsch et al., "Applying Indices Post-Grutter to Monitor Progress towards Attaining a Diverse Student Body," *Northwestern Journal of Law and Social Policy* 7 (2012): 385.
58. Ibid., 388.
59. Brian Sullivan, "Your World with Neil Cavuto," *Fox News*, September 24, 2010.
60. Samela Harris, "Race to Topple Obama," *Advertiser* (Australia), October 4, 2011.
61. Shannon McCaffrey, "Tea Party Favorite Sets Sights on White House: 'Hermanator' Has Grassroots Support," (Newark, NJ) *Star-Ledger*, May 22, 2011.

62. James Oliphant, "Herman Cain Drops out of Presidential Race," *Los Angeles Times*, December 3, 2011.

63. William Jelani Cobb, "Herman Cain's Race-Free Campaign," *Washington Post*, October 9, 2011; Andrea Peyser, "He Won't Be Stereotyped," *New York Post*, October 20, 2011.

64. Jason L. Riley, "Cain's Post-Racial Promise," *Wall Street Journal*, October 7, 2007, A13.

65. Herman Cain, *This Is Herman Cain! My Journey to the White House* (New York: Simon & Schuster, 2011), 18.

66. Douglas A. Blackmon and Neil King Jr., "Herman Cain's Political Education," *Wall Street Journal*, November 25, 2011, A1.

67. Ibid.

68. Fredricka Whitfield, "Jobs Bill Looms in Senate," *CNN Newsroom*, October 9, 2011.

69. Eric Deggans, "Is This High-Tech Lynching? Hardly," *St. Petersburg* (FL) *Times*, November 6, 2011.

70. William Jelani Cobb, "The GOP's Cynical Embrace of Herman Cain," *Washington Post*, October 7, 2011.

71. Joy-Ann Reid, "Cain Playing the Race Card," *Miami Herald*, November 2, 2011.

72. Clarence Page, "Cain's Racial Offense," *Chicago Tribune*, October 16, 2011.

73. Ibid.

74. Sandhya Somashekhar, "Cain Plays the Race Card and Plays It His Way," *Washington Post*, October 22, 2011.

75. Ibid.

76. Eugene Robinson, "Raising Herman Cain," *Washington Post*, October 14, 2011.

77. Page, "Cain's Racial Offense."

78. Darryl E. Owens, "Blacks Can't Afford Cain's Painful Antics," *Orlando Sentinel*, December 3, 2011.

79. Annette John-Hall, "Cain's Civil Rights Movement Alibi Not So Fast," *Philadelphia Inquirer*, October 14, 2011.

80. Somashekhar, "Cain Plays the Race Card and Plays It His Way."

81. Tony Norman, "Black GOP Candidate Missing Right Words," *Pittsburgh Post-Gazette*, June 24, 2011.

82. Vanessa Williams, "In Claims on Black Vote, Rose-Colored Glasses?" *Washington Post*, November 25, 2011, C1.

83. Jesse Holland, "The Return of Racial Politics," (Arlington Heights, IL) *Daily Herald*, November 7, 2011.

84. Ibid.

85. Hermene Hartman, "The Making of Herman Cain," *Huffington Post*, November 7, 2011, http://www.huffingtonpost.com/hermene-hartman/the-making-of-herman-cain_b_1077076.html.

86. Holland, "The Return of Racial Politics."

87. Merlene Davis, "When Herman Cain Cries Racism, He's Really Crying Wolf," *Lexington* (KY) *Herald-Leader*, November 6, 2011.

88. Tony Norman, "Whites in GOP Find Comfort in Cain," *Pittsburgh Post-Gazette*, November 4, 2011.

89. Armstrong Williams, "Can Cain Explain?" *Washington* (DC) *Times*, November 7, 2011.

90. Holland, "The Return of Racial Politics."

91. Jerry Z. Muller, "Conservatism: Historical Aspects," in *International Encyclopedia of the Social and Behavioral Sciences*, edited by Neil J. Smelser and Paul B. Baltes (Oxford: Elsevier, 2011), 2624–28; Fred N. Kerlinger, *Liberalism and Conservativism: The Nature and Structure of Social Attitudes* (Hillsdale, NJ: Erlbaum); Samuel P. Huntington, 1957, "Conservatism as an Ideology," *American Political Science Review* 51.2 (1984): 454–73.

92. Paul W. Eastwick et al., "Is Love Colorblind? Political Orientation Moderates Interracial Romantic Desire," *Personality and Social Psychology Bulletin* 35.9 (2009): 1258–68.

93. "Colin Powell: Sununu and GOP Dark Vein of Intolerance," *Miscellany Blue*, Jan. 13, 2013.

94. Mike Vilensky, "Trump Roasted and Skewered at White House Correspondents' Dinner," *New York Magazine,* May 1, 2011.

95. Ibid.

96. "How Obama Trumped Donald . . . with a Joke," *Daily Mail*, May 2, 2011.

97. Tim Perone, "Obama Mocks Trump at White House Correspondents' Dinner," *New York Post*, May 1, 2011.

Matthew W. Hughey, Ph.D., is an Associate Professor of Sociology at the University of Connecticut and the author of over forty peer-reviewed research articles and seven scholarly books. His research examines racial identity formation, racialized groups, and the production, distribution, and reception of mass-mediated racial representations.

Gregory S. Parks, J.D., Ph.D., is an Assistant Professor of Law at Wake Forest University School of Law, where he teaches courses in civil litigation, race and law, and social science and law. Dr. Parks has published eight scholarly books on topics ranging from black Greek-letter organizations to race in America to social science and law.